Faith in the Marketplace

American Society of Missiology Monograph Series

Series Editor, James R. Krabill

The ASM Monograph Series provides a forum for publishing quality dissertations and studies in the field of missiology. Collaborating with Pickwick Publications—a division of Wipf and Stock Publishers of Eugene, Oregon—the American Society of Missiology selects high quality dissertations and other monographic studies that offer research materials in mission studies for scholars, mission and church leaders, and the academic community at large. The ASM seeks scholarly work for publication in the series that throws light on issues confronting Christian world mission in its cultural, social, historical, biblical, and theological dimensions.

Missiology is an academic field that brings together scholars whose professional training ranges from doctoral-level preparation in areas such as Scripture, history and sociology of religions, anthropology, theology, international relations, interreligious interchange, mission history, inculturation, and church law. The American Society of Missiology, which sponsors this series, is an ecumenical body drawing members from Independent and Ecumenical Protestant, Catholic, Orthodox, and other traditions. Members of the ASM are united by their commitment to reflect on and do scholarly work relating to both mission history and the present-day mission of the church. The ASM Monograph Series aims to publish works of exceptional merit on specialized topics, with particular attention given to work by younger scholars, the dissemination and publication of which is difficult under the economic pressures of standard publishing models.

Persons seeking information about the ASM or the guidelines for having their dissertations considered for publication in the ASM Monograph Series should consult the Society's website—www.asmweb.org.

Members of the ASM Monograph Committee who approved this book are:

Margaret E. Guider, OSF, Associate Professor of Missiology, Boston College School of Theology and Ministry

Susan L. Maros, Affiliate Assistant Professor of Christian Leadership, Fuller Theological Seminary

RECENTLY PUBLISHED IN THE ASM MONOGRAPH SERIES

Emily Ralph Servant, *Experiments in Love: An Anabaptist Theology of Risk-Taking in Mission*

Vinod John, *Believing Without Belonging?: Religious Beliefs and Social Belonging of Hindu Devotees of Christ*

"How should faith, work, and economics conspire together to promote Christian missions? Dr. Samuel Lee's *Faith in the Marketplace* seeks to answer this question by studying three sites of the Entrepreneurial Church Planting (ECP). What emerges from this investigation is three foundational principles: relationality, emphasis on growth and development, and a focus on holistic transformation. While most other Christian missiologists do not use the language and concepts of the ECP, they would do well to read this book carefully as it has a lot to teach them about what is central in Christian missions and how to bring God to the public square."

—**Peter C. Phan**, Georgetown University

"Change is all around us. We live in an increasingly post-Christian world where Christianity is no longer the dominant force in our culture. This new context has created one of the greatest missionary moments in the history of the church. More than ever before, we need new contextual churches for an increasingly multicultural, secular, and global context. With thoughtful research, Dr. Lee has written an accessible introduction to a fresh new movement of entrepreneurial church planting in the marketplace. If you want to know what God is doing through this movement and how you can join in, *Faith in the Marketplace* is a must-read."

—**Winfield Bevins**, author of *Marks of a Movement*

"Samuel Lee's wonderfully researched book opens the way for deeper intellectual understanding of how entrepreneurs create synergies between business startups and church planting initiatives. Lee provides vivid case studies of how such initiatives can have transformative results. He also introduces innovative spiritual metrics to evaluate such initiatives. All of this makes the book a must-read for those interested in church-planting in the twenty-first century."

—**Stephen Offutt**, Asbury Theological Seminary

"This is a thoughtful study about how you measure the impact of church-based entrepreneurial mission. Using case studies, Samuel Lee opens up a sophisticated relational approach. The study deserves careful reading by all those interested in the growing and important field of missional entrepreneurship."

—**Michael Moynagh**, author of *Church in Life: Innovation, Mission and Ecclesiology*

"*Faith in the Marketplace* is a great book and Christian leaders must read it. . . . Ministries of the church today have experienced lots of changes in an effort to reach out the ever-changing world. However, the way they measure the success and effectiveness of their ministries has remained almost the same. It has got to change. And now we have an effective alternative. Samuel Lee's new measurement is so contextual and practical. . . . It pays attention to the details of the practical side of the church's ministries while remaining focused on God. Lee offers a measurement with eternal perspective as well as present perspective."

—**Hansung Kim**, Asian Center for Theological Studies and Mission, South Korea

Faith in the Marketplace

Measuring the Impact of Church Based Entrepreneurial Approaches to Holistic Mission

SAMUEL LEE

FOREWORD BY
W. JAY MOON

American Society of Missiology Monograph
Series vol. 53

☙PICKWICK *Publications* · Eugene, Oregon

FAITH IN THE MARKETPLACE
Measuring the Impact of Church Based Entrepreneurial
Approaches to Holistic Mission

American Society of Missiology Monograph Series 53

Copyright © 2021 Samuel Lee. All rights reserved. Except for brief quotations in critical publications or reviews, no part of this book may be reproduced in any manner without prior written permission from the publisher. Write: Permissions, Wipf and Stock Publishers, 199 W. 8th Ave., Suite 3, Eugene, OR 97401.

Pickwick Publications
An Imprint of Wipf and Stock Publishers
199 W. 8th Ave., Suite 3
Eugene, OR 97401

www.wipfandstock.com

PAPERBACK ISBN: 978-1-7252-8517-0
HARDCOVER ISBN: 978-1-7252-8518-7
EBOOK ISBN: 978-1-7252-8519-4

Cataloguing-in-Publication data:

Names: Lee, Samuel, author. | Moon, W. Jay, foreword.

Title: Faith in the marketplace : measuring the impact of church based entrepreneurial approaches to holistic mission / by Samuel Lee ; foreword by W. Jay Moon.

Description: Eugene, OR: Pickwick Publications, 2021 | American Society of Missiology Monograph Series vol. 53 | Includes bibliographical references and index.

Identifiers: ISBN 978-1-7252-8517-0 (paperback) | ISBN 978-1-7252-8518-7 (hardcover) | ISBN 978-1-7252-8519-4 (ebook)

Subjects: LCSH: Missions—Theory. | Entrepreneurship—Religious aspects | Entrepreneurship—Cross-cultural studies

Classification: BV2061 L4 2021 (print) | BV2061 (ebook)

Manufactured in the U.S.A.   04/08/21

Carol Mitchell (deceased), who had served as a missionary to Koreans for over thirty-five years and guided my wife (Elaine Kim) and me as our spiritual mentor. We owe an incalculable debt of love to her. Even though she is not with us any longer, we remember her in our hearts. She showed us what a missionary's life should look like.

Contents

List of Tables and Figures | viii
Acknowledgments | xi
Foreword | xiii

1. Introduction and the Overview of the Research | 1
2. Three Church Planting Models of Integrating Faith, Work, and Economics | 21
3. Methodology | 45
4. Case Study of Redeemer Community Church and Dayspring Technologies | 63
5. Case Study of Blue Jean Church and Arsenal Place Accelerator | 86
6. Case Study of Meridzo Ministries | 110
7. Models of Holistic Transformation | 135
8. Conclusion | 159

Appendix A: Informed Consent Letter | 179
Appendix B: Interview Questions | 181
Appendix C: Entrepreneurial Church Planting Questionnaire | 187
Appendix D: Description of Interviews | 196
Appendix E: Operational Indicators of Four Relational Changes | 222

Bibliography | 225
Index | 237

Tables and Figures

Table 1: Characteristics of Tentmaking, BAM, FXC, and ECP | 16

Table 2: Three Models for Missional Practice | 32

Table 3: Comparison of Characteristics of Three Examples of Faith/Work Interaction | 40

Table 4: Comparison of Characteristics of Three Examples of Faith/Work Interaction | 43

Table 5: Description of Selection Criteria | 50

Table 6: Site Visits and Interviews | 54

Table 7: Key Issues and Responses of Danny Fong, Founder and Pastor of Dayspring Technologies and Redeemer Church | 71

Table 8: Operationalization of ECP Outcomes | 80

Table 9: A Percent Change for Selected Counties in Alabama, 2000–2015 | 91

Table 10: Description of Subjects | 95

Table 11: Description of Subjects | 115

Table 12: Clemens Sedmak's Kinship Model | 130

Table 13: Transformation between Levels | 131

Table 14: Application of Clemens Sedmak's Kinship Model | 131

Table 15: Application of the Holistic Transformation Model | 140

Table 16: Research Findings of the Goals of Three American ECPs | 141

Table 17: Research Findings of the Outcomes of Three American ECPs | 143

Table 18: Research Findings of the Metrics of Three American ECPs | 145
Table 19: ECP Performance Assessment Factors | 154
Table 20: ECP's Indicators of Change | 155
Table 21: Indicators for Evaluating Outcomes | 171

Figure 1: Tentmaking Model | 34
Figure 2: Business for Economic Development Model | 36
Figure 3: Holistic Transformation Business Model | 39
Figure 4: The Goal and Outcomes of the Redeemer and Dayspring Technologies | 77
Figure 5: Percentage of Parishioners Who Live within One Mile of BJC | 102
Figure 6: Three Holistic Praxes of Meridzo Ministries | 152
Figure 7: Key Principles in Making ECP Effective | 129

Diagram 1: Church Attendance, Selected Years | 66
Diagram 2: Network of Affiliations of BJC, APA, and CPC | 93
Diagram 3: Basic Diagram of the Operation of Entrepreneurial Church Planting Four Factors | 165
Diagram 4: Operation of Entrepreneurial Church Planting | 169

Chart 1: Percentage Income Distribution: 2013 Comparison of Selma with the State of Alabama | 88
Chart 2: Juvenile Incarcerations, Selected Counties in Alabama, 2000–2015 | 90

Acknowledgments

Even though my name appears as the author of this dissertation, everyone knows that I cannot take credit for everything in it.

First of all, I offer my deepest gratitude to the Triune God who has guided me down my life's path, has given me the opportunity to study at Asbury Theological Seminary, and sustained me through six long years of the Doctor of Philosophy program. His grace and love enabled me to complete this dissertation.

I am also deeply grateful to God for allowing me to get to know the following wonderful people who have supported me through the journey of this dissertation. I offer my gratitude to:

My beloved wife, Hyeonjeong, who deserves more than I can ever give her as she has joyfully helped me get through these six years. Without her prayers and support, I could not have finished this long journey.

My children, Daniel and Gideon, who have always brought me great joy and have been a great source of motivation.

My grandmother, Jang Munrye, and my parents, Jaenam Lee and Dongshim Kim, who led me to faith in Jesus Christ and taught me diligence, honesty, and courage.

My parents-in-law, Kwankoo Kim and Gyeonghee Lim, who entrusted me with their beautiful daughter and continually supported us financially and spiritually. I am deeply grateful to them for taking care of my children whenever help was needed.

My dissertation committee members, Drs. W. Jay Moon, Stephen W. Offutt, and Gregg A. Okesson.

Dr. Moon, who helped me find my dissertation topic, guided me with his keen scholarly insights, and mentored me in a way that only a caring father could. His teaching has been foundational to this project.

Dr. Offutt, my reader, who supported me with his knowledge of social science and provided me an understanding of holistic transformational development that has shaped my life and this project.

Dr. Okesson, my examiner, whose teaching and encouragement have been essential in writing this dissertation.

Dr. Robert Danielson, who welcomed me warmly whenever I visited his office and gave me valuable advice on my dissertation.

Dr. Dale Walker, who willingly proofread my dissertation and gave me great counsel.

Dr. Mary Conklin, who took me step-by-step through the dissertation journey from the beginning, who guided my dissertation, and edited it.

Howard Biddulph, who proofread my papers for countless hours with his missionary vision and lifelong experience in Colombia, South America.

Manki Hwang, who discipled me in my spiritual journey and accompanied me in many struggles since the university.

Without these people of God, I could not have completed this dissertation. I praise God for all of them. I know I cannot repay their immeasurable favors, but I want to repay them by participating in *missio Dei* to those in need the rest of my life.

Foreword

THIS IS NO ORDINARY book. Combining robust research with a missionary heart, Samuel Lee provides much needed insight to guide holistic ministries. The author is no ordinary man. Drawing upon his previously published works and own missionary experiences, Lee addresses the topic of mission to the marketplace that is even more relevant now than when he first started this research journey. He both understands common mission practice and also challenges long held assumptions.

"What gets measured, gets done." This maxim is as valid in ministry as it is in business and other areas of life. What business does not have particular metrics to gauge their success? Similarly, what church planters do not use measures to gauge how they are doing? Samuel Lee challenges the traditional metrics of success for businesses (single financial bottom line) and churches (how much, how many, and how often) to provide missional insight for churches that are engaging the marketplace. In this insightful book, he guides ministry leaders to consider effective ways to measure their own holistic ministries.

In particular, Samuel is encouraged by ministries that are engaging the marketplace. These Entrepreneurial Church Plants (ECP) are finding that work spaces are not simply secular gathering venues; rather, these can become vibrant and vital mission outposts to connect unaffiliated people to Jesus. This project is very timely. For example, American twenty somethings are increasingly indifferent to religious affiliation. Lee documents the tremendous potential, however, of using entrepreneurial approaches to church planting. Through three case studies, he demonstrates the significant missional potential that can result when ministries intentionally eschew the sacred/secular divide and plant churches in the marketplace.

This book is not satisfied with quick formulaic answers though. Lee dives into the complexities of both operating a business and planting a church. While each one of these are significant endeavors, Lee recognizes the synergies within each that can promote ECPs. This is not easy—but when was mission ever easy? This is not simple—but hasn't mission usually been more messy than neat and tidy? Instead of providing easy and simple answers, Lee provides the foundational questions to ask in order to guide holistic ministries. After all, aren't good questions often much better than easy and simple answers? Lee provides the right questions to ask in order to spark innovative and relevant approaches to mission in the marketplace.

This book is even more timely as many churches are facing financial pressures and are looking to alternate financial models that do not rely upon tithes and offerings alone. When tithes and offerings are not sufficient to financially support a church, ECP becomes one vital approach for churches to remain both missionally vibrant and financially viable. The growth of ECP's is testament to this assertion. Lee takes us one step further, though, and demonstrates that this approach has been a significant force for mission in the history of the church. He documents the historical approaches whereby the church integrated faith, work, and economics. Along the way, he picks up "gold nuggets" to demonstrate that contemporary applications of ECP are really nothing new—this is more of a renaissance than an innovation in mission.

Lastly, this book is written for both the practitioner and the theoretician. While Lee provides robust research and builds upon solid theoretical grounding, he also provides practical insight for those engaged in holistic mission. Through the voices of the ECP leaders in the case studies, readers will encounter real people in various contexts with one common mission—participate in the missio Dei. Instead of ivory tower academics disconnected from the struggles of life, these ECP practitioners have all rolled up their sleeves and opened their hearts to engage a needy world through their marketplace endeavors. Their stories will provide fresh hope for readers to consider their own opportunities in holistic mission.

Let me say it again. This is no ordinary book. This is no ordinary author. I have been privileged to know Samuel Lee and his research. This book will provide readers both unique insights and new hope to fulfill the missio Dei in fresh ways in the marketplace.

Dr. W. Jay Moon

Professor of Church Planting and Evangelism, Asbury Theological Seminary at Wilmore, and author of *Intercultural Discipleship: Learning from Global Approaches to Spiritual Formation* and co-editor of *Entrepreneurial Church Planting: Innovative Approaches to Engage the Marketplace*

1

Introduction and the Overview of the Research

HUDSON TAYLOR, THE WELL-KNOWN missionary of the nineteenth century, understood missions as being primarily rooted in saving souls; yet, experiences with the hungry, the weary, and the sick eventually expanded his missional scope to include physical care.[1] Missions have developed in ways that Taylor never anticipated, and many practitioners are now in agreement that holistic ministry is required to share the Gospel by "word and deed."[2] However, it is not enough to agree on the merits of holistic ministry. The next step is to describe the content of holistic ministry. Several writers such as Ron Sider[3] have endeavored to map out the activities of holistic ministry.

The identification of programs and policies to undergird holistic ministry is no guarantee that it happens or that the programs mission groups have developed achieve holistic ministry. What is lacking is some way to assess what is actually achieved or how does one determine when a given mission's approach has produced a good return.[4] Without such a tool and its use, ministries are simply replicated and/or perpetuated without a demonstration of effectiveness. The mission harvest is too valuable to simply assume effectiveness is attained.

Very few practitioners have provided markers for gauging holistic ministry success, and consequently ministries have tended to bifurcate goals

---

1. Walls, *Cross-Cultural Process in Christian History*, 241.
2. Sider, *Churches That Make a Difference*, 64.
3. Sider, *One-Sided Christianity?*
4. Collins, *Good to Great and the Social Sectors*, 5–9.

based on an evangelistic-economic continuum.[5] While some organizations measure success based on evangelistic outcomes such as conversion rates,[6] others go in different directions with a focus on financial stewardship.[7] What is needed is a measuring system, perhaps a scale, that includes both ends of the continuum in order to offer an approach more in sync with the theological vision of holistic missions.

One expression of holistic missions is Entrepreneurial Church Planting (ECP), which focuses on social development.[8] Within this term (ECP) is the concern to reach people incarnationally[9] with energy to create what is needed to advance the kingdom, i.e., being entrepreneurial. Max Weber in his *Spirit of Capitalism* identifies a collection of characteristics associated with a successful capitalist[10] or entrepreneur who "gets nothing out of his wealth [his accomplishments] for himself, except the irrational sense of having done his job well"[11] and "the chances of overcoming traditionalism,"[12] i.e., a willingness to try new approaches. These significant tendencies have been appropriated as the meaning for entrepreneurial in ECP efforts.

This Christian mission approach utilizes a combination of economic strategies along with church planting to engage the marketplace or the number of potential customers of a product or service defined by some boundary, e.g., geography or neighborhood. This study will examine the unique data trends that emerge in three case studies of US ECPs. Each case study of an ECP provides a unique opportunity to investigate the possibilities of holistic transformation. In order to assess the stewarding capabilities of ECPs, this research addresses: How do we determine when a given mission's approach has produced a good return and how do we measure the effectiveness of that approach? To that end, this study reviews what each selected ECP has done and how that ministry might be instructive in thinking about outcomes relative to the quality of relationships engendered. Based on an analysis of current praxis of ECPs, this study compares them with one another in order to discover existing metrics and suggests new metrics with the goal of developing effective metrics for vital and holistic religious expression.

---

5. Swarr and Nordstrom, *Transform the World*.
6. Johnson, *Business as Mission*, 202.
7. Yamamori and Eldred, *On Kingdom Business*, 287.
8. Long and Mood, *Entrepreneurial Church Planting*.
9. Lingenfelter and Mayers, *Ministering Cross-Culturally*, 14–16.
10. Weber, *Protestant Ethic and the Spirit of Capitalism*, 47–78.
11. Weber, *Protestant Ethic and the Spirit of Capitalism*, 71.
12. Weber, *Protestant Ethic and the Spirit of Capitalism*, 63.

BACKGROUND OF THE PROBLEM

Globally, the ECP movement is an emerging phenomenon with examples appearing in Asia, Africa, Latin American, North America, and Europe.[13] One of the main appeals of ECP is that it incorporates a broad approach to include people and activities still outside of the formal church as well as those who are unreached. By combining both entrepreneurship or finding nonchurch places where people gather and church planting, ECP has sought to reach both the unchurched and the dechurched by creating a "third space."[14] A "third space" refers to neutral spaces that are more inviting to strangers than traditional ecclesiological models. Such a space might be a café or a general store used for bringing the gospel to people.

ECP models want to provide culturally sensitive economic and social environments to nurture nascent Christians and to reach people who mistrust traditional evangelical approaches. Several churches have attempted to reshape ecclesiology through socio-economic engagement[15] by integrating business and church planting. Some examples are bi-vocational ministers, Business as Mission practitioners,[16] Fresh Expressions of Church (FXC) entrepreneurs,[17] and mission organizations that have sought outreach opportunities with spiritual, economic, and social dimensions.

An additional appeal of ECP in foreign contexts is the creation of communities for seekers and/or converts who otherwise may not be accepted by the neighborhood. In situations where conversion causes ostracism, the community fostered through an EPC can provide both an economic and a social home. Furthermore, foreign governments are often open to business enterprises that are inherent in ECP activities. In less developed countries, economic opportunities for the disenfranchised are often welcomed.

---

13. Moynagh, *Church In Life*, 2; Lee, "Eschatological Framework," 95–109.

14. Fitch, *Great Giveaway*, 63.

15. There are several examples, such as Campus House in Tennessee, Ebenezer Café in DC, and Real-Life Church in Virginia to name a few. Churches that attempt to reshape ecclesiology through socio-economic engagements are growing.

16. The models of Business as Mission (BAM) utilize business enterprises to fulfill the Great Commission and are focused on setting up businesses among unreached people groups.

17. A fresh expression of church is defined as "a new gathering or network that engages mainly with people who have never been to church" (Fresh Expressions, "Starting Our Journey"). Michael Moynagh uses the term "new contextual churches" to describe the Fresh Expression movement as follows: "Christian communities that serve people mainly outside the church, belong to their culture, make discipleship a priority and form a new church among the people they serve. They are a response to changes in society and to the new missional context that the church faces in the global North" (Moynagh, *Church for Every Context*, ix–xxi).

However, consideration of ECP also demonstrates that a combination of business and church planting has the potential for problems. A focus on multiplying profits may reduce the attention to church planting, produce a poor witness, and result in a decline in spiritual interest.[18] In contrast, focusing primarily upon church planting results in a division whereby the business merely becomes a platform for church planting such that the business is not valued for its inherent good, thus resulting in shoddy work. Thus, planting a church combined with operating a viable for-profit business presents significant challenges, especially when the creation of a spiritual community is also a desired end.

In view of these advantages and disadvantages of ECP as well as the general need to monitor growth, evaluation becomes necessary. Specifically, while it may be conceptually inviting for spiritual and economic forces to co-mingle in reaching the lost, dechurched, and unchurched, activities need to be evaluated as to whether they are accomplishing the goals of the Great Commission (reconciliation/discipleship), the Creation Commission (stewardship), and the Great Commandment (social transformation).[19]

As mentioned before, while the relatively limited number of ECPs provide few choices for study, the situation is confounded by the lack of research done on these ECPs. There is no indication of their ability to assess their operation and to determine their ability to formulate goals in the economic, spiritual and social domains with measurable outcomes. In general, the lack of assessment tools for the holistic operations and outcomes of ECP provides little guidance for developing a systematic way to evaluate ECP outcomes. Suitable pre-existing measures to evaluate the holistic dimensions of ECP activities have not been found. Even though there are several attempts to measure the economic and spiritual impact,[20] the social outcomes have not been scrutinized, despite the interest in and implementation of social endeavors, a conclusion substantiated by David Bronkema and Christopher M. Brown.[21] The paucity of evaluation of the social dimension may be explained by a lack of appreciation for the benefits of assessment and the prevalence of evaluation of the two dominant domains: spirituality and economic profitability.

---

18. Steffen and Barnett, *Business as Mission*, 167–80.

19. For more information on three terms (the Great Commission, the Creation Commission, and the Great Commandment), see "Definition of Key Terms" below.

20. See BAM Global, "Current State of Business as Mission Research," which reviews various existing Christian and non-Christian assessment tools, with analysis on what they do, how they do and why they might be helpful.

21. Bronkema and Brown, "Business as Mission," 83.

If holistic praxis is the desired model, however, ECP needs to include the social arena as well. Few ECPs measure the multi-dimensional goal of the Great Commission, the Creation Commission, and the Great Commandment. As Andrew Kirk points out:

> The Christian community needs a standard by which to measure its own performance—a standard which is able to call into question its own policies, programs, and practices. Without this, mission simply becomes an arbitrary response to whatever a particular culture or moment of history throws up.[22]

New measures are thus needed to evaluate the holistic dimensions of ECP activities. The value of holistic transformative metrics is that all three dimensions can be measured simultaneously, and the interactive effects of the three components can be assessed. ECP has been implemented in a sufficient number of places to generate data for an evaluation of this strategy more thoroughly and determine its effectiveness. Metrics would be helpful because ECP provides many good opportunities regarding reconciliation, financial stewardship and social transformation. Given the time required and money invested in finding appropriate people with the needed skill sets, language proficiencies, abilities to identify appropriate locations, obtain government permits, do demographic research of the target community, etc., Christian leaders and ECP practitioners need to use strategies that are proven to produce these outcomes.

For example, Larry Stoess, pastor of the United Methodist Church of the Promise,[23] and his ministry team began a new contextual church plant in Louisville, Kentucky in 2012. This church has a community development corporation that launched a pay-what-you-can restaurant scheme called *The Table Cafe*. Their mission at the Promise includes training and mentoring church planters who want to use business as ministry and discipleship as the organizing principle for their expression of church. According to Stoess, as he planted the café church, he built social capital and a community. Consistent with my inability to find assessment tools, when I asked him how to assess the performance of the Promise in terms of community development, he could not provide suggestions for specific measurement; he and his staff did not know how to measure their outcomes in the holistic transformational areas such as economic, social, and evangelical realms. What this example suggests is the need for ECP practitioners to develop a holistic

---

22. Kirk, *What Is Mission?*, 39.

23. Even though the Promise and *Table Café* were using ECP program, they were not selected as a case study for this project as they did not meet the five specific criteria that I set out in chapter 3.

framework for tracking and measuring evangelism, business effectiveness, and social development of an ECP.

STATEMENT OF THE PROBLEM

I am studying three American ECPs to see how ECP practitioners are currently measuring the performance and the effectiveness of church-planting efforts combined with business models in order to develop a holistic framework for metrics to aid in assessment of ECP outcomes.[24]

The previous section argues for the holistic potential of ECP, but potential must be supported by proper metrics to determine periodically the status of the ECP if it is to mature and blossom into reality. ECPs continue to rise in popularity and are a global phenomenon, but the global nature of these ventures only increases the importance of metrics. If ECPs fail to manifest their promising ability of uniting evangelism, creation care, and neighborly love, missional witness is once again thrown off balance. In addition, this study explores further the deficiencies present in ECPs and investigates each ECP's metrics which help develop holistic commitments and imagination. Accordingly, ECP practitioners are asked the following sub-research questions which serve as the basis for determining the appropriate theoretical framework for the research:

1. What is the primary goal of each ECP?

2. How do practitioners of ECP activities broadly define success? This will identify theoretical definitions of success.

3. What are the metrics (implicit or explicit) that ECPs employ presently to gauge their performance? This question will reveal operational definitions of success of ECPs.

THEORETICAL FOUNDATION

While researching the ECP ministries, this study explored them through three theoretical perspectives—Tentmaking, Business as Mission, Fresh Expressions of Church—in defining the primary goal of each ECP, gauging its performance, and studying factors that may bring about the multiple bottom-line goals of reconciliation, financial stewardship, and social transformation.

Specifically, since the 1970s, many churches have become interested in presenting the entire Gospel in a holistic manner through

---

24. Here performance implies how ECP practitioners are doing. On the other hand, effectiveness refers to how ECP practitioners are doing in order to reach their goals.

evangelistic-socio-economic engagement. This orientation brings us to the above-mentioned three theoretical perspectives which undergird the research reported on ECP. ECP is still too new a concept to have a solitary theoretical basis. ECP's unique contribution is its acknowledgement of evangelism and economic development incorporated in a social transformation framework so as to produce spiritual, economic, and social fruits. Given that the components of ECP are interwoven, aspects of its full operation are overlooked if explanations emanate from a single theory.

Consistent with the emphasis on doing something to participate in God's mission, the earliest paradigm developed was Tentmaking. Closer scrutiny of New Testament teaching saw Paul, the great missionary, working as a tentmaker to support his mission.[25] Ronald Hock notes, "Paul's letters and Acts provide good evidence for placing the apostle in workshops wherever and whenever he was doing missionary work and teaching."[26] Given Paul's zeal for telling others about Christ, it is not generalizing beyond the evidence to suggest it occurred in his workshop.[27] Accordingly, we find that the first modern tentmakers were professionals with multinational corporations and as English teachers, students, and those who established NGOs to provide social services in the community.[28] Whatever work they did, allowed them to be self-supporting, but at the same time providing "the lost a good look and often a first look, at who Jesus really is."[29] As more sites were added, the strategy became legitimated.[30] Despite its economic origins, Tentmaking is often described as an approach associated with evangelism and discipleship.

From this theoretical perspective, attention has been focused on what are the types of business that are more likely to flourish, how to enter a country, development of suitable training programs, etc. The site of God's mission has moved from the sanctuary to the workplace. What has made Tentmaking acceptable to countries, otherwise closed to the gospel, is its veneer of providing economic opportunities.

The model that evolved from Tentmaking in some parts of the world is business as economic development or more commonly, Business as Mission. As governments began to demand an organized business as opposed to

---

25. Hock, "Paul's Tentmaking," 14.
26. Hock, "Paul's Tentmaking," 15.
27. Hock, "Paul's Tentmaking," 18. Hock discussed a few philosophers who taught in various venues, including a work site.
28. Lai, *Tentmaking*, 4
29. Lai, *Tentmaking*, 3.
30. Lai, *Tentmaking*, 6.

the start-ups, characteristic of Tentmaking, in order for groups to enter the country. Business as Mission brings attention to the role of the marketplace and asserts that Christian mission and the marketplace can work conjointly. To be more specific, it is "for-profit commercial business venture that is Christian led, intentionally devoted to be used as an instrument of God's mission to the world, and is operated in a cross-cultural environment."[31] The business attracts people—whether workers, clients, or suppliers, etc.—where they are then ministered to. The ministry is more than spiritual as it includes holistic community development.[32] This perspective introduced, developed, and emphasized the holistic development which had been underdeveloped in the Tentmaking model. Business is transformed from personal employment to a venue where others are employed and shown God's love. With the operation of a true and fully developed business all who are involved with the business are also connected to kingdom business.[33]

The third theoretical paradigm has a transformational development focus. The economic aspect, common to the earlier theoretical approaches, is retained with an emphasis on entrepreneurial activity. People within a community are assisted as they start businesses that provide employment for themselves and other local people, teach job skills, create socializing venues to solidify social bonds with customers, and support other local retailers and wholesalers that provide goods and services to the fledgling businesses. Thus we see grass-root economic activity that simultaneously heals and feeds people spiritually, socially, and emotionally.

Within this larger view, there is one approach that begins to capture the complex interweaving of gospel and economics with a goal of transforming people: it is the new monasticism. There is no attempt to present a one-approach-that-fits-all, but rather to identify attitudes and orientations that work with existing circumstances and skills to create "incarnational Christian communities who embody and demonstrate the spiritual in the everyday life."[34] Another essential element that the new monasticism promulgates is interpersonal relationships where those serving "live and work with the people they connect with"; reference is made to the need "to build a positive hospitable relationship with whomever comes along."[35] Thus, people are not just seen as souls, but individuals, alive and breathing, who

---

31. Johnson, *Business as Mission*, 27–28.
32. Johnson, *Business as Mission*, 23.
33. Johnson, *Business as Mission*, 29.
34. Cray et al., *New Monasticism as Fresh Expressions of the Church*, 149.
35. Cray et al., *New Monasticism as Fresh Expressions of the Church*, 147, 149.

need to be loved as they are and cared for. Divinely inspired hospitality is a high standard.

Rather than implement an action plan developed elsewhere, Mark Berry talks about the need for ruptures or "when perceptions of the norms that exclude the spiritual suddenly burst with potential."[36] We recognize the need to do or be in new ways that are guided by the Spirit as we seek to serve others. Mission then becomes a divine activity—an activity conceived and guided by the triune God—"in which we participate—the *missio Dei*."[37] As Shane Claiborne notes about the activity, "There should be a bias towards goodness rather than away from it, so that we can pick up new habits, holy habits, as we become new creations transformed by God."[38] Ministry is not necessarily conducted along standard business procedures, but reflect practices that give God the glory.

Within this paradigm of transformational development, we find attention to "Fresh Expressions of Church" or new approaches, relationships with people in the present covered with prayer that result in transformations of people into being active followers of Christ, cultivation of community where new believers are nurtured and hurts are healed and vision is developed, with an economic basis so individuals involved with the ministry become productive citizens of the larger society. Attention is given to the process of incarnational restoration rather than the bottom line or the number of church members.

In this way, my research was done using these three lenses. The three theoretical perspectives would aid in alluding to novel church based entrepreneurial approaches to holistic mission. However, in a dissertation whose primary focus is on measurement and the development of metrics, theory simply serves as a guide to what concepts and activities are incorporated into models and later operationalized. The step into praxis is what enables the refinement of understanding of how various factors work and influence the outcomes.[39] The theories, then, provide a departure point for analysis rather than to be a continuing guiding force in the discussion and analysis. The case studies instruct us about the actual way the components or variables work together to achieve the desired outcome of growth of God's kingdom.

---

36. Cray et al., *New Monasticism as Fresh Expressions of the Church*, 149.
37. Cray et al., *New Monasticism as Fresh Expressions of the Church*, 150.
38. Cray et al., *New Monasticism as Fresh Expressions of the Church*, 152.
39. For the Church's early forms of praxis, see chapter 2.

PURPOSE OF THE STUDY

The objective of this study is to research current practices of fruitful ECP ministries, identify desirable outcomes, and assess the overall effectiveness of ECP, and develop a metric to evaluate this holistic transformational approach. To accomplish this goal, the dissertation examines three ECP sites and compares them with one another in order to articulate effective metrics for vital and holistic religious expression. Using various ministries within the US, this study investigates goals, activities, and evaluative metrics for ECP outcomes that do not merely rely on the common assessment standards of the number of conversions or financial success. This evaluative strategy will reflect the components of holistic transformation, echoed in the elements of the Kingdom of God on earth.

Beyond the recognition of elements contributing to the operation of an ECP and the more obvious outcomes, this study seeks to identify what practices, orientation, ministries constitute effectiveness. Ultimately, I would like to create metrics to assess the holistic operation of an ECP. Several books and articles have presented the practical aspects of ECP,[40] but few have tackled the problems of identifying what constitutes effectiveness.

METHODOLOGICAL APPROACH

To address the issues of determining when success and effectiveness have been achieved, it is, first of all, important to consider what has been written about the goals of ECP and what suggestions have been made by actual ECP examples. With the collection of this information, a method to collect data on actual ECPs was an issue. To accomplish the assessment of ECP, a case study approach is used for this analysis, where there is an "in-depth examination of a single instance of some social phenomenon such as a village, family or a juvenile gang."[41] This research methodology is the most effective for this type of assessment[42] of this kind because it provides a contextual methodology integrating theory with praxis. Another advantage of the case study approach is that it enables the study of process—how an ECP is established, ministries introduced, development of a community feel to the ministry, etc. In the operation of an ECP, the ebb and flow of conversations, planting an idea and allowing it to become established can be studied. Realizing the limitations of a single case, multiple cases were used. Despite

---

40. Moynagh, *Church for Every Context*; Moynagh, *Church In Life*; Joo, "Entrepreneurial Church Planting (ECP)"; Long and Moon, *Entrepreneurial Church Planting*; Lee, "Holistic Framework for Measurement of Entrepreneurial Church Planting."

41. Babbie, *Practice of Social Research*, 309.

42. Babbie, *Practice of Social Research*, 309–10.

the inability to generalize based on the limited number of cases, the insights gained from intensive study will more than compensate.

Research using the case study approach, investigates a definition of goals for ECP activities and the process of identifying concepts to measure ECP outcomes. Based on this, the research attempts to identify what factors result in economic sustainability, church planting, and social development and what effectiveness in ECP looks like.

SIGNIFICANCE OF THE STUDY

This research project offers significant contributions, both academically and practically regarding the vitality of religious life, especially related to church planting and evangelism for the unchurched and dechurched. There are four academic objectives for this research. First, this is an exploratory study in the field of Entrepreneurial Church Planting (ECP) metrics. Because ECP is an emergent stream of Christian missional praxis, this study advances the conversation about measuring outcomes and the impact of ECP endeavors. Second, by examining the unique data trends that emerge in each ECP case study completed, this research contributes to a better understanding of the relevance of contextual expressions of the Christian faith. Third, the research findings can increase an understanding of how non-governmental organizations (NGOs) collaborate with church planting projects in order to generate human, social, and spiritual capital. Lastly, the research findings help us understand how effective ECP is in meeting holistic transformation in community and society.

Regarding practical goals, the study can be significant for field-based missiological practitioners in at least two ways. First, the research findings can help global church leaders evaluate factors affecting the integration of faith, work, and economics by providing suggestions on how to pursue an effective combination. Second, the research findings can enhance the quality of ministry in global churches through a holistic picture of God's working in the world that allows Christian communities to more faithfully live out the Gospel in everyday life.

DELIMITATIONS AND LIMITATIONS

This research is restricted to addressing the factors that achieve the interconnected goals of economic fruitfulness, broadly defined as profitability, but also includes job creation, a redeemed work environment, and job preparatory activities; church planting; and the relationships that emerge in the process. Environmental performance of the company is not specifically addressed in this study. This does not imply that environmental factors are unimportant, but limited time and space, however, do not permit further discussion here, even though this area is mutually dependent upon the subject matter addressed throughout.

Additionally, this study is delimited to America. This is because the US appears to have a larger number of ECPs compared to other countries, the sites were readily accessible, and facilitated comparison of ECPs without confounding factors of national differences and concomitant cultural differences.[43] Furthermore, since a limited budget barely allowed for US travel, it was better to focus on emerging ECP trends in the US exclusively. Thus, no data is presented to confirm whether the US trends hold up in other countries. It is assumed, however, that this pattern may point to useful measures in other locales.

Although research was done in areas that were racially diverse, especially Selma, Alabama, and San Francisco, no specific consideration of racially-related issues were discussed. The topic of race-related factors is too complex given the exploratory type of research done to delve into this issue. By tapping ministries in racially varied settings, the results of the research will be suggestive of the effectiveness of ECP with racially diverse groups. Similarly, with the decision to study three separate ministries, there is not an adequate basis to speculate about urban/suburban/rural distinctions. A characteristic of the ECP approach is its community focus. Thus, as a ministry seeks to serve a bounded area, generalization to large urban or suburban areas would be inappropriate.

DEFINITION OF KEY TERMS

A list of terms and their definitions is provided below for purposes of clarity in this study.

The Creation Commission, the Great Commission & the Great Commandment

The *missio* Dei is a Trinitarian mission, with each person of the Trinity uniting and interacting together. For example, John 4:34, John 5:30, and John 8:29 demonstrate an interconnected Trinity in that the Son is sent to do the Father's will and the Spirit, proceeding from both the Father and the Son, highlights the life of the Son and continues to function on earth.

Yet, each takes the lead in the Trinitarian activity for their special part in salvation history. For purposes of discussion, this study focuses on God's

---

43. Second only to the UK.

Trinitarian work. For instance, the Creation Commission primarily represents the work of the Father (stewardship); the Great Commission primarily reflects the work of the Son (reconciliation/discipleship); and the Great Commandment is primarily symbolized by the work of the Holy Spirit (social transformation). In other words, God the Father works in creational stewardship (the Creation Commission); God the Son works in reconciling human beings with God and others and furthering the Kingdom of God by making disciples (the Great Commission); God the Holy Spirit works in transforming and completing our relationships to God, humanity, and the earth (the Great Commandment).[44] R. Paul Stevens expresses the idea that God assigned us two tasks: the Creation Commission (Gen 1:27–30) and the Great Commission, also known as the New Creation Commission (Matt 28:19–20).[45] It is through these two different but similar mandates[46] that persons serve, love, and live for God and others (the Great Commandment).[47] In this way, human beings are called to participate in a Trinitarian mission—that is, both the extrinsic value of the Creation Commission (the work of the Father) and the intrinsic value of the Great Commission (the work of the Son). This culminates with a deeper communal appreciation for the impending New Creation (the eschatological, in-breaking work of the Spirit). In my research, I draw upon these Trinitarian taxonomies.

Entrepreneur

In generally, entrepreneur is defined as a person who "gets nothing out of his wealth [his accomplishments] for himself, except the irrational sense of having done his job well"[48] and "the chances of overcoming traditionalism,"[49] i.e., a willingness to try new approaches. In this study, I adopt Michael Volland's definition. He defines entrepreneur as a visionary who challenges the status quo by energetically creating something of kingdom value.[50]

---

44. Stevens, *Other Six Days*, 118–23.

45. Stevens, *Other Six Days*, 89.

46. Two mandates appear to be different, but they are essentially two aspects of the same coin.

47. A number of Christian leaders and theological educators committed to the Oikonomia Network call this whole-life discipleship. You can find out their names and articles in Oikonomia Network, "Christian Vision for Flourishing Communities."

48. Weber, *Protestant Ethic and the Spirit of Capitalism*, 71.

49. Weber, *Protestant Ethic and the Spirit of Capitalism*, 63.

50. Volland, *Minister as Entrepreneur*, 3.

Marketplace

The marketplace is a place where people get their income, self-identity, social contacts, and a sense of purpose. It is also a setting where relationships are formed and people exchange value with one another. Consequently, in this study, the marketplace is "used as a broad term to describe the network of relationships whereby people exchange value with one another."[51]

Church

Moynagh identifies a church as an entity that focuses on relationships with the Trinity, relating to others in the body, with other religious groups, and telling others of God's love. He elaborates on these relationships. He describes the essence of church as *relationships* rather than differentiating churches by how they observe practices such as sacraments and prayer.[52] In the book entitled *Mission-Shaped Church* (2009),[53] the church consists of "UP relationships" through participating in the inner life of the Trinity (communion of the immanent Trinity), "IN relationships" through intimacy within members of the local church (as reflected in *the mutual love of the divine persons*), "OF relationships" through interdependence with the wider church (κοινωνία), and "OUT relationships" through proclaiming the good news, teaching, baptizing, and discipling new believers, serving the world, seeking to transform society, and striving to safeguard the creation (missionary nature of the economic Trinity).[54] These four-relationships echo the Trinity—*koivonia* and mission. Even though this four-relationship approach looks different in form, the relational nature of the church coincides with the historical four marks of the church (One, Holy, Catholic, and Apostolic)[55] and a variety of practices of the church such as word, social justice, and worship. Therefore, defining the church by its key relationships will make space for differences and diversity, leading to the desirable integrated outcomes of ECP practitioners.

---

51. Moon, "Entrepreneurial Church Planting."

52. Moynagh, *Church for Every Context*, 112.

53. Moynagh is one of the members of research team. See MPAC, *Mission-Shaped Church*, 99.

54. MPAC, *Mission-Shaped Church*, 99; Walls and Ross, *Mission in the Twenty-First Century*, xiv.

55. MPAC, *Mission-Shaped Church*, 96–98; Moynagh, *Church for Every Context*, 104–14.

Church Planting

The *Mission-Shaped Church* report defines church planting as "the process by which a seed of the life and message of Jesus embodied by a community of Christians is immersed for mission reasons in a particular cultural or geographical context."[56] Even though some are concerned that the notion of church planting is imperialistic and ecclesiocentric,[57] this study advocates for this term because (1) the imagery of church planting has deep biblical roots (Eph 1:3–14; Phil 4:3; 1 Cor 3:6–10; Peter 2:4–10; 3 John 1:8), and (2) the language of church planting has been widely used in diverse cultures and contexts.[58]

Tentmaking

This missionary model was originally inspired by the examples of Paul, Aquila and Priscilla, and came into the scholarly spotlight by the late 1980s.[59] Based on Paul's mission strategy, Christians used their professional (business) skills to establish a business as a means of contact and witness with locals and eventually to plant a church. This model permits access to countries where traditional missionaries have been denied entry.

Business as Mission (BAM)

According to Mark L. Russell, "The term business as mission was first coined in 1999 by a small group of leaders meeting at the Oxford Center for Mission Studies in the United Kingdom."[60] Business as Mission (BAM) is "intentional about the 'to all peoples' mandate, and seeks out areas with the greatest spiritual and physical needs."[61] Russell defines BAM as "business as a vehicle of the mission of God in the world."[62] Some people such as Tetsunao Yamamori and Kenneth A. Eldred focus on groups of least access for BAM ministry.[63] More information will be provided below on how BAM, Tentmaking, Fresh Expressions of Church, and ECP differ and are alike.

---

56. MPAC, *Mission-Shaped Church*, 32.
57. Murray, *Planting Churches*, 6.
58. Poll and Appleton, *Church Planting in Europe*, 29; Murray, *Planting Churches*, 6–9.
59. See BAM Global, "Current State of Business as Mission Research."
60. Russell, *Missional Entrepreneur*, 133.
61. Tunehag et al., "Business as Mission."
62. Russell, *Missional Entrepreneur*, 23.
63. Yamamori and Eldred, *On Kingdom Business*, 7–10.

Entrepreneurial Church Planting (ECP)

As noted earlier, according to Jay Moon, entrepreneurial church planting can be defined as "entrepreneurial approaches to form communities of Christ-followers among unchurched people through business in the marketplace."[64] Simply put, it describes the birth and growth of the new expressions of churches through entrepreneurial approaches. In the field of church planting, ECP can be regarded as a subset of FXC.[65] This is because, even though ECP adopts a fresh expressions approach, its context is often reduced to the marketplace and it always has to do with entrepreneurial approaches. Additionally, while FXC underlines the connection with the existing church or denomination, EPCs sometimes break away from established churches or denominations. Table 1 shows the distinct contributions of FXC, Tentmaking, BAM, and ECP. One thing to note is that Table 1 is a typology with permeable lines instead of hard and fast categories to see how and why Tentmaking, Business as Mission, FXC, and ECP are used in different ways.

Table 1. Characteristics of Tentmaking, BAM, FXC, and ECP

Characteristics	Models			
	Tentmaking	BAM	FXC	ECP
Priority	Evangelism & discipleship	Business & econ development	Kingdom extension	Holistic transformation
Target group	Foreign activity	Unreached business people	Existing church groups, unchurched, and de-churched via 4 relationships	Anyone and everyone
Planter: strong laity	X	X	X	X
Founder: expat or outsider	X	X		X
Local organizer			X	X

---

64. Long and Moon, *Entrepreneurial Church Planting*, 6.
65. See footnote 12 on page 2.

	Models			
Characteristics	Tentmaking	BAM	FXC	ECP
Purpose: strong faith, work, kingdom integration	X	X	X	X
Focus on church planting			X	X
Mission Context:				
Post-Christian			X	X
Foreign mission	X	X		(possibly)
Business		X		X

As depicted in Table 1 above, ECP is similar to BAM, Tentmaking, and FXC in regard to both the integration of faith and work, and its openness to laity having an expanded role in ministry.[66] Additionally, all these models are used as a vehicle for the kingdom of God. While ECP shares a common purpose with BAM, Tentmaking, and FXC endeavors, its focus slightly differs. Specifically, compared to tent-making, we realize that tent-making was developed as a missional enterprise. Consequently, it does not always have an entrepreneurial dimension and is involved with other disciplines or activities. Moreover, it focuses on evangelism and discipleship in foreign missions. BAM utilizes business endeavors to fulfill the Great Commission and is focused on setting up businesses among unreached people groups. These two models do not exclusively focus on church planting. On the other hand, FXC and ECP seek to form communities of Christ-followers among unchurched people through business in the marketplace in post-Christian contexts and to unite the Creation Commission (stewardship) and the Great Commission (evangelism & discipleship) by emphasizing loving relationships—with God and with others (the Great Commandment) rather than a bifurcated focus on economic development or spiritual growth. However, all FXCs are not exclusively entrepreneurial like ECP. Furthermore, the public marketplace is ECP's venue. Given this difference, I have chosen to make comparisons throughout my study with only Tentmaking and BAM models.

In an effort to differentiate the three approaches in a rough way, BAM tends to be predominantly business-oriented (the Creation Commission),

66. Joo, "Entrepreneurial Church Planting (ECP)," 211–23.

Tentmaking veers more toward a church-oriented (the Great Commission) approach, and ECP is inclined more towards a Kingdom-orientation (the Great Commandment), although this does not keep other models from having a Kingdom-oriented approach. These basic tendencies do not preclude the presence of other tendencies. In chapter 2, I will explain in more detail some distinct characteristics between Tentmaking, BAM, and ECP.

Kingdom Transformation

Kingdom Transformation is a guiding principle for this research. Bryant Myers offers a definition: "The twin goals of transformation: changed people who have discovered their true identity and vocation; and changed relationships that are just and peaceful."[67] Myers includes the physical, psychological, and social arenas[68] in that Kingdom transformation is to bring people and societies into restored relationship with God, with others, with creation, as well as restored self-understanding.[69] From a Wesleyan perspective, Howard Snyder defines Kingdom transformation as the restoration of the image of Christ, the mind of Christ and true community.[70] Interestingly, most commentators agree that the ultimate goal of Kingdom transformation is relational success (loving relationships with God and others, including creation) and the formation of a true community by way of true shalom.[71]

All things taken together, in this research, the theoretical definition of Kingdom transformation includes two critical components: (1) relational restoration, and (2) participation in true community. The aspect of relational reconciliation refers to the reconciliation of four broken relationships (God, self, other people, and creation).[72] The aspect of participation in true community, on the other hand, refers to participation in "community of faith" in relationship with the *missio Dei*.[73] Here true

---

67. Myers, *Walking with the Poor*, 202.

68. Yamamori and Eldred, *On Kingdom Business*, 202–4; Myers, *Walking with the Poor*, 181.

69. Steffen and Barnett, *Business as Mission*, 76; Getu, "Measuring Transformation," 92; Myers, *Walking with the Poor*, 202; Snyder, *Yes in Christ*, 25–26.

70. Snyder, *Yes in Christ*, 25–26.

71. Offutt, "New Directions in Transformational Development," 44; Snyder, "Salvation Means Creation Healed," 27; Snyder, "Babylonian Captivity of Wesleyan Theology," 30; Myers, *Walking with the Poor*, 181.

72. Corbett and Fikkert, *When Helping Hurts*, 59.

73. South African missiologist David Bosch defines the *missio Dei* as "God's activity, which embraces both the Church and the world, and in which the Church may be privileged to participate" (Bosch, *Transforming Mission*, 391). Another definition is given by Enoch Wan: "*Mission Dei* is the Triune God" (Wan, "Paradigm of 'Relational Realism'").

community represents a deep spiritual connection to the church leading to participation in the *missio Dei*.

SECTION SUMMARY

Contemporary missions, regardless of the sending country, often includes evangelistic-socio-economic dimensions. One application of the socio-economic aspect is Entrepreneurial Church Planting (ECP), which uses business entrepreneurs such as the laity and clergy members to launch spiritually and economically integrated communities of faith. The business activities may spawn a variety of programs that support the larger community socially and spiritually. In a missions world that frequently measures success economically or spiritually, how is success being measured in ECP endeavors? For too long in missions including church planting, financial stewardship (the Creation Commission) or evangelical fruit (the Great Commission) such as the number of baptisms and disciples have sufficed as the sole measuring tools for missional effectiveness. Increased economic pressures, however, such as the triple bottom line (e.g., financial, social, and spiritual) have enlightened us to the need not only to be governed by the quantifiable elements of reconciliation or financial flourishing, but also to evaluate outcomes of social transformation, i.e., to be accountable.

To accomplish the assessment of ECP, this dissertation is presented in eight interrelated chapters. The first three chapters lay the foundation of the study. Thus far, the first chapter has discussed the rationale for undertaking the study and a brief background on its theoretical underpinnings. Chapter 2 examines a literature review of Tentmaking, Business as Mission, Fresh Expressions of Church, and social entrepreneurship. It identifies three models of ECP, noting deficiencies in each model and the need for a new holistic framework. And chapter 3 deals with methodology, addressing the following topics: the key research questions and method, the research process, and ethical concerns.

While these three chapters provide both theoretical foundations for this study, chapters 4–6 move into praxis with three case studies, each of a different ECP site. These studies consider various contexts for ECP endeavors, and they also demonstrate the necessity of holistic metrics for measuring success. Chapter 4 explores Redeemer Community Church and Dayspring Technologies in San Francisco, California. These two settings provide insight on how to work with the emerging generation of millennials, and with their concern for holistic transformation in a low-income area of the city. Chapter 5 examines Blue Jean Church in partnership with Arsenal Place Accelerator and the Children's Policy Council in Selma, Alabama.

The analysis of Blue Jean Church serves as a significant entry point to the theoretical groundwork and theological consideration of the church as an agent of transformation in society.

And chapter 6 investigates Meridzo Ministries in Lynch, Kentucky. Meridzo, started by a missionary couple in the late 1990s, emphasizes spiritual renewal, relational flourishing, and social impact in the heart of the Appalachian Mountains. The study of Meridzo offers a grassroots understanding of success based on holistic transformation encapsulated in Kingdom relationships ("loving God and our neighbor").

Chapter 7 does cross-case analysis of the data findings of the three case studies of American ECPs in order to facilitate the development of a holistic framework for metrics to aid in assessment of ECP outcomes. In doing so, it gives an overview of the data and identifies the similarities and differences of three case studies.

Chapter 8 concludes this study by seeking to move beyond existing models of measurement in order to offer a way forward that engages the Creation Commission, the Great Commission, and the Great Commandment. This chapter also addresses achievements and limitations of this study, and it offers ideas and suggestions for future practice and research.

In short, this study seeks to uncover the metrics (implicit or explicit) that ECP practitioners use presently to gauge their performance and outcomes. As the metrics are reviewed, thoughts are offered for issues or topics overlooked by these ministries, realizing that many leaders are not trained in program assessment. Based on that, it aims to develop a framework for tracking ECP's holistic transformational approach. As such, this research contributes to renewing our definition of success and effectiveness through measuring outcomes and impacts of Christian ministries.

In order to accomplish this project, let us first review the relevant literature.

2

Three Church Planting Models of Integrating Faith, Work, and Economics

INTRODUCTION[1]

THE INTEGRATION OF ECONOMIC activity with church planting and missions is not new. A careful study of the Apostle Paul shows that his missionary strategy combined manual work, discipleship/teaching, as well as church planting.[2] Paul used his workplace as a mission field, thereby creating opportunities for the formation of new churches. In so doing, he showed how work could be a form of ministry. Additionally, he practiced his faith by demonstrating love in the daily affairs of the workplace and marketplace.[3] In this way, the Apostle Paul provides a helpful basis for what would later emerge as ECP.

While a plethora of others throughout Christian history[4] have used Paul's approach of work as a site for missions, we find that the type of work has varied across time. The early forms of work occurred without payment nor did they generate surplus; various manual jobs were done simply to sustain a family or group. With the emergence of markets in the Medieval period, crafts had developed to the point where artisans had a few extra items

---

1. Part of this material is adapted from my "Historical Perspectives on Entrepreneurial Church Planting."

2. In much of this, Paul was following the Jewish Rabbinic traditions of labor and trade along with teaching. See Pocock et al., *Changing Face of World Missions*, 230–32.

3. Danker, *Profit for the Lord*, 55.

4. See, for example, Danker, *Profit for the Lord*; Pocock et al., *Changing Face of World Missions*; Steffen and Barnett, *Business as Mission*; Lowery, *Case Histories of Tentmakers*.

to sell/barter.[5] It would not be until the eighteenth century and the emergence of the Industrial Revolution and the accompanying societal changes (acquisitiveness, regular hard work, reinvestment of profits) that capitalism and entrepreneurial activity would become widespread.

A brief historical overview into the diverse Christian traditions illustrates these changes in the understanding of work. The missional movements and historical figures presented offer useful examples of the integration of economic activity with missions, including church planting. Furthermore, they exemplify how the concept of church has changed across time. We note the Pauline practice of establishing house churches to serve the neighborhood. In the sixth and seventh century, churches were constructed to serve primarily the clergy found in monasteries. By the time of the Industrial Revolution and later, villages had central churches that operated in the heart of the community. Later in the chapter, business models suitable for entrepreneurial activity will be presented where churches are located wherever to serve the local people.

HISTORICAL OVERVIEW OF BUSINESS AND THE CHURCH

In the history of Christianity, theological innovators within different Christian traditions have implemented various combinations of church activities and business. This section provides a brief survey of Christian movements and figures that engaged in their faith economically, socially, and evangelistically. By examining these historical examples, we discover that the ECP approach has a faint, but viable track record that emerged more fully during the eighteenth century and remains relevant for contemporary praxis. These groups provide evidence of a process occurring from work as sustenance to work with the intent of generating excess products for sale.

The Celtic Missionaries (Sixth Century)

Columba, an early Celtic missionary, was a premodern example of a zealous witness. He and his monks travelled from Ireland to the Scottish Highlands in order to spread the gospel in the kingdoms of the Northern Picts in the sixth century.[6] When Columba and the Celtic missionaries arrived, they first sought close relations with powerful political leaders and authorities; after that, they found favor with the local kings and then established spiritually and self-supporting monasteries that would often include some local

---

5. Forster, *Joy for the World*, 13.
6. Terry and Gallagher, *Encountering the History of Missions*, 45–48.

people. Their daily activities at the monastery included prayer, meditation, Bible study, crafts, and physical work tending fields and livestock. They were active evangelists among the Pict people.[7] Columba was known for his willingness to care for sick animals and poor neighbors. Columba and the Celtic missionaries established a loving relationship with local people. These activities exposed the Picts to Christianity and often led them to believe in Christ.[8] In this way, the Celtic missionaries, motivated by the Great Commandment, sought to usher in a new era of caring human interaction through the operation of monasteries.

The Benedictines (Seventh Century)

Although the Celtic monks from Ireland brought their version of Christianity to continental Europe beginning in the sixth century, Italian monks were travelling in the opposite direction.[9] Augustine[10] of Canterbury and a group of forty Benedictine monks were sent by Bishop Gregory of Rome to evangelize the English.[11] Their approach to ministry was in line with the "Rule of St. Benedict," which united spirituality with manual labor.[12] The Benedictines particularly stressed the importance of work in their missional outreach. The Benedictines' main goal of their work activities was to meet the needs of the monastery, in terms of foodstuffs and any monetary requirements, to facilitate a prudent lifestyle.[13] Like the Celtic missionaries, Augustine also made contact with the local leader, King Ethelbert of Kent and gained his favor. The King allowed Augustine and the monks to proclaim the gospel freely and to establish churches. In the first year of their ministry, they reported baptizing ten thousand Anglos.[14] Benedictine monasteries later became great centers of learning, trade, and community.[15] Rich families would sometimes establish monasteries overseen by abbots. As a result of their position in the monastery and the professions that some monks assumed outside the monastery,

---

7. Bruce, *Spreading Flame*, 386–93.

8. Hunter, *Celtic Way of Evangelism*, 54.

9. Gascoigne, "History of Monasticism."

10. This is not Augustine of Hippo, whom people are used to thinking about with the name "Augustine," but another Augustine, who lived in an earlier era.

11. Bevans and Schroeder, *Constants in Context*, 123.

12. Keplinger et al., "Entrepreneurial Activities of Benedictine Monasteries," 1.

13. Martin and Feldbauer-Durstmuller, "What Can the Corporate World Learn," 51–73.

14. Neill and Chadwick, *History of Christian Missions*, 58–59.

15. Smither, *Mission in the Early Church*, 39–43.

e.g., scholars, doctors or lawyers, some within the monastery became wealthy during the medieval period.[16]

The Nestorians (Seventh Century)

As attention moved eastward from Europe, Christianity spread to central Asia and China through a movement of Nestorian merchant missionaries.[17] Beginning in the third century, Christianity was introduced in Persia, while the Arbela Kingdom and Edessa served as missionary training centers. Although monasticism occasionally was characterized by extreme asceticism, the Nestorian church stressed geographic mobility and mission, establishing monasteries in a hundred cities in ten provinces. Their monasteries were self-supporting, self-governing and self-propagating. In the fifth century, Sassanid Persia had opened trade connections with China.[18] When Nestorians entered into China, the missionaries identified with the local community by using their medical knowledge and surgical skills and sharing their faith.[19] In 635, the Nestorian missionary Alopen arrived in the Tang dynasty's capital, Changan, on the old Silk Road. After Alopen's third year (638 AD) in residence, the King decreed religious toleration; the first church was dedicated soon after.[20] An important monument dating from 781, unearthed near the ancient capital in 1623, substantiates Alopen's arrival. Consequentially, the Nestorian missionaries' evangelistic and missional efforts significantly contributed to the growth of churches in China from the seventh to the tenth centuries.[21] Moreover, these efforts were combined with business acumen as manifested by their trading activities.

In sum, these three monastic movements (the Celtic missionaries, the Benedictines, and the Nestorians) demonstrate a combination of work and spirituality in various locales. Despite their characteristic "separation" from the world, they did go out and evangelize. Because monasticism is regarded as a solitary vocation of prayer and asceticism, it is often assumed that the Great Commission was buried under the contemplative goal of becoming righteous before God.[22] Although the hermit school of monasti-

---

16. Seasoltz, "Benedictines," 96–98.
17. Moffett, *History of Christianity in Asia*, 291, 297, 461.
18. Moffett, *History of Christianity in Asia*, 290.
19. Villagomez, "Fields, Flocks, and Finances of Monks," 104.
20. Moffett, *History of Christianity in Asia*, 288; Steffen and Barnett, *Business as Mission*, 133–46.
21. Aprem, *Nestorian Missions*, 18; Irvin and Sunquist, *History of the World Christian Movement*, 278.
22. Fanning, "Brief History of Methods and Trends of Missions."

cism emphasizes an isolated spiritual journey, given the groups reviewed, the majority of the monks were coenobitic, i.e., communal. Thus, as we saw above, the Celts, the Benedictines, the Nestorians built communities of monks as a viable means of spiritual growth and for service to the common good. They demonstrated neighborly love to unbelievers, provided education, and in China, pursued trade. Wealth was understood as a grace bestowed upon the community by God and seen as a useful tool for the purpose of spreading the faith. They felt it was incumbent that they were good stewards of the excess they developed. Thus, spiritual asceticism was expressed in their communal economy because members subordinated their own interests to those of the community.[23] As a result, these monastic communities became instrumental in bringing about significant social transformation in Ireland, England, and Asia.[24]

Martin Luther (Sixteenth Century)

As we move forward chronologically, the Protestant Reformation of the sixteenth century brought about noteworthy changes both in the church and in the expectations of believers. It is understood to have recovered the notion of the priesthood of all believers, thus transforming the understanding of vocation.[25] Since Martin Luther accentuated the universal call of all Christians to service in the world, the theological impetus was on calling and vocation. Luther taught that all Christians, whether carpenters, farmers, or homemakers, were to act as ministers serving their neighbors as they needed assistance,[26] i.e., one's calling is to serve in one's station in life.[27] This theological perspective deconstructed the pervasive sacred/secular distinctions of the Medieval Ages, in which a calling only applied to the priesthood or the monastic life.[28]

Instead, Luther's doctrine of vocation relocated religious life into the realm of ordinary life.[29] These insights also recast Luther's own life and ministry; he rejected the monastic lifestyle and subsequently, married. To facilitate his efforts to publish his writings and spread ideas associated with the Protestant Reformation, Luther established a printing shop.[30] As a result

---

23. Villagomez, "Fields, Flocks, and Finances of Monks," 104.
24. Winter et al., *Perspectives on the World Christian Movement*, 280.
25. Ramachandra, *Recovery of Mission*, 117.
26. Veith, *Working for Our Neighbor*, 13–14.
27. Witherington, *Work*, 32.
28. Bainton, *Here I Stand*, 156.
29. Bainton, *Reformation of the Sixteenth Century*, 246.
30. Tillmanns, "Lotthers," 261.

of his teachings, the formation of diverse Reformed churches occurred. Eventually, due to Luther's biblical rediscovery of the priesthood of all believers and his perspective on work as a holy calling, the sixteenth century was a time of gaining greater confidence in ordinary callings.[31] However, the association of calling to one's station in life partly had the negative effect of inhibiting spiritual mobility and reducing the willingness among believers to participate in cross-cultural missionary service.[32]

Matteo Ricci (Seventeenth Century)

The emergence of Protestantism further revealed the need for ecclesial reform within the Catholic Church. Of particular importance for this study was the creation of new religious orders to expand Catholic witness in the world. Ignatius Loyola helped form the Society of Jesus (the Jesuits) in 1540 partially motivated by cross-cultural missional aspirations.[33] The seventeenth century was an outstanding triumph for Jesuit expansion: Roberto Nobili in India, Matteo Ricci in China, and Alexander de Rhodes in Vietnam.[34] Among these, Matteo Ricci is a good example of a marketplace witness.[35]

Ricci is well-known as one of the first contextualists, adopting the look of Confucian scholars seeking to win the Chinese intelligentsia and to make Christianity understandable in the Confucian culture. To do so, he adapted indigenous cultural forms into his Christian witness. For example, he chose the existing Chinese terms for God (*T'ien* and *Shang Ti*).[36] He allowed the context to influence the forms of the Christian faith. Additionally, he combined his highly contextualized missionary tactics with his marketplace skills as a "mapmaker, translator, watchmaker, and general scientist,"[37] which helped him plant a church that stood the test of time. At his death, there were four hundred converts. Within fifty years, another one hundred fifty thousand were added to the Catholic fold. Ricci made a difference in the Chinese understanding of Christianity that continues to influence Christianity in China today.[38] Thus we note movement from little emphasis on work to Luther's call to serve in one's present position to active use of skills to accomplish the spread of the gospel.

31. Taylor, *After God*, 65–66.
32. Stevens, *Other Six Days*, 74–75.
33. Irvin and Sunquist, *History of the World Christian Movement*, 112–23.
34. Banchoff and Casanova, *Jesuits and Globalization*, 175.
35. Pocock et al., *Changing Face of World Missions*, 233.
36. Kim, *Strange Names of God*, 29.
37. Pocock et al., *Changing Face of World Missions*, 233.
38. Latourette, *History of the Expansion of Christianity*, 339–42.

The Moravians (Eighteenth Century)

In the Protestant world after the Reformation, there was little thought of cross-cultural missionary activity outside of Europe.[39] A popular view of Lutheran orthodoxy in the sixteenth and seventeenth century among the Protestants was that the command of Christ to preach the gospel to all the world was satisfied by the apostles.[40] However, the Moravians presented a contrast to these trends. During the eighteenth century some missional movements arose in terms of integrating self-supporting economic activity and missions, including evangelism and church planting. These developments included the Moravians, the Wesleyan/Evangelical revival, and later, Hans Nielsen Hauge's work. These movements served as a "launching pad for Protestant missions."[41] At the close of the nineteenth century, due to the influence of these groups, the European colonies, North America, and Norway witnessed a phenomenal growth of converts as new Christian communities came into existence.

Perhaps the Moravians were the best-known eighteenth century example of integrating faith, work, and economics.[42] In the wake of the Reformation, Protestants tended to emphasize the Creation Commission (stewardship and human development), but on the eve of the Evangelical Revival, the Moravians began to spread cross-culturally as they faithfully sought to live out the Great Commandment in obedience to the Great Commission. Influenced by the mission of Hans Egede to Greenland, beginning in 1732 the Moravian churches stepped into missionary work. The Moravian community sent out their missionaries to the island of Saint Thomas, in the Caribbean, to establish a mission for African slaves.[43] After one of the missionaries used his carpentry skills to support himself, other missionaries soon followed his example. Later all Moravian missionaries were expected to support themselves financially and give any profit they earned from their endeavors to the mission;[44] this was an early example of tent-making.

The Moravian economic model for missions eventually resulted in the establishment of a large commercial operation in Suriname, on the northern

---

39. The reasons were (1) the disputes among the Protestants, (2) consolidation of doctrines and stabilization of the church, and (3) *Cuius regio, eius religio*, which means that in each area the ruler is responsible for the spiritual welfare for his people. Winter and Snodderly, *Foundations of the World Christian Movement*, 370; Scherer, *Gospel, Church & Kingdom*, 67.

40. Bosch, *Transforming Mission*, 249.

41. Winter et al., *Perspectives on the World Christian Movement*, 370.

42. Pocock et al., *Changing Face of World Missions*, 233.

43. BAM Global, "Business as Mission and Church Planting."

44. Danker, *Profit for the Lord*, 34.

coast of South America. The Moravians discovered that business could function as a means of gospel proclamation via a relational connection. To illustrate this concept, the missionaries found it easy to talk about the gospel with African slaves who worked in a tailor shop. Later, in Suriname, the establishment of seven churches (with a total worshipping attendance of thirteen thousand) and a department store fostered holistic transformation.[45] In this way, the Moravians skillfully combined evangelistic efforts with trade and industry, not only providing for their own support, but also employing the local people and teaching them spiritually.

John Wesley (Eighteenth Century)

Through the influence of the Moravians,[46] John Wesley also pursued a public society, i.e., having churches accessible to all—clergy, lay people, and unbelievers—and he promoted economic justice in order to form Christ-following communities. Yet, when Wesley realized there were large groups of people who were not coming to church, he went to where the masses gathered—the market place, the brickyards, and the coal mines—in order to bring them the gospel. For Wesley, the spread of the gospel included the practice of what Theodore Jennings calls "evangelical economics,"[47] or having/earning money to assist our neighbor, reflecting Wesley's teleological "inward and outward holiness." Thus, Wesley emphasized proper stewardship of money as a means to care for the poor and the marginalized. He exhorted the early Methodists "to gain all one can, save all one can, and yet give all one can"[48] in order to glorify God through the sharing of goods. His own business life and ministry illustrated this. For example, Wesley operated his own successful printing shop to disseminate spiritual writings and pamphlets along with his famous book on medical care called "Primitive Physick."[49] He also "set up apothecary shops so that they [Methodist communities] could buy the best available treatments of the day at the affordable prices."[50] One estimate proposed that Wesley earned as much as thirty

---

45. Spaugh, "Short History of the Moravian Church."

46. Wesley admired Moravians: "You are not slothful in Business, but labor to eat your own Bread, and wisely manage the Mammon of Unrighteousness, that ye may have to give to others also, to feed the Hungry, and cover the Naked with a Garment." (Wesley, *Works*, 5:166).

47. Jennings, *Good News to the Poor*, 111–16.

48. Wesley, *Works*, 10:150.

49. Wright, *How God Makes the World a Better Place*, 71.

50. Wright, *How God Makes the World a Better Place*, 71.

thousand pounds (six million dollars today) from his business.[51] Almost all of this money Wesley invested in the broader Methodist movement, an example of using business profits to support a mission.

The spark generated by Wesley's entrepreneurial approach or because he owned various businesses, eventually spread rapidly to the American frontier. Methodist circuit riders, such as Francis Asbury, traveled to locations where pioneers lived and worked, and, consequently transformed people's lives for the better, politically, socially, and spiritually.[52]

Hans Nielsen Hauge (Nineteenth Century)

A lesser-known example of the integration of entrepreneurship and holistic Christian outreach is Hans Nielsen Hauge (1771–1824). Hauge, a Norwegian, was instrumental in transforming his homeland into a more modern and economically thriving Christian nation in the eighteenth century and early-nineteenth century.[53] In 1796, at the age of twenty-five, Hauge's journey to faith began when he suddenly felt assured of his salvation. This spiritual encounter spurred him to act: he began sharing his message of assurance with others.[54] Traveling through Norway and Denmark for eight years, he preached about the importance of having a personal commitment to the Lord. His preaching resulted in the creation of several spiritual societies relationally connected with Hauge as senior leader.

In addition to emphasizing spiritual renewal, Hauge also saw the need to educate and equip people for employment. For Hauge, running a business and preaching were inseparable; both were helping people. He had an

---

51. White, "Four Lessons on Money," 24.

52. One good example is that Wesley and nineteenth-century Wesleyanism argued against the vile practice of slavery. In his sermon "Thoughts Upon Slavery," he put slavery in a historical context but then quickly spoke against the common myth that people are saved through slavery by bringing them out of a terrible place. He did this by describing Africa before the slavers came. He spoke about how the Africans were procured, making sure to talk about how appalling it was and was nothing like Christian salvation. In order to abolish slavery, Wesley not only published letters against the evil of slavery but also assisted the abolitionists in their cause to have Parliament outlaw slavery. Wesley's argument had a considerable impact on the evangelical movements of nineteenth-century America. According to Dayton, Charles Finney continued the movements begun in England by Whitefield and Wesley (Dayton, *Discovering an Evangelical Heritage*, 88). Wesley was a great evangelist who called for the reformation of humankind. He not only fought against slavery, but he also brought a great deal of impetus to the female role in social and Christian ministry through his revivalism (Dayton, *Discovering an Evangelical Heritage*, 92–93).

53. Arntzen, *Apostle of Norway*, 5.

54. Wee, *Haugeanism*, 22–24.

amazing capacity to identify potential business opportunities and for the work required to establish the business. All this business acumen combined with his pioneering spirit, made him an entrepreneur par excellence.[55] During the years 1800 to 1804, he established one hundred fifty industries across Norway, including "fishing industries, brick yards, spinning wheels, shipping yards, salt and mineral mines, waterfall harnessing, paper mills and printing plants."[56] These innovative industries not only were a source of employment for a modernizing people, but also taught them how to support themselves by doing something other than farming. In turn, Hauge's religious zeal and aptitude for business resulted in Norway becoming the foremost model for spiritual, social, and economic transformation.[57] Hauge's work serves to illustrate the interconnectedness between entrepreneurial activity, spiritual renewal, and pathways for holistic transformation.

SUMMARY OF THE HISTORICAL OVERVIEW

The way that economic activity has been incorporated with church planting has changed across time, in part influenced by the level of economic development. What is readily apparent in consideration of Celtic missionaries, The Benedictines, and the Nestorians was their willingness to travel to evangelize and to establish long-term residences. They seemed to have valued work and were good stewards of what they produced as well as showed concern for their neighbors.

A significant shift is notable when we reflect on the spiritual and economic activities in the sixteenth century and beyond. One of the notable achievements was Luther's elevation of the concept of calling, i.e., everyone is to serve in one's station in life. Thus, calling was expanded to include more than just priests and monks. Luther illustrated the value of secular employment with his print shop business as it provided the means to distribute his writings more widely and offered a few jobs. Although a Jesuit, Ricci expanded the realm of Catholic witness by going to China. But more notably, Ricci laid the groundwork for a contextual ministry by adapting indigenous cultural forms into his evangelizing efforts with great success. In the world of work, he used various skills, *viz.*, mapmaker and watchmaker, to reach out to the local community.

Of the remaining three groups and individuals singled out for consideration, the Moravians are significant missionaries and churchmen. Their ministry was distinctively cross-cultural, going into the Caribbean and into

55. Yates and Eijnatten, *Churches*, 264.
56. Saxby, "Revival-Bringer."
57. Lim, "Norway."

South America; there was clear emphasis on the Creation Commission. Besides, they were early practitioners of tent-making; and they demonstrated a clear concern for social remediation as businesses were open to provide employment opportunities. Similarly, both Wesley and Hauge funded their ministries through good stewardship of the money their businesses earned and both sought to help needy neighbors. These three illustrate how the door to various forms of missionary work, from evangelism to the creation of jobs for the poor to increased literacy, was opening more broadly.

THREE EMERGENT MISSIONS/BUSINESS MODELS

The historical discussion revealed occasions where groups or individuals participated in the *mission Dei* by being marketplace workers, as well as being involved with the community economically, evangelistically, and socially. We note that elements of the models associated with business and evangelism/missions are found: Tent-making where earnings/profits fund church planting and evangelistic activities; Business for Economic Development of what has become known as Business as Mission; and the Holistic Transformation Business model. These models draw upon R. Paul Stevens's work, *The Other Six Days: Vocation, Work, and Ministry in Biblical Perspective* and Stephen B. Bevans and Roger Schroeder's work, *Constants in Context: A Theology of Mission for Today*.

Stevens in his book connects human work to God's work and His three great callings: The Creation Commission or Cultural Mandate (Gen 1:26–28), the Great Commission (Matt 28:19–20), and the Great Commandment (Matt 22:37–38). He depicts this connection as a three-layer cake of callings. The first layer is the Creation Commission as God the Father works in creational stewardship which is foundational as it addresses the issues of creation and human development. The second layer is the Great Commission as God the Son works in reconciling human beings with God and others, furthering the Kingdom of God by making disciples. As man violated the relationship with God in the garden, redemption for man was needed or a way to effect reconciliation of man to God. The third tier is the Great Commandment that represents God the Holy Spirit working to transform and complete our relationships to God, humanity, and the earth.[58]

Additionally, models that emerge from Bevans and Schroeder's book summarize the theology of mission under three models: (1) mission as saving souls and extending the church, (2) mission as discovery of the truth, and (3) mission as commitment to transformation. As the labels suggest, the orientation of each model is different. The focus on saving

---

58. Stevens, *Other Six Days*, 118–23.

souls and extending the church reflects the fundamental belief that mission is subject to the church. This view places a significant emphasis on the church.[59] This model is suggestive of the earliest held view of missions. Mission as discovery of the truth recognizes that as new approaches are tried and new locales are visited, truth also is learned. We find in this model the belief that people can learn if the right circumstance is created. Thus when missions in the form of businesses (as this is the most common option used) are established, people have the opportunity to learn a skill and to become a more productive individual. Thus as Christ's redeeming love is accepted by individuals, it allows people to realize their potential.[60] For missional work in the twenty-first century, the last model indicates awareness that transformation is needed in missional work as social injustice and poverty are so widespread.

These models postulate that even though the church received and participated in the same three mandates (the Creation Commission, the Great Commission, the Great Commandment) throughout history, communities of faith and Christian innovators addressed these three commissions differently with varying emphases (economic development/stewardship, evangelism/discipleship, social transformation). These three emphases are found in some of the popular mission's models currently being practiced, see Table 2. Additionally, these elements contribute to an expansion in the number of churches and mission societies, reaching out to people in non-Christian lands for purposes of gospel proclamation, conversion, and church planting.[61] These approaches/models will be discussed below.

Table 2. Three Models for Missional Practice

Model	Emphasis
Tentmaking	Evangelism/Discipleship
Business for Economic Development	Economic Development/Stewardship
Holistic Transformation Business	Social Transformation

---

59. Bevans and Schroeder, *Constants in Context*, 31.
60. Bevans and Schroeder, *Constants in Context*, 59, 61.
61. Scherer, *Gospel, Church & Kingdom*, 36.

Tentmaking Model

Luther pushed the envelope when he advocated all believers have a calling to witness wherever they are. Wesley similarly did not limit his preaching to the pulpit, but rode a horse to reach areas unchurched or walked to the nearest gathering of lost souls. Wesley realized the people he sought were not commonly going to be found in church pews. This continues to be true as a growing number of Americans are unchurched and, especially since about 80 percent of countries won't let avowed missionaries enter their country.[62] Tent-making "is using daily-life strategies to tell people about Jesus."[63] Given the economic developments that have occurred world-wide, life for most people revolves around the marketplace where they get their income, self-identity, social contacts, and a sense of purpose or in other settings where relationships are formed where people exchange value with one another.[64] Consequently, the marketplace is an ideal place to meet people where they can see Jesus in action. However, what tent-making keeps front and center, is that their activity is not solely about money, it is also about God. It permits tent-makers "to put Jesus in front of those who have never had an opportunity to hear the truth about Him"[65] without stepping inside a church.

Whether we think of the Apostle Paul, Ricci, the Moravians, Wesley or Hauge, we see people doing work that provides their livelihood, but also being on the front line where Jesus is visible. In 1985, the Lausanne Tentmaking Statement was written, recognizing the role of Christian lay people in the operation of tent-making as they possess the skills and abilities to operate a business.[66] Since then, many mission agencies have used the "tent-making" model. The relationship between business and the church is illustrated in Figure 1 where church planting is nested within the business activity.

---

62. Siemons, "Vital Role of Tentmaking," 121.
63. Lai, *Tentmaking*, 4.
64. Moon, "Entrepreneurial Church Planting."
65. Lai, *Tentmaking*, 3.
66. See Lausanne Movement, "Lausanne Statement on Tentmaking."

Figure 1. Tentmaking Model

Despite their income generating activity, personal conversion and a viable indigenous church planting program were regarded as the goals of Tentmaking endeavors.[67] Tentmakers place a high premium on the importance of helping others to develop a personal relationship with Jesus and with other Christians. They have focused upon evangelistic labor or the realization of the Great Commission by means of reconciliation or discipleship.

While there are many aspects that commend tent-making, there is a downside to this model. This approach can be less holistic as less attention and fewer resources are applied to economic sustainability, structural problems and social justice concerns in the larger society where one's work is located. Furthermore, this view does not appreciate the world as the place where God is active; rather, the world is seen as having degenerated into "a sort of ecclesiastical training-ground"[68] and was defined as "not-yet-church, already-church, still-church and no-longer-church."[69] Finally this model may impede work performance because work itself is only seen as a means to an end;[70] thus, there is less motivation to do one's work with excellence as a means in and of itself to honor God. This false distinction

---

67. Winter and Koch, "Finishing the Task," 71–72.
68. Hoekendijk, "Church in Missionary Thinking," 324.
69. Hoekendijk, "Church in Missionary Thinking," 324.
70. Ott and Wilson, *Global Church Planting*, 324.

has historically had a deep impact on Christian views of wealth, faith, economics, and mission.[71]

Business for Economic Development Model or Business as Mission

The next model that emerged chronologically was the Business for Economic Development. Late in the twentieth century this model joined the tentmaking model as a way to use business in missions. The theme of Business for Economic Development was simply economic development done by Christians in an area; these words were taken as its definition. The thought was that in less developed and least-reached countries, which are often hungry for business acumen, jobs and income, Christian business people would enter. One of the distinguishing characteristics was that once businesses for economic development were established, other businesses would follow to add to the markets of economically challenged parts of the world.

During this time, the concept of *missio Dei* rose in popularity, undoubtedly due in part to the Willingen Conference (1952). The pendulum of theological understanding of Christian mission has swung from the church-centered view to the theocentric view of mission. In the *missio Dei* concept, mission is no longer subject to the church alone; mission has its source in the Triune God. The church is viewed as an agent for God's universal outreach as the mission becomes the church's reason for being. However, interpretation of the theocentric conceptualization of mission has varied. On one hand, some have proposed that, even though the church should be neither the starting point nor the goal of mission, the church, as a foretaste and of the kingdom, is the agent of God's mission.[72] On the other hand, others, supporting the world-centered view of mission, argued that the true context for mission was the world and not the church. So the correct sequence is "kingdom-gospel-apostolate-world."[73] Consequently, the church and the kingdom of God were viewed as separated from each other, especially in ecumenical circles.[74]

Alongside this ecumenical mission thinking, the concept of Business as Mission (BAM) came on the scene, espousing similar views. BAM has been broadly defined as business ventures led by Christians that are for-profit and are intentionally designated to be "used as an instrument of God's

---

71. Stevens, *Other Six Days*, 75.
72. Newbigin, *Gospel in a Pluralist Society*, 233.
73. Scherer, *Gospel, Church, and Kingdom*, 97.
74. Hoekendijk, "Church in Missionary Thinking," 334.

mission to the world."[75] In countries seeking established businesses to bolster their economy, BAM's unique approach has created doors for missions. Many BAM practitioners understood that the world was regarded as the locus of God's mission. As a result, the church was increasingly relegated to a marginal position within the BAM community.[76]

Different from most tentmakers, BAMers intentionally focus on working through an organized business to find meaning in what they do. Thus, work itself is seen as a calling[77] and BAMers describe the economic activities as being missional. Practitioners are missional in the way they are involved in the community, because it is at this local level, where economic, social and spiritual transformation occurs. They not only find economic enterprises that draw on local strengths, enabling people to become financially independent, but in the process creatively expose others to the Gospel, e.g., Dayspring Technologies discussed in chapter 4, resulting in financial, social, and spiritual growth. Other BAMers seek to model biblical values in the marketplace by focusing on ethical business practices and providing jobs to women and other marginalized groups.[78] Figure 2 presents the framework for BAM by depicting the business as the central core, and from the center comes wider social and spiritual development.

Figure 2. Business for Economic Development Model

SPIRITUAL **BUSINESS** **SOCIAL**

---

75. See Johnson, *Business as Mission*, 28.

76. Scherer, *Gospel, Church & Kingdom*, 108.

77. Stevens, *Other Six Days*, 77; Johnson, *Business as Mission*, 485; Sherman, *Kingdom Calling*, 102.

78. Tunehag et al., "Business as Mission."

From these considerations, it can be inferred that many BAMers focus initially on ensuring the foundations of business effectiveness such as financial sustainability[79] and the realization of the Creation Commission. Miroslav Volf describes it as a "vocational understanding of work developed within the framework of the doctrine of creation"[80] or stewardship. In other words, BAM practitioners place church planting as just one part of the larger role of serving greater human development needs. Consequently, many BAM practitioners have a financial focus, emphasizing financial sustainability, profitability, and larger scale operations—the typical financial metrics of success such as return on investment, return on assets, compound annual growth rate, or internal rate of return.[81]

One problem in BAM's approach is that it might downplay the importance of the church. The church is relegated from its status as the mystical body of Christ to that of *a* body of Christ, meaning that it is only one of several sacred venues advancing the Kingdom of God. Additionally, the Business for Economic Development view tends to campaign strongly for individual calling over against the conceptual framework of being a people of God. In this way, individual calling is placed above the embodied community. More specifically, this model so closely identifies one's specific job as his or her calling that it may result in identity crisis if, for some reason, one loses his or her job or skills, be it through dismissal, retirement, or medical disability.

Holistic Transformation Business Model

The focus shifts to a form of ministry that is more inclusive, one that includes social, spiritual and developmental activities, in addition to the business or economic orientation of the Holistic Transformation Business Model. The church in the Holistic Transformation Business model (HTB) intends to offer loving relationships—with God and with others, in contrast to the client-based, market-driven relationships found in the world and in other models.

---

79. Yamamori and Eldred, *On Kingdom Business*, 73, 75; Tunehag et al., "Business as Mission."

80. Most discussions of work in the "business for human development" view have tended to focus on seeing work as one's vocation, as one's calling, because most Christians start with the creation account in Genesis where God is seen as at work, and we, as bearers of God's image, are called to work as well (Volf, *Work in the Spirit*, ix).

81. See Ready Ratios, "DuPont Formula." Many businesses also have a set of key metrics such as the "DuPont formula" that they keep a close eye on. The DuPont ratios are helpful in business to explain how the return on equity (ROE) is obtained by using the following equation: ROE = Return on Sales x Asset Turnover x Financial Leverage. Businesses can focus on this combination in order to predict positive Return on Equity (ROE).

The HTB model pursues on-going contact with potential believers and emphasizes the need to listen to what they are saying.

In recent years, Volf's pneumatological understanding of work[82] has been influential resulting in the view that Christian business in partnership with the community of faith can be a means to overcome materialism, individualism, and self-centeredness.[83] We find activities that combine lean startup business principles[84] and a church planting vision. A mounting body of literature is developing regarding Holistic Transformation Business, categorized by various expressions: Fresh Expressions of Church and missional communities. Holistic Transformation Business model is freshening the religious landscape of the global North with an ever-increasing variety of sites and approaches to reach the unchurched, from sport gyms to neighborhood groups.

One core theological principle of the Holistic Transformation Business model is the belief in a "kingdom-shaped church" that emerges from the interaction between the church planting activity and business activity as shown in Figure 3. The kingdom of God gives rise to the church, which is taken to be a sign of the coming kingdom. Here the essence of the church can be defined as four interlocking sets of relationships: (1) participation in the *perichoretic* (mutual indwelling) Trinity, (2) fellowship within the local church, (3) joint participation in the Trinity with the whole body of the church, and (4) the mutual giving and receiving between the church and the world.[85] Because the Holistic Transformation Business model contains interactions among these four relationships, it highlights the realization of the Great Commandment by means of social transformation of a community/society.

---

82. Volf suggests an alternative, a "pneumatological one developed within the framework of the doctrine of the last things" (Volf, *Work in the Spirit*, ix). He proposes that we frame the way we think about work in terms of the centrality of eschatology in Christian faith and that we think of work in terms of the Spirit inspiring us in every step of our lives as we walk forward toward the full coming of the Kingdom, the New Creation.

83. Moynagh, *Church In Life*, 14.

84. Lean start-up, led by Steve Blank and Eric Ries, is a revolutionary methodological shift in entrepreneurial practice that makes starting a business far less costly. Lean start-up is unconventional in that it favors experimentation over elaborate planning, customer feedback over intuition, and iterative design over a large development policy (Blank, "Why the Lean Start-Up Changes Everything," 66).

85. MPAC, *Mission-Shaped Church*, 96–98; Moynagh, *Church for Every Context*, 104–14.

Figure 3. Holistic Transformation Business Model

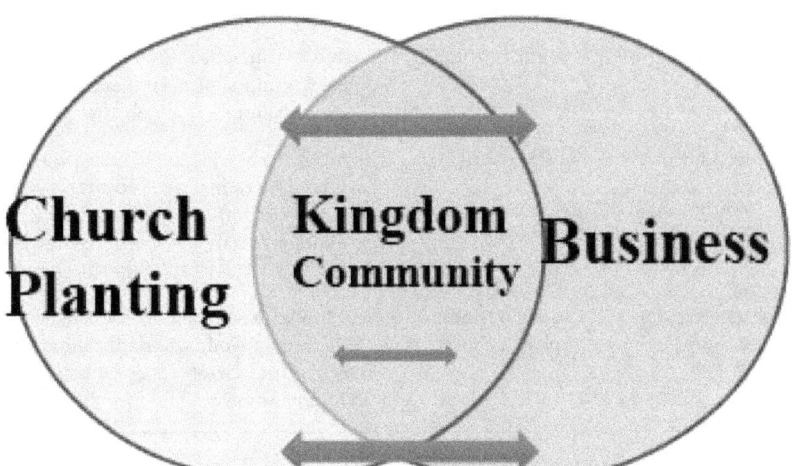

In short, the Holistic Transformation Business model recognizes that God's reign in the world is unthinkable without the church.[86] The church can help build an ethos of mutual civic responsibility and accountable communities of discipleship where temptations of greed, self-centeredness, and materialism are confronted. Additionally, at the core of Holistic Transformation the Business model is a focus on spiritual, social, and economic transformation. Transformation happens as churches are planted and businesses are established that create an environment where people can connect with God, others, and the rest of creation. There is one risk with this model that Snyder has identified: there are differing understandings of God's kingdom with accompanying differences in the ideas of the calling of the church.[87] He presciently remarked that the forces of "globalization/glocalization" call for a renewed model of the Kingdom of God with regard to ecology and economics.[88]

Thus far, we have reviewed the literature on three models of economic-social-ecclesial engagement: (1) Tentmaking, (2) Business for Economic Development, and (3) Holistic Transformation Business in the recent application of ECP. A summary of similarities and differences among these three analytical lenses is reflected in Table 3 below:

86. Engen et al., *Good News of the Kingdom*, 73.
87. Snyder, *Models of the Kingdom*, 13–17.
88. Snyder, *Models of the Kingdom*, 140–41.

Table 3. Comparison of Characteristics of Three Examples of Faith/Work Interaction

Models	Archetype	Orientation	Activity
Tentmaking	tent-making	church-centered, Great Commission, cross-cultural	Christians use a professional skill for job, disciple people
Business for Economic Development (BED)	business-oriented	theocentric/ world-centered, Creation Commission, Cross-cultural	Create profitable businesses with concern for public corporate responsibility & eco justice
Holistic Transformation Business (HTB)	sustain business & plant a church	foretaste of Kingdom of God, Inter-cultural, Great Commandment	Establishing good relationships whether for business or for the church

Scrutiny of the table reveals several ideas. The tent-making model is the only model that is decidedly church-centered, while the others have broader-based spiritual concerns, *viz.*, foretaste of the Kingdom of God, Creation Commission and the Great Commandment. Tent-making is more individually oriented than is BED with its focus on an entire business entering the market place. HTB is radically different from the other two models with its emphasis on the establishment of relationships in business or in the church. Proponents of each model claim cultural sensitivity, but it would be insightful to ascertain the level of cross-cultural awareness actually demonstrated.

IMPLICATIONS FOR ASSESSMENT

With an overview of their defining characteristics and operation as well as any drawbacks of a model, I want to consider how each of these models would be evaluated, i.e., how their outcomes are measured. For the Moravians, the focus was simply on the number of converts and that the businesses remain viable. Three hundred years later assessment has become more refined. Evaluation is seen as a tool to keep ministries fruitful by being able to identify stagnant or ineffectual ministries. Now, there is more emphasis on ways to measure outcomes or goals of the various components of a ministry.

As we turn to consider assessment of tentmaking endeavors, there is a focus on personal conversion and a viable indigenous church planting movement.[89] Tentmakers place a high premium on the importance of

---

89. Winter and Koch, "Finishing the Task," 71–72.

Three Church Planting Models of Integrating Faith, Work, and Economics 41

helping others so as to lead them to develop a personal relationship with Jesus and with other Christians. They have focused upon evangelistic labor or the realization of the Great Commission by means of reconciliation or discipleship, often measured by numbers of converts. As a result, many tentmaking ministers use spiritual metrics of success: (1) how many people have heard the Good News, (2) how many people have been converted, (3) how many have been baptized and joined the church, and (4) how many converts have been disciple.[90] However this last question is emphasized less. One of the reasons is that many ministers focus on membership (quantitative metrics) rather than discipleship (qualitative metrics), which is the core of Jesus's Great Commission to his disciples (Matt 28:19).[91]

Another assessment tool that many tentmakers use is the three-self principle developed by Henry Venn (1867) and Rufus Anderson (1869) for guiding the development of church plants; three "selves" refer to self-governing, self-financing, and self-reproducing.[92] Typically the three-self principle has been used as a yardstick for all church planting initiatives, and success is measured based on the level of indigenous leadership, financial viability, and church reproduction. The three-self principle, however, focuses more on inculturation and vitality of church plants, i.e., qualitative issues, rather than on mirroring the social, cultural, and economic outcomes.[93] As a qualitative measure is a more subjective measure, data collection, and the results must be carefully examined.

With regards to the Business for Economic Development, we find a different emphasis in assessment. BAM leaders mainly adopt existing financial reporting systems such as the ISO 2600, the Global Reporting Initiative, or Global Compact.[94] These standards emphasize measuring economic, social, and environmental goals alone, leaving the spiritual aspect untouched.[95] Consequently, Yamamori and Eldred note that profit-making and humanistic achievement become the primary standards of assessment for BAMers.[96]

The last model to consider in terms of its evaluation approach is Holistic Transformation Business. Given the holistic emphasis, measures of the activities of the church/business are compared with measures of the relationships found within the ministry. For example, the following relational

---

90. Rundle, "Does Donor Support Help or Hinder Business," 24–25.
91. Rendle, *Doing the Math of Mission*, 12.
92. Kim and Kim, *Christianity as a World Religion*, 40–43.
93. Rendle, *Doing the Math of Mission*, 9; Moynagh, *Church in Life*, 375.
94. See Bimba, "Business as Ministry Assessment."
95. Eldred, *God Is at Work*, 202.
96. Yamamori and Eldred, *On Kingdom Business*, 287.

questions are asked: "Does the Bible study help the members of the church walk beyond the church's walls and get connected to the lost?"; "How far would our business help the non-churched cultivate their relationships with God?"; "How do you relate to other churches/businesses?"; "How do you know members of the church relate with others outside the church?"; "How far, would our church advance a foretaste of the kingdom?"

Thus, the church in the Holistic Transformation Business model (HTB) intends to offer loving relationships—with God and with others, in contrast to the predominate consumer-oriented relationships found in the world and in other models. As the HTB model pursues on-going contact with potential believers and emphasizes the need to listen to what they are saying, measures of these activities are also used. Relationship becomes the central concept because business and church planting occur within the contexts of relationships in the larger community. The primary standards of assessment for the Holistic Transformation Business model are levels of interpersonal connectedness and relationship with the neighborhood.

To help pull the discussion together, the models are identified along with their primary archetype, their orientation, and activity, consistent with the discussion on each of the models in Table 4 (see the next page). Overview of the key issues in evaluation are listed in the column entitled "Success Metric." The table reveals some similarities and differences among the models with regard to the success metric. It needs to be recognized that in reality, more indicators than those listed, would actually be used to determine success. To begin with, we note a similarity between Tent-making and BED. Both reduce their assessment to quantitative elements. Of course, it is not as easy to count souls saved or the number disciple as it is to detect closing a business year in the red or black. However, quantitative approaches may miss the imperceptible elements of those in the process of transformation.

On the other hand, the HTB model emphasizes intangible components such as transformed lives and community. However, HTB is uncertain concerning the pathway to achieve its success, that is, it is not sure how to measure success. In sum, there are problems for finding metrics to evaluate ECP since the metrics for Tent-making, BED, and HTB presently are not effective or clear nor do they address the issue of relationships; Tent-making uses mostly spiritual metrics of success; BED tends to employ financial metrics of success; and HTB regrettably is not sure how to measure its success and performance. Furthermore, we see the integrated place of the church in both tent-making and in HTB related to success metrics. While implicit, all three of these models open the door for laity to have a full role in the outreach activities, even to the point of discipling and leading a church.

Table 4. Comparison of Characteristics of Three Examples of Faith/Work Interaction

Models	Archetype	Orientation	Activity	Success Metric	Problems
Tentmaking	tent-making	church-centered, Great Commission, cross-cultural	Christians use a professional skill for job, disciple people	# hear gospel, # saved, # discipled	limits God's reach to just the church, doesn't deal with structural financial, & social justice issues, work as means to end
Business for Economic Development (BED)	business-oriented	theocentric/world-centered, Creation Commission, cross-cultural	Create profitable businesses with concern for public corporate responsibility & eco justice	profitability and financial sustainability	church relegated to edge of the world, job = calling
Holistic Transformation Business (HTB)	sustain business & plant a church	foretaste of Kingdom of God, Intercultural, Great Commandment	Establishing good relationships whether for business or for the church	sustain financial and church activities, build relationships	Uncertain pathway to achieve Success, not sure how to measure success

In sum, these three church planting models of engaging faith, work, and economics have helped us to understand the utility of a joint venture—church planting and a business enterprise. Common to Tent-Making, BED, HTB is the need to reach out to others, and, hopefully in doing so, establish relationships with people. None of these models indicate how to maintain balance between church planting and business activities, so this issue continues to be a discussion point. The different goals lead to different outcomes making comparison of models more difficult. To actualize the goals of economic fruitfulness and church planting, a literature review revealed that we might need to take into account aspects of all three types (Tent-Making, Business for Economic Development, Holistic Transformation Business). The assumption is that these models need each other for the creation of a truly novel church that is economically sustainable; a conglomerate is thus needed to liberate these models from leaning too closely on a one-sided goal of economic fruitfulness or church planting to the detriment of the other. In this way, it is anticipated that balance may be achieved by the integration of three theological emphases (the Creation Commission, the Great Commandment, and the Great Commission).

SECTION SUMMARY

This section examined ECP's historical and theoretical underpinnings. The historical sampling reveals that a characteristic method of engaging the unchurched and unreached peoples has been through community contact, although after the Industrial Revolution marketplace witness became more common. In other words, in the overall history of the Christian movement, God has used critical individuals, movements, and ideas in each era for the creative expansion of His Kingdom by combining economic activity with church planting and missions. These historical perspectives are now re-emerging at the cutting edge of God's global mission.

As the historical basis of ECP was investigated, we discovered three models of integrating faith, work, and economics in church planting. This section helped us understand that there are problems for finding metrics to evaluate ECP, the amalgam of the three models, since the metrics for Tent-making, BED, and HTB presently have not been clearly operationalized. Specifically, tent-making uses mostly conventional measures of spiritual success; BED tends to employ business-based metrics of success; and HTB is still in its infancy in terms of identifying and measuring components it equates with success. Thus, the historical review demonstrates why this study is needed to evaluate the holistic dimensions of ECP activities. Furthermore, this historical basis directs us to know where to collect data and what data to collect. This will be the topic of the next chapter about data collection.

3

Methodology

INTRODUCTION

THIS SECTION DETAILS HOW the research was conducted. Included are the key research question and assumptions, the research design, and ethical considerations.

RESEARCH METHODOLOGY

The research question that is the focus of my study is: What metrics are ECP practitioners currently using to measure the performance and the effectiveness of church-planting efforts when combined with business models to develop a holistic framework. Furthermore, this research question seeks to know: how are practitioners combining business models, social development, and spiritual transformation statistics into a holistic framework.

The research question was based on three assumptions influenced by the literature on church planting:

1. Pastors and ministry leaders including many ECP practitioners tend to define success by quantitative measurements, such as the number of people attending services, financial collections, and number of programs offered.[1]
2. People tend to work toward what gets measured (and reported). Currently, those who use ECP as their mission model tend to utilize business metrics with a focus on profits or mission metrics with their emphasis on spiritual fruit, such as converts or attendance at church or church programs.

---

1. McNeal, *Missional Renaissance*, xvi–xvii.

3. The holistic nature of the gospel message associated with ECP, however, cannot be captured with business or mission metrics alone. Attention to interpersonal relationships and any changes in the relationships, conscious attempts of ECP personnel to interact with the neighborhood, and the occurrence of community transformation must also be noted.

These assumptions generated the following questions: (1) what is the primary goal of each ECP; (2) how do practitioners of ECP activities broadly define success; and (3) what are the metrics (implicit or explicit) that ECPs employ presently to gauge their performance?

With these questions in mind, I chose the case study method as a way to study both the surface manifestations of the operation of ECPs as well as the underlying processes. The section below details how the research was conducted to yield data so I could answer these questions. Discussion of the research method, the sample including both specific ECPs and the individuals surveyed and interviewed, data collection and analysis of the data, and ethical considerations are provided.

Research Design

Research design incorporates several aspects of doing research: methodology and the requisite steps to implement the method, unit of analysis, sampling procedure, and sample selection—both site and interviewee selection. The use of a case study approach frequently is complemented by the use of other methodologies, such as surveys and interviewees.[2] The Methodology section is concluded with a discussion of data collection and data analysis. In particular, data analysis and findings will be discussed in chapter 7 on Model of Holistic Transformation.

Case Study

For my research, I employed a multiple-case study embedded design based on the methodological ideas of Robert Yin.[3] "The two primary characteristics of this design are constant comparison of data with emerging categories and theoretical sampling of different groups to maximize the similarities and the differences of information"[4] As Creswell notes, this design fosters the analysis of the interplay among the multiple units of analysis of ECPs, *viz.*, financial, social and spiritual foci, as well as the

---

2. Merriam, *Qualitative Research and Case Study*, 26–43.
3. Yin, *Case Study Research*, 40.
4. Creswell, *Research Design*, 14.

on-going comparison of findings as new cases are studied. These three key aspects of ECP are identified repeatedly in the literature as pivotal points in the operation of ECPs.

The multiple-case study embedded design allowed me to select cases in geographically diverse areas: San Francisco, California; Lynch, Kentucky; and Selma, Alabama. The opportunity to use three sites and in different regions of the country increases my external validity over a single-case study. The multiple-case approach is based on a "replication logic" and not "sampling logic."[5] Additionally, I can compare and analyze the three cases in relation to both church planting and business profitability as well as the degree of movement toward a holistic framework.

The decision to do a case study only creates the general framework without specifying the details of the research endeavor. Below is discussion of the unit of analysis, the stratified sampling procedure and the resultant sample, key variables and their operationalization, and explanation of survey and interview schedule development.

STEP 1: UNIT OF ANALYSIS AND SAMPLE SELECTION

Given the focus of my research question, the unit of analysis for my research was the individual ECP program. With the increasing number of ECP ministries in operation, it was necessary to narrow my attention to a few programs to find diversity in the ministries and locations as Yin noted:

> When using a multiple-case design, a further question you will encounter has to do with the number of cases deemed necessary or sufficient for your study. However, because a sampling logic should not be used, the typical criteria regarding sample size also are irrelevant. Instead, you should think of this decision as a reflection of the number of case replications. . . . For example, you may want to settle for two or three literal replications when the rival theories are grossly different and the issue at hand does not demand an excessive degree of certainty.[6]

To implement Yin's ideas, I looked for exemplary ministries that clearly incorporated holistic praxis, or had spiritual, economic, and social dimensions, as it is the desired model I wanted to study. Thus, the ECP programs needed to possess five specific criteria: (1) a Kingdom of God outlook; (2) economic sustainability; (3) small size of the business enterprise; (4) relational investment; and (5) social responsibility.

5. Yin, *Case Study Research*, 47.
6. Yin, *Case Study Research*, 51.

The criterion of having a Kingdom of God outlook was that the ECP endeavor sought to create an environment where people can connect with God, others, and the rest of creation across economic, social, and spiritual lines. Economic sustainability refers to a ministry that had survived for at least three years so it was capable of affecting and benefitting the community. The literature suggests that small to medium enterprises (SME)[7] have sufficient size to survive and account most significantly for job growth, so ECP practitioners tend to target this segment to allow them to grow their businesses and expand their influence. I wanted small businesses; The SME's in my research employed from three to thirty people. Beside size, previous research has indicated that personal relationships within the business are an important factor in the development of holistic ECP ministries.[8] Consequently, a potential ECP program had to have a structure and company culture where all employees intentionally invested in interpersonal relationships, e.g., mutual care between staff and clients, proper and early training for employees, etc. Lastly, the ECP program needed to demonstrate social responsibility by expressing a desire to help people in every aspect of their lives, be it financial, social, or spiritual, or a *Blessing orientation*.[9]

Beginning in 2015, I conducted a snowball search for anything and everything associated with innovative church planting through business. I searched the Internet using the keywords *the integration of business and church*, *Entrepreneurial church planting*, *bi-vocational ministers*, *business as mission*, and *Tentmaking*. My preliminary research revealed that there were sixty churches in the US operating as ECPs. However, the exact number using ECP program was unclear as there might be as many as one hundred other ministries using a tent making approach or a bi-vocational approach which might or might not use the ECP model. At the end, using the above criteria for ECPs, I found six sites that were suitable for study. The six sites were as follows: Copper River Grill in Nicholasville, Kentucky; The Table Café in Louisville, Kentucky; Meridzo Ministries in Lynch, Kentucky; Blue Jean Church and Arsenal Place Accelerator in Selma, Alabama; The Camp House, Chattanooga, Tennessee; and Redeemer Church in San Francisco, California.

Next, I explored whether the ECP was willing to participate in my research given the detailed study of their operation that would be required. Security concerns and other commitments eliminated three communities of

---

7. Eldred, *God Is at Work*, 167.

8. Lee, "Assessing the 'Success' of Business as Mission," 56–64; Lee and Conklin, "Conceptualization of the Relational Proximity Framework," 17–40.

9. Russell, "Use of Business in Missions," 247–48.

faith. I set up interviews with the three remaining ministries. The interviews confirmed that these three sites fit my criteria and demonstrated their willingness to participate in my research. The three mission endeavors selected using ECP represent three different inter-denomination organizations.

Consequently, the three sites selected are as follows: Meridzo Ministries in Lynch, Kentucky; Blue Jean Church and Arsenal Place Accelerator in Selma, Alabama; and Redeemer Church in San Francisco, California. Their characteristics with regard to the selection criteria are reported in Table 5 below.

Table 5. Description of Selection Criteria[10]

Name	Affiliation	Type of Ministry	Sustainability	Size	Employees	Relational Investment	Social Responsibility
Meridzo Ministries	Southern Baptist Convention	Holistic manner through socio-economic engagement	19 years	SME	30	Hedge trimming, Cookie give-aways	Food bank, Black Mountain Exchange gas station
Blue Jean Church & Arsenal Place Accelerator	Independent	Church planting that is integrated with business in such a way that a synergetic revelation of the kingdom of God is provided.	11 years	SME	15	Community fellowship opportunities, Solidarity and representation in court	Business incubation, Drug rehabilitation, Job training,
Redeemer Community Church & Dayspring Technologies	The Presbyterian Church of America	The integration of business and church planting for the purposes of holistic transformation of the individual and the community	15 years	SME	20	The Isaiah 40 policy, Embodying the gospel through Sabbath remembrance	The Neighbor Fund, Job training & coaching

10. Given the security concern, their family names were not used. SME stands for Small and Medium Enterprises.

1. Redeemer Community Church and Dayspring Technologies in San Francisco, California. Danny Fong and Chi-Ming Chien began a new contextual church plant in a low-income area of the Bayview neighborhood on September 28, 2003, as part of the Presbyterian Church denomination. Shortly, a web development company, Dayspring Technologies, was founded by three church members of Redeemer Community Church with a vision of opening up work opportunities to empower and motivate local youth to aspire to higher education and jobs. The company presently hires sixteen employees and has a revenue of $1.7 million. Redeemer Community Church also currently gathers a very diverse group of one hundred people each Sunday. The collective vision of the business and church has been to demonstrate the redemptive qualities of the workplace and economic exchange in order to bear witness to God's work in the world. Specifically, a combination of business and church planting provides ways of blessing others such as a policy of a 2:1 employer-to-employee salary scale or the Isaiah 40 policy, which binds people to one another, and eventually to God, in beautiful ways.[11] In addition, the business and the church express love to its neighbors in the community through the "Neighbor Fund"; this is relationship-based investing or relationship-based small business loans. These loans apply the principle of socio-economic reconciliation as a way of bearing witness to the reconciling power of Christ. The loan committee is participatory, meaning that borrowers sit on the committee and recommend loans to be made to other borrowers. They want to break down the barriers that exist between borrower and lender. A distinctive is that they want borrowers and lenders to become friends. This is done through the sharing of a meal in order to promote an atmosphere of camaraderie. Something unique happens as people fellowship around the table. In this way, Dayspring and Redeemer believe that God is actually at work reconciling all things to himself through Jesus for his Kingdom. Further, they are blessed by getting individuals to walk forward toward the full coming of the Kingdom through evangelism and discipleship. In particular, Redeemer Church and Dayspring Technologies provide some insight on how to work with the emerging generation of Millennials with their concern for holistic transformation.

---

11. The Isaiah 40 policy (2:1 employer-employee salary structure) will be discussed in more detail in chapter 4.

2. Blue Jean Church in Selma, Alabama. Blue Jean Church (BJC)[12] is addressing racial tensions and poverty by using multifaceted capital in its holistic outreach to the community; their public witness includes business incubation, drug rehabilitation, job training, and community fellowship opportunities. By embracing a model of church life that goes beyond the four structural walls, BJC seeped out into the marketplace, the neighborhood and the public space. In this way, BJC provides a unique case study to investigate the possibilities of social transformation in American religious life. Furthermore, it reveals an ecclesiology of public life in the context of multicultural neighborhoods.[13] BJC gathers a very diverse group of two hundred people each week. Services are held in the same building.[14] Bob Armstrong, a founder of BJC notes, "We are black, white, rich, poor, middle class, addicts, bank presidents, the mentally handicapped, doctors, lawyers, blue collar workers, unemployed, young, and old. We are fully integrated."[15] BJC is currently trying to extend their vision and recruit interns through academic partnerships with Asbury University, Asbury Theological Seminary, and University of Alabama. Twenty-two interns have already participated with BJS over the last three years.[16] The vision is to foster more partnerships of holistic transformation and Kingdom expansion.

3. Meridzo Ministries in Lynch, Kentucky. Struck by the poverty and economic limitations characteristic of Lynch during a visit, the Rileys returned in 1999.[17] After a period when their only action was to simply show kindness to their neighbors, they slowly established various businesses and ministries. A church plant was established in 2005. What started off as a meeting of the Meridzo Ministries staff has evolved into a friendly public place for people from all walks of life to gather together for praise and worship, Bible study, and fellowship. This church gathers a group of thirty people at 11:00 a.m. Sunday Services. Non-believers are encouraged to come together and seek a better understanding of who God is. The fundamental goal of the Rileys in their ministry in Lynch was to address both the spiritual hunger and physical needs they found. The Rileys realized that sharing

---

12. Henceforth, BJC will be used in place of Blue Jean Church.
13. Hull, "Come Back, Christianity," 86–88.
14. Moon, *Intercultural Discipleship*, 200–201.
15. Armstrong, "Proposal for the Millennial Project," 1.
16. William, personal conversation with the author, June 13, 2018.
17. Riley et al., *Miracle in the Mountains*, xv.

the gospel was going to be more effective than presenting the gospel. As few opportunities developed for broad-based sharing the gospel, the Rileys implemented a one-on-one approach as they trimmed hedges and passed out cookies. These actions demonstrated human caring, empathy, and love of the Rileys for their neighbors. One of the first activities they pursued was to address the physical needs of the people, since the people were already aware they had these needs. The establishment of a food bank was a larger and more concrete act to alleviate people's hunger. Addressing the food needs of people could be initiated by the Rileys and required little personal investment of the people of Lynch, except to stop by and collect food. All of these activities fostered the establishment of relationships that were formed from one-on-one contact. Additionally, the lives the Rileys lived out reflected hope and transformation; their embodied narrative showed their continued connections to Lynch.

Another dimension of the Meridzo Ministries was that the Rileys were lively participants in the life of the community. People saw them daily as they sought to become integral members of Lynch. As they related sensitively to people in their context, authentic participation was taking place. So Meridzo Ministries' effectiveness can be summarized by a neighbor who thought that Lonnie had "put feet on Jesus." Currently, Meridzo Ministries has thirty employees, which they call "missionaries." While Meridzo Ministries has been in operation for nineteen years, economic revitalization has been accompanied by spiritual renewal, relational development, and social support in the heart of Appalachia. For example, Meridzo Ministries offered several outlets for sharing the gospel such as a functioning local church called Community Christian Center. It also created businesses such as Lamp House Coffee Shop, Black Mountain Exchange gas station, Faithfully Fit fitness center, and Agribusiness Center. Remarkably, the ministry has resulted in significant transformation of the Lynch community. In particular, Meridzo Ministries offers a grassroots understanding of success based on holistic transformation encapsulated in Kingdom relationships ("loving God and our neighbor"). In light of an emphasis on relational development (love for God and neighbor), the collective work of Meridzo Ministries demonstrates an effective ministry centered on holistic networks of stewardship and whole-life discipleship. People who initially responded to friendly gestures recognized in time the transformative power of God's love. In sum, Meridzo Ministries started with one solitary act, but the continuing response to local needs done in a God-glorifying way helped turn despair into hope, economic need into jobs, and inadequate income into good stewardship.

This small but varied sample, along with the data collection, provided substantial depth of information about each site. Table 6 contains information about my visits and interviews. I visited each of the three sites multiple times. Most of the visits occurred in the warmer months, so the type of activities would be comparable.

Table 6. Site Visits and Interviews

Site	Redeemer Church San Francisco, CA	Blue Jean Church Selma, Alabama	Meridzo Ministries Lynch, Kentucky
Visits	January 28–31, 2016 January 26–28, 2019	May 10, 2015 June 25–July 1, 2016	April 15, 2017 June 6–11, 2017 October 29, 2017

For the next strata of my sample, individuals within the ministry, I used nonprobability based sampling; I intentionally selected individuals who served at different levels and in various aspects of the ministry to complete the survey. This approach guaranteed responses providing comprehensive coverage of the ministry. When the chosen individuals signed their Consent Form, I asked them to complete the survey. Subsequently, I intentionally selected administrative leaders, volunteers, and community members to complete my sample. The same process was repeated at each ECP site. In all, thirty-five surveys were completed, and thirty-five structured interviews were done. The use of both surveys and interviews yielded responses from more people. As interviews provide an opportunity to ask follow-up questions and clarify answers, I preferred interviews over surveys as a way to collect information. Analysis of the data collected confirmed the value of interviews for the insights they furnished. I considered surveys as more supplemental sources of data. More specifically, I was able to complete thirty-five interviews in all: ten from the Redeemer Church, eleven from the Blue Jean Church, and fourteen from Meridzo Ministries. With repeat visits to each of the sites, some people were interviewed more than once.

Methodology 55

Step 2: Variables and their Operationalization

Dependent Variables

It is commonly recognized that case studies do not revolve around the operation of variables, but primarily focus on the operation or process of the unit being studied. Most of the information collected is simply background information or a description of how the enterprise operates. Similarly, this study of ECPs is not variable oriented. The exception are the metrics the ECPs use to evaluate their outcomes in the areas of business, mission and social concerns. As these metrics are self-defined, there is no way to operationalize them at this point.

Similarly, a significant goal of this research is the development of a multi-dimensional scale to measure the outcomes of ECP holistic ministries: spiritual/mission, business, and social. As the discussion continued four growth factors are identified that fostered activities in the evangelistic, economic, and social domains. Discussion and identification of indicators is the subject of chapter 7, where the indicators are operationalized. In turn, these domains nurture the relational outcomes of: becoming a good neighbor, becoming a part of God's family, economic vitality, and enhancing human capital. These concepts are discussed and located within the larger operation of entrepreneurial church planting in chapter 8. Indicators are provided for the measurement of the outcomes in Table 21 of chapter 8. It would be premature to define these concepts at this point.

Independent Variables

Given the high reliance on verbal description as opposed to statistical description in a case study, there are few independent variables. The literature I used made few suggestions on what were essential independent variables to include in a study.

- Number of Years of Operation [of the ECP]—Response to Question 11 in the survey will be used: "For how many years has this business been operating? ____ years." The number supplied by the respondent is the value used in the analysis. If there is no response, ninety-nine will be entered.
- Initial source of startup capital [for the ECP]—Response to Question 13 in the survey will be used: "Where did the startup capital come from?" Eight responses were provided. The responses were coded as follows: 1—My own personal funds; 2—The founder's personal funds;

3—Loans from donors and other friends; 4—Equity stakes sold to investors; 5—My mission agency; 6—Grants/donations; 7—Not sure; 8—Other; 9—No response. For options 6 and 8, space was provided for a written answer as to the source of the funds.

- Length of time at the ministry (at the time of data collection)—Information collected during the interview will provide a numeric response to this question. The categories and coding will be as follows:
- 1—from the start of the ministry; 2—more than ten years; 3—more than five years to ten years; 4—four or five years; 5—two or three years; 6—six months to one year; 7—less than six months; 9—no information. These categories will be collapsed for analysis given the sample size, but greater precision in actual data collection will permit this variable to be used in statistical analysis, such as correlation.
- How did you become involved in this ministry? From journal and interview notes the response will be determined. The information will be coded as follows: 1—I was a founder or worker at the beginning of the ministry; 2—the ministry invited me to work for them because of my skills or abilities; 3—I applied for a job and was hired; 4—I came as a volunteer and was subsequently hired; 5—I came as a volunteer and I'm still a volunteer; 9—no information is available.
- Paid/Unpaid Worker—Not all workers at a ministry are paid; many volunteers come to assist the ministry for various lengths of time. The variable will be coded: 1—paid (I receive a paycheck from the ministry); 2—my income is provided by my supporters; 3—not paid; 9 = no information is available.
- Type of Work—While some of the ECP ministries strive to down play the presence of a hierarchical structure, it is inevitable that there are different types of work done to keep the ministry functioning. Information about the individuals job type will be determined from their interview. The variable will be coded as follows: 1—manager or supervisor; 2—staff (support workers to managers or supervisors); 3—worker; 9—no information.

It may be as data is collected, other variables are identified as helpful to study variations in responses. These will be introduced and discussed in chapter 7 in the analysis section.

Methodology 57

STEP 3: THE USE OF TRIANGULATION OF METHODS

The case study method permits both the collection of a lot of information as well as considerable depth of information about each ECP. However, there is nothing implicit in the case study method about how information is collected. Thus, I used surveys, interviews and participant-observation to collect data. Below is a discussion of the specific steps I took to do this study. Incorporated in the discussion is the use of other methodologies, surveys and interviews. The triangulation of methods provided offsetting perspectives, broad coverage of the ministry and helped to neutralize any of my research biases.

   a. *Survey Construction*: I was able to find many survey questions from existing research on the topic of Tentmaking and Business as Mission. Based upon this literature review, I wanted to use survey questions developed by Steve Rundle for ECPs in order to compare my findings with what other researchers discovered.[18] So I reworded existing questions and added questions to tap other topics.

   To ensure that I had questions to cover all essential topics, I identified key areas on which I wanted to collect information, e.g., theological focus, practical experience, performances in assessment, and their informal ministry. Then within each general area, I listed the specific information I needed. Next, I determined the demographic information needed to categorize respondents, such as gender, ethnicity, educational background, amount of training in the business/ministry they were trying to do. Other relevant information not included in other sections of the survey I developed questions for are length of time involved in the ministry/business, their understanding of kingdom-based business/ministry.

   In the actual survey, the first section dealt with background information such as family, education, and business experience. The next section addressed respondents' business/ministry such as level of financial support for business/ministry, steps for setting up the business/ministry, and their goals. The last part consisted of questions on economic, social, and spiritual performances. I pretested the group of questions in The Asbury Marketplace Summit[19] and queried subjects

---

18. See Rundle, "Does Donor Support Help or Hinder Business."

19. The Asbury Marketplace Summit is a conference open to the community that unites students, pastors, business and community leaders, and academicians to discuss faith, work, and economics in the marketplace and how social entrepreneurship carries out Kingdom-minded initiatives using the business approach. See http://www.asbury-project.org.

about what they thought the questions were asking. [I later realized that seminarians were sufficiently dissimilar to my study participants, and that several of my subjects did not understand the questions nor why some questions were asked. Supplemental introduction at the beginning of the survey and the addition of an explanation of the importance of various sections might have improved my completion rate.]

b. *Interview Development:* As I did for the survey, I drew upon Mark Lowery Russell's existing interview questions[20] and modified a few questions to be more appropriate for my research. Especially, I added questions specific for people who had differing relationships to the ECP ministry, e.g., such as founders, workers, and supervisors as well as community people external to ECP programs. My hope was that these questions would provide both an insider's perspective and an outsider's perspective of the ECP's operation. I put the questions on different colors of paper to help me differentiate between the different sets of questions. The interview questions were ordered to enhance the participant's recall of the sequence of events in the establishment of the business/church activity, respondent's motivation and goal of the ECP model, their definition of success, and ways of measuring success. Some of the questions address their businesses philosophy and their theological focus and their operating philosophy. Lastly, other questions handle the perceptions of people toward the ECP program and the impact of the ECP program on local people.

c. *Participant Observation:* Participant observation represents a continuum from fully involved as a participant, but observing to a full observer with minimal participation. My vantage was closer to being a full observer with little involvement. This orientation let me to observe each of the ECP programs and from these observations to further explore the ministry. First, through observation, I sought to discover if the ECP organizational structure reflected their stated goals. For example, do they say they want local involvement but operate with paternalistic attitudes? Additionally, during periods of observation I intentionally noted the relationships between Christians and non-Christians and between managers and subordinates. For example, if an ECP practitioner has the stated goal of investing in people's lives so that they become a Christian, does she or he spend valuable on-the-time job with other people or does he or she spend very little time with people in the community? If so, why? Finally, I participated and

---

20. See Russell, "Use of Business in Missions."

observed church worship service and other religious gathering related to each ECPs. The goal of this observation was to understand the relationship between the ECP program and spiritually oriented activities. Additionally, I wanted to know if they had a worship service at the place of business and whether other local Christians, affiliated with the business, were involved in the worship service.

Step 4: Data Collection

From the time I arrived at each of the three sites, I was making observations about the site, from its appearance to the neighborhood it was located in to my reception when I arrived. These observations I recorded in my journal consistent with being an observer. I continued to make journal entries during each of my visits to each site. Together with the interviews, this information informed my discussion of each site.

Surveys were administered during the first visit I made to each site. The survey I used is in Appendix C. Previous correspondence had alerted me to who the founder was and the organizational leaders of each site were. At Redeemer Church in California, I administered ten surveys, eleven at Blue Jean Church in Selma, and fourteen at Meridzo Ministries in Lynch, Kentucky.

Interviews were my primary data collection tool. Each potential interviewee was given a Consent Form to read and sign. The questions that guided the interview are found in Appendix B. Interviews were conducted with the founder(s), organization's leaders, volunteers, and community members outside the operation of the ECP. When the ECP had established relationships with community organizations, as was the case in Selma, Alabama, I interviewed the founders about the nature of the relationship between their organization and the church, including the positives and negatives of the relationship.

Obviously, each interview would not generate equally useful information, but I sought to collect contextual information, attitudes expressed, noted attitudes manifested, and impressions I had of each ECP. Information from the interviews, corroborated from my journal notes, is the basis of my discussion of each specific site or chapters 4–6.

Lastly, the data from my observations vary, but primarily fall into three categories: contextual information, attitudes expressed or manifested, and impressions I have of the operation of each ECP. Journal notes enhanced my interpretation of the interviews. I have over 200 pages of journal notes.

Step 5: Data Analysis

Given the nature of the data I planned to collect, I intended on calculating descriptive statistics on the data from the surveys and any codified data from the interviews. However, with a moderate response rate from those completing the survey, my goal to analyze the survey data was set back as I cleaned and coded the often-incomplete surveys. With so few completed surveys, the results would not be representative of the entire group of subjects. Journal notes and the use of cross-case analysis served to cross-check my identification of key themes and reduce the occurrence of researcher bias.[21] Given the interview questions I asked, the themes that emerged were: goals and vision associated with the ECP, definitions of success, and ways of measuring success. Specifically, utilizing Anselm Strauss and Juliet Corbin's coding process: (1) open coding, (2) axial coding, and (3) selective coding),[22] I first transcribed all interviews. Transcriptions facilitated content analysis of the comments, particularly to identify statements that address goals and visions associated with kingdom-based activities that would lead to desired outcomes. I then manually coded every transcription through line-by-line analysis and discovered 1,702 codes in the process of open coding. In the analytical process or axial coding, I continuously looked for patterns and recurring themes across the respondents. At times I grouped the responses based on the relationship the individual had with the ECP. I then compared responses. Content analysis enabled me to note any patterns of action and recurring themes. With the written text of the interviews, comparison of statements based on the relationship the individual has with the ministry (e.g., primary organizer, managers, workers/volunteers, etc.) could be made. As a result, I came to categorize twenty subcategories. In the process of selective coding, several themes or categories in each case study were emerged. The key characteristics among the three ministries will be presented on chapter 7 on Model of Holistic Transformation.

ETHICAL CONSIDERATIONS

Regardless of the type of information collected, it must be collected in an ethically responsible manner. The primary ethical considerations are: guarantee of anonymity or confidentiality to the respondent, informed consent for participation, no physical or emotional harm to participants and some positive benefit for participating in the research, respect for privacy,

---

21. Bryman and Bell, *Business Research Methods*, 300.
22. Strauss and Corbin, *Basics of Qualitative Research*, 57.

accurate recording and reporting of the data and debriefing of respondents. These concerns guided the conduct of my research.

Institutions provide an additional level of protection to respondents by requiring approval of research by the Institutional Review Board. I applied and my research was approved by the Asbury Theological Seminary Institutional Review Board. As was required by the IRB, I prepared a Consent Form for all respondents in which they gave their permission for me to use their information. The Consent Form provided a clear and concise description of my research, so each participant knew the type of information to be collected and how it would be used. A copy of the Consent Form is in Appendix A. I have a signed consent form from each of the research participants.

An important provision mentioned in the Consent Form is the guarantee of anonymity or confidentiality. I promised each respondent anonymity. I have provided this by assigning each participant another name. Situations and contexts have been adequately disguised so their identity cannot be determined from the discussion. Recordings of interviews and transcriptions of interviews are kept secured. All data are kept on my personal computer which is password protected. Upon the approval of my dissertation, I will secure all recordings that include identifying information on my computer and any digital recordings.

I did not feel that the information I was collecting was emotionally charged so that any psychological harm would occur to a respondent. The IRB concurred with this assessment in the form of their approval of my research. Concerns about physical harm were not germane to this research.

To guarantee that no harm come to my subjects, I did not report observations of respondents to their superiors nor did I let anyone read the comments of other respondents. In this way, no one could be directly or indirectly harmed by their comments. Additionally, I doubt anyone would feel guilt or shame for the observations they made during interviews as there were no consequences occasioned by their comments. Benefit from their comments came in the form of providing me a more thorough understanding of what makes for a successful ECP and what to include in a metric to measure a holistic transformation.

As noted in the section on research methods, I have sought to process answers to interviews in a way to retain the true content of what was said. By double checking the transcriptions I have sought to reflect accurately what people said. In this way, I have tried not to subtract from or add to the information from interviews. Subjects were not formally debriefed, but I permitted them to ask me questions about the nature of my research and how I would use the results.

SECTION SUMMARY

This chapter addressed the research methodology I used in my study of three ECPs. I have tried to describe and explain the various steps I took as I implemented my research. The sites were chosen based on their overall effectiveness with regards to their economic, social and spiritual activities. Doing a case study of each of the three ECPs endeavors, I supplemented the information I collected from observation with surveys and interviews. The discussion concluded with the ethical guidelines that governed my research.

What follows in the next chapter is an analysis of a case study of Redeemer Community Church and Dayspring Technologies in San Francisco, California that integrates business with mission. This will be followed by two other case studies that demonstrate the use of various paths to narrow the gap between the Kingdom of God and "a not-yet-redeemed world."[23]

---

23. Hays, *Moral Vision of the New Testament*, 198.

4

Case Study of Redeemer Community Church and Dayspring Technologies

IN THIS CHAPTER, THE discussion moves from a consideration of the theoretical (chapter 2) and methodological (chapter 3) to current ECP activities. Even though there are numerous non-profit organizations standing in solidarity with the disenfranchised, one area that has not been as widely studied is holistic transformation tied to an entrepreneurial church plant. This chapter and the two following chapters seek to identify and discuss the factors that result in economic development and sustainability, church growth, and social development, along with consideration of ECP effectiveness. Simply put, the hermeneutic that is used for these three chapters is to ascertain how each ECP operates and measures its success. For our analysis, less emphasis and attention are given to other elements of ethnographic information.

INTRODUCTION[1]

Our first case study is an ECP located in San Francisco, California: Redeemer Community Church/Dayspring Technologies, a joint venture of both a church and a business. As we consider its goals and accomplishments, what becomes evident is the importance of interpersonal relationships. This ministry illustrates one of many paths to achieve the ultimate goal of an entrepreneurial church plant: effective evangelism.

The approach used in the study of the first of three ministries is to identify basic elements of the financial, social, and spiritual components

---

1. A part of this case study was previously published in Lee, "Can We Measure the Success and Effectiveness."

that contribute to its functioning. As our study becomes more comprehensive in chapters 5 and 6, these elements are then discussed more thoroughly. As noted in chapter 3, Yin suggests this approach when doing a multiple-case study.[2] Thus as subsequent ministries are analyzed and more specific information is provided, comparisons are encouraged and new factors relevant to the operation of an ECP are identified.

BACKGROUND INFORMATION

To approach this joint ministry historically, Dayspring Technologies, a successful Web development company, started in 1997. The firm is located in the Bayview/Hunters Point neighborhood of San Francisco, CA. Ethnically diverse and with the highest concentration of youth in the city, Bayview/Hunters Point is in the southeast corner of the city where unemployment and households below the national poverty level are nearly double, compared to the rest of the city; the poverty line is $23,000 for a family of four. The economic disadvantages of the area are accompanied by high crime rates. The rate of violent crime in assaults was 444.9, compared to the national average of 282.7. The coming of a business looking to hire local people was viewed positively.

Redeemer Community Church (RCC) started in 2002 and shared the Dayspring location. Their first thought was how they might share space and address the welfare needs of the local neighborhood. They moved ahead together establishing both the church and the business with a common address and an united desire to be a blessing to the area.

Groundwork for the founding of a church had been laid by Danny and Chi-Ming when Grace Fellowship Community Church developed a non-profit community development program, Grace Urban Ministries, in Bayview/Hunters Point. With an abundance of young people, they led a youth group in the community. RCC pastored by Danny Fong came to the neighborhood as an outgrowth of Grace Fellowship Community Church. Both Danny and Chi-Ming were also co-founders of Dayspring Technologies. Thus, from the beginning the leaders had a vision and an understanding of how the joint ministry could work. They wanted to demonstrate the redemptive qualities of the workplace and the economic exchange in order to bear witness to God's work in the world.

With close to half (47 percent) of the community having only a high school education or less, Danny and Chi-Ming recognized that the young people contacted through Grace Urban Ministries had a distinct social and cultural ceiling to their goals. The duo wanted to raise the aspirations

2. Yin, *Case Study Research*, 40.

of the teens to consider college and enter into professional jobs. Dayspring Technologies had a vision of opening up work opportunities to empower and motivate the youth to seek higher educational and jobs. So RCC was planted in the Bayview/Hunters Point neighborhood to work with the community's youth and families.

RCC was not laboring alone in the neighborhood. The church was able to fellowship and share ministry with Cornerstone Missionary Baptist Church, Shekinah Christian Fellowship, and Providence Baptist Church.[3] In 2005, RCC was first introduced to the Ekklesia Project whose goal was to connect the church's scholars to area pastors and laity to strengthen the church and encourage one another. Members from RCC have served on its board and planning committees.[4]

Involvements more directly linked to the neighborhood include Open Door Legal—"pioneering the country's first system of universal access to legal help"[5]—and Jubilee Immigration Advocates in San Francisco. Reflecting the ethnic diversity of the neighborhood, RCC supports ECWA Theological Seminary in Nigeria, Justo Mwale Theological University College in Zambia, and Seed and Light International Sunrise Ministries in Cambodia.

To promote fellowship and integration of the community, the church runs six Life Groups, smaller communities where people seek God and one another, located throughout the Bayview/Hunters Point area. Additionally, RCC created several groups specifically for middle and high school students: small groups are held Friday night and, on Sunday, there are several groups that meet at 9:15 a.m. There are additional groups to serve adults. Besides these sessions, there is a Sunday worship service.

All the activities the church has started with the original sixty people in attendance plus those who have been added as time passes, especially the Sunday activities, revolve around the church. Yet, evangelism and spiritual growth are not limited to just the church, but occur in a variety of settings, including Dayspring Technologies. The minimal growth in the sanctuary doesn't disturb the leadership, as the church itself is just one evangelistic site.

The church started with sixty people in 2002; in 2019 there were one hundred and twenty people. Diagram 1 shows church growth from its inception. To fight the tendency to evaluate the church solely in terms of attendance, little attention and time are devoted to monitoring this statistic. In the last four years for which information exists, steady growth is evident.

3. http://www.redeemersf.org/about.
4. http://www.ekklesiaproject.org/about-us.
5. http://www.opendoorlegal.org.

In fact, when I asked for annual church attendance figures, there were no known figures from 2003 to 2015, except for 2013!

Diagram 1. Church Attendance, Selected Years

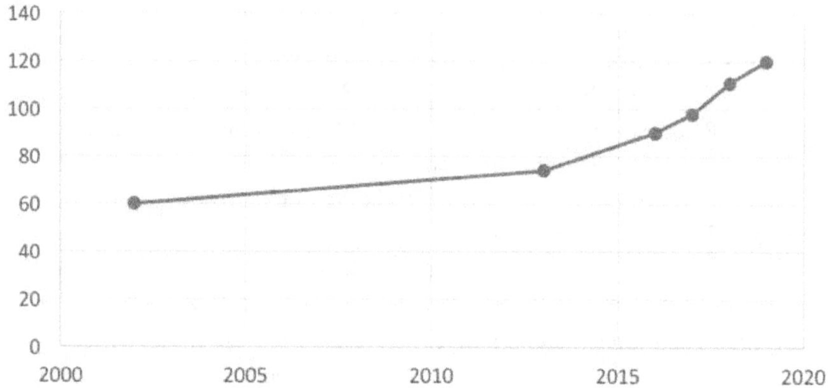

Evidence that the ministry has not stagnated, a new ministry was started in 2017, Rise University Preparatory, an independent Christian school serving grades six to twelve. Some of the teachers are also church members and many of the children have an affiliation with the church. The school day runs from 9 a.m. to 5 p.m., so despite the socio-economic level of the home, all children can have access to extracurricular activities and homework tutors. What further integrates the school with the neighborhood is their academic program is based on partnerships with local businesses. The tie to local businesses allows the school to offer unique educational opportunities in project-based science, technology, engineering and mathematics or STEM. With an 8:1 student to teacher ratio, the academic program, and parental involvement, factors associated with student success are in place.

In an analysis of an ECP, we need to consider the place of the church when economic activities also exist. In this ministry we see the joint operation of church and business, although the business was established five years earlier than the church. The founders of both the business and the church came from within the Grace Fellowship Community Church, so they understood what the inclusive ministry would be run and what they wanted to achieve. As the business became established and was able to be a true partner of a church, i.e., able to offer employment opportunities and operate the Neighbor Fund, i.e., makes small loans to local people, we note their joint operation; both are involved in evangelism.

Deeper consideration of Dayspring Technologies reveals the operation of a redeemed work environment. This milieu is evident from day one of employment for an employee. Dayspring has intentionally organized its salary scale to better reflect a scriptural vision of economic distribution. A policy of a 2:1 employer-to-employee salary scale or the Isaiah 40 policy, has been implemented by Dayspring. As Scripture speaks of valleys lifted up and mountains brought low, the Isaiah 40 policy smooths the peaks in salaries throughout the company. They reduce the high-end salaries and boost the bottom end salaries. This practice specifically illustrates the love of neighbor in the workplace (The Great Commandment).

Additionally, a transformed work space is conveyed by the creation of a positive work environment. Staff comments have consistently pointed out that Dayspring lacks the political environment so common in the working world. For example, one employee said:

> Dayspring care about their clients, the people in the community that we serve, but they also care about their employees. One of the things that I've liked most about Dayspring is that before I even joined, they set up this structure that every Friday, they have half an hour of company time for people to reflect on how they're doing. Sometimes it's half an hour of individual time. You can go somewhere and think about how the past week has been. It's an intentional slowing down. No company in Silicon Valley would say, "I'm just going to give half an hour free time to my employees," because they're losing money. That's just one of the things that I've seen them intentionally set aside as a structure to look out for the well-being of their employees. I think it makes me appreciate work more when I have a chance to pause and reflect like, "Why am I working?" It's because God gave this for me to enjoy or He blessed others. It gives you a chance to slow down.

In this way, workers were aware of the altered or redeemed environment. The practice of "rank and yank" is not found at Dayspring; in the "rank and yank" workplace structure, all the people on a team are ranked and the bottom 10 percent are yanked, meaning they are laid off. Dayspring rejected this practice. Of course, Dayspring Technologies pursues excellence, but brutal competition is a mark of the worldly market, and not of the kingdom of God.

A lack of divisiveness generates the feeling that you do not need to stand watch to guarantee your own well-being. One anecdote showcases this. A new staff person was assigned to a project that entailed working with a new client. As the employee worked, he accidentally deleted most of the production database; all the e-commerce orders, going back for about decade were deleted. All the teams stayed late working alongside this staff person. While the worker was devastated and thoroughly dejected, the teams were actually able to recover most of the data from backup, but there were still some lost orders. The client was informed about the mishap.

This was another way of practicing trust in God. Afterwards, Chi-Ming had a conversation with the staff person. They were standing, waiting for the elevator, and the staff person was completely depressed. He basically said, "I feel completely worthless." By the grace of God, Chi-Ming was able to reassure the staff member. He helped him to recognize that the staff member's own well-being, and the well-being of the company were not tied up in what had happened. It was ultimately in the hands of a sovereign and loving father who knows all that we need. And so, by the grace of God, Chi-Ming was able to tell that person, "Your worth is not tied up in your work. Who you are is not your work. Who you are is that you're a beloved child of God." The staff person ended up working with the company for another seven years until he took a job elsewhere. The client remains with the Dayspring Technologies eight years later. In this way, Dayspring Technologies shows that if Jesus is Lord, we are freed from the need to secure our own well-being. Thus, Christian business leaders are capable of nurturing an environment where people do not feel the need to watch their own backs. Instead, a generous community can be formed in which neighbors flourish by having their needs met as a reflection of the holistic gospel.

Beside the workplace, similar ideas of Kingdom-oriented thinking also govern the marketplace. Dayspring attempts to embody the gospel through Sabbath remembrance. While the company esteems the value of work, the Sabbath boundary serves to prevent the idolization of labor. In this way, employees are encouraged to spend Sundays with their families and churches, resulting in a more balanced and spiritually vibrant schedule. To guarantee that the workload stays controlled, they structure their business in a way that attempts to limit the work week to forty hours and not require staff to work evenings or weekends. To enable this practice, Dayspring executives at times would turn down business opportunities in order to protect their staff and prevent over extending themselves. This is reflected in one employee's comment about how the management would respond to a client's request that would overburden the Dayspring workforce:

> Another company might value that relationship [with the client] so much that they would be willing to do anything in order to keep that relationship because if Dayspring says, "Sorry, we can't do that work for you because we don't have time." Then

that company might go somewhere else. We are open to say, "We can work with you on your projects on how to get it done, and maybe not all at the same time or whatever, but this is what we have to offer."

This practice honors God by resting on the Sabbath. In this way, an environment of righteousness and justice is cultivated. Thus the "rules" of produce more, work harder and longer do not determine the operating principles of this business.

Moving from reflections on the internal operations of the business, we want to determine the impact of Dayspring Technologies and Redeemer Church has on the broader community. From the start, the business and the church were concerned about how they could express love to its neighbors. One of the ways to support the neighborhood was to establish the Neighbor Fund (this is relationship-based investing or relationship-based granting of small loans). These loans apply the principle of socioeconomic reconciliation as a way of bearing witness to the reconciling power of Christ. The loan committee is composed of Danny and a few others who have already received loans. By involving previous borrowers there is an attempt to incorporate some neighborhood people making the committee more participatory, where existing borrowers make recommendations about loans to be made to other borrowers. Their goal was to break down the barriers that exist between borrower and lender and to see each other as people, perhaps even friends. To promote relating to each other as equals, the loan committee members and borrowers share a meal. Something unique happens as people fellowship around the table. Two committee members said as follows:

> Instead of requesting financial numbers, we ask borrowers, "Who referred you to Neighbor Fund? Who will say that you will pay for the fund?" In this way, we ask for the relationship. The value is to continue with the relationship as long as there is communication and relationship, then the money is a secondary thing.

> Because these people have [the] worst credit but believe that relationships are strong and that honoring the relationship will cause people to pay it back as opposed to [a decision based on] their credit score or something.

As this process occurs, borrowers and lenders become friends rather than two ends of an exchange. The practical dimension is that over a meal any difficulties in repayment can be identified and a remedy can be discussed.

In these ways, Dayspring and Redeemer believe that God is actually at work reconciling all things to himself through Jesus for his Kingdom.

In sum, Dayspring Technologies and Redeemer have reflected the Kingdom of God by embodying redeemed economies such as Isaiah 40 or in essence, shared access to the land and resources,[6] creating a supportive environment where people get connected, loved, and reconciled to Jesus and the community of faith so that the Holy Spirit may work to bring about a new creation. In other words, Dayspring Technologies and Redeemer use the integration of business and church planting for the purposes of holistic transformation of the individual and the community. As the light of the gospel radiates and business practices are centered on relationships, the combination where the Creation Commission, the Great Commission, and the Great Commandment meet for the New Creation occurs. This is reflected well in one of the employees of Dayspring Technologies' comment:

> I think . . . within the first six months . . . we got broken into and had some computers stolen. They broke in that fence, they smashed the glass, they broke in there. It started like that. Now we've got a school here where kids are walking to school. Later, the people who robbed us, their kids are in the school. It's not like that, but still just being in a place, staying there, getting to know the neighborhood. I think the fact that we get to do what we do with the school is the best thing, because our partnership with the church is great.

Thus, this study clearly shows that a combination of business and church planting can provide ways of blessing a local community, binding people to one another, and eventually to God, in beautiful ways, by getting individuals to walk forward toward the full coming of the Kingdom, the New Creation.

OUTCOMES OF THE OPERATION OF REDEEMER CHURCH AND DAYSPRING TECHNOLOGIES

Now to move beyond the operation of this ministry, we seek to analyze what has been achieved. Insight about their accomplishments came from Danny, the cofounder of Dayspring Technologies and the pastor of the Redeemer Community Church, as he considered the five questions listed below.

---

6. Christopher Wright uses the term "Redeemed Economies" (Wright, "Biblical Reflections on Land," 161).

Table 7. Key Issues and Responses of Danny Fong, Founder and Pastor of Dayspring Technologies and Redeemer Church

Questions	Response
What is the primary goal of the ministry of the Redeemer Community Church and Dayspring Technologies?	Bring glory to God and create a space where people can experience God's grace.
With regards to the business enterprise you have established, how do you define success?	Faithfulness in our business and the outflow of God's blessing into the neighborhood.
How do you measure success?	Living wage for Dayspring workers
	Create more jobs
	Ability to return money and time to the local community
	Equipping underserved adolescents
How do those metrics help you achieve the objectives you set out?	They provide standards whereby we evaluate our activities
What kind of story do you want to share with your denomination or friends?	Partnership built with the community

Earlier the link between the goals and visions associated with kingdom-based activities and outcomes was made. The goals of Redeemer and Dayspring are, according to Danny, to bring glory to God and create a space where people can experience God's kingdom through *relational reconciliation* with Jesus Christ based on the *relational expression* of love for God and others, occurring in *transformed business practices*.[7] Relational reconciliation refers to restoring relationship to self, to others, to the rest of creation, and to God through Jesus and the church (2 Cor 5:18).[8] The relational expression of love for God and others refers to the action that flows in the aftermath of spiritual reconciliation.[9] When our other relationships have been transformed, what emanates are behaviors and practices

---

7. Danny Fong, interview with the author, January 29, 2016. Their vision statement reflects the goal as well. See Redeemer Community Church, "Vision Statement."
8. Corbett and Fikkert, *When Helping Hurts*, 75.
9. Preece, "Threefold Call."

that reflect our right relationships to creation through stewardship,[10] or in the case of Dayspring and Redeemer, transformed business practices and socio-economic reconciliation.

Beyond the establishment of goals and activities, it is important to consider their theoretical definition of success. Unlike most church planters, Danny is critical of the thinking that equates success with quantities with kingdom advancement. He said:

> There is a way in which churches are evaluated by those markers such as the heads or the attendance of how many. The denomination asks me, I have just filled it out: how many baptisms, how many professions of faith, how many new members, how many in Sunday school, how many active members. They have all these numbers they want you to mark. In that kind of report, you don't know whether any of these people are growing in faith or how many of these people are true worshippers.

Most church planters assume that if they keep an eye on these three analytics—how much, how often, and how many—then their business/church plant will be successful. Instead, at Redeemer Church and Dayspring Technologies success is thought of in terms of "faithfulness" and "blessing." As Danny notes:

> We prefer the language of "faithfulness" to the language of "success." If people see what we do and notice it as "different" and "good" and "a blessing" and ask why, we tell them that it is Jesus and his church, the in-breaking of the kingdom. We would want friends and neighbors to see Redeemer and Dayspring as a blessing, that if we were not here, we would be sorely missed, that our presence makes a positive difference in the community.

Another also reported:

> I think for Redeemer one of the values is being faithful. Redeemer is not trying to grow bigger or to attract more numbers. Instead, they're trying to be faithful to what they believe the Gospel is, which is to be a testament to the world, to show what God's kingdom can look like. It's not about numbers, because that's what the culture of today cares about.

Thus, we find a greater focus on how peoples' lives are transformed by the integration of the church and business. There is concern to count success as Jesus did: seeing the lost redeemed and transformed. Too many times

---

10. Preece, "Threefold Call," 284.

entrepreneurial church planters can have large congregations and even have significant offerings, but as Reggie McNeal points out, there may be virtually no impact for the kingdom in the neighborhoods surrounding the church.[11] However, the intangible indicators of success suggested by transformed lives is not deemed relevant when seeking outcomes that can only be tracked or counted.

As we move to establish an operational definition of success, Danny helps when he says:

> With Daypsring we do have some measurements. We work hard so that the highest salary is not much more than twice the lowest salary in the company, meaning that the CEO is [paid] just a little more than twice the salary of the secretary. We want to pay a living wage, so that every worker can live in San Francisco. In order to do that, those at the top end of the salary scale need to be willing to take a lower salary than they might receive elsewhere doing the same work. We count it a "success" in your language, when we are able to add three employees a year for the last couple of years. Folks who are willing to choose us "despite" or "because of" this salary structure [are valued]. We give away 10 percent of our net income to the community. We give away 5 percent of our time that would otherwise be given to paying-client-work. Currently, the ministry focus of Dayspring is three fold: pro-bono work, supporting local small business, and equipping underserved youth [basic work etiquette, job etiquette, and work ethic]. Redeemer partners [with Dayspring] in the latter two.

Dayspring once again moves away from the typically used discrete, measurable concepts to determine success. The qualitative approach guided by the Holy Spirit manifests itself as Danny elucidates on their guiding principles for business assessment.

> Our metrics for Dayspring are business metrics [but] . . . we use them differently. Redeemer and Dayspring operate using a fourfold relational approach: (1) Are we operating in a way that manifests the love of God?; (2) Do our products and services provide healthy benefits to customers, the community at large, and the creation?; (3) Are the values of the Kingdom of God reflected in all business procedures (hiring, training, evaluating, rewarding, and dismissing employees)?; (4) Are the values of

---

11. McNeal, *Missional Renaissance*, xvi–xvii.

the Kingdom of God present in relationships with suppliers, distributors and contractors?

To take the analysis a step further, what drives their definition of success is relational righteousness where people are transformed through loving relationships with God and others. Relational righteousness is alluded to when Danny spoke about "work hard," "be willing to take a lower salary," "give away 5 percent of our time," "pay a living wage," "a policy of a 2:1 employer-to-employee salary," and "give away 10 percent of our net income to the community." Here Danny's focus is with the employees, but it is also in the supply chain and distribution channels. Along with that, another founder of Dayspring Technologies also said:

> [Our metrics are] justice, generosity, integrity, and mercy, partnership in the Gospel, dependence on God. Are we being faithful to those things? We think of the dependence on God and partnership in the Gospel as these foundational values. The books on the bookshelf justice, generosity, integrity, mercy, those were things we thought of what are the things that are important to us that if we weren't acting out of those [metrics] that we would no longer be Dayspring?

In this way, we see that there is a premium place on relational righteousness even at the cost of typical profit maximization strategies used by businesses. Yet this business thrives and is able to expand.

The common theme found in the four criteria Danny cited is relational connections: between *missio Dei* and human participation, between company and the creation, and between business and clients. There is intent to have business practices that reflect the basic relationship with God as they deal with other people and creation.

More revealing about the significantly different orientation of Dayspring is found in its non-business activities. When asked what story he wants to tell with regards to Dayspring, he responds with "partnership built with the community." He then talked about the Neighbor Fund.

> We want the relationships that form around the Neighbor Fund to be different than that of the typical bank or financial institution, not based on credit score and not just on whether you are making your payments. We want *partnership to be built up* within the community. Recently one of our loan recipients received a contract to deliver snack packs to the media for Super Bowl 50. She is a two-person shop, just she and her daughter. She did all the baking but needed help packaging. She called Dayspring to ask for help. Three Dayspring employees went

> over to help. When the media wanted to come out and take pictures of her, she called Dayspring and the other "supporters" to be part of the photo op because we were a part of her success. This is the kind of story that excites us. Not just that loans are made, but *the community is being built up*, neighbors are working together, *friendships are being formed*, and if it does so *across racial boundaries*, as it is in this case, we see all this as a sign of God's redeeming work.

The italicized expressions convey the relational connections to the community, especially to the community of faith, where trust and cooperation for the common good occur. A case in point is reflected in one subject's comment:

> I really do think [the neighbor fund] is developing relationships. For example, there's an African-American businesswoman who basically was one of our borrowers from Neighbor Fund. We were having dinner together with her. She basically said, "I initially got this. Somebody had forwarded the email about the Neighbor Fund saying, lending money, no interest. She along with her African-American other small business people, friends, looked at that and kind of laughed. Like what are they trying to pull? She was actually like I don't trust you because you're not from here. To me, you're a foreign entity, outsider and you're inserting yourself into this neighborhood and you're claiming to help. I don't trust that. I think we were through just meeting with her and actually ended up giving her a loan. We changed her mind set on her view of us. It turns out that her experience was that in this community. It's a very interesting community. There's poverty. It has come out of poverty. Also, home prices throughout the city are just skyrocketing. In this particular community, there were Chinese investors or representative Chinese investors going around and having done research on tax distressed properties to essentially offer cash your check the fire out the property way below market value, but to take care of the tax problem. There's a lot of mistrust from the African community towards people that look like me. I thought that that was a beautiful picture of the gospel in a gospel of reconciliation, that the four of us were sitting around a table eating dinner and that she was willing to share that story. I think there's concrete steps of trust and relationships that are being built or folks are willing to say these people are not trying to pull a fast one on you. There's a power that's different than the power of money that is working what they're trying to do.

From these relationships lives are being transformed to partner for living together well and to stand in solidarity with the people in need.

What emerges as the answers to the five questions about goals and outcomes are considered make it clear that success for this ECP is the focus on the relationship between Kingdom values and business operations in the workplace and marketplace, their relational connections with others through Jesus and the church, and their relational righteousness through God and others and for God and others.

DISCUSSION

Analysis of Redeemer Church and Dayspring Technologies was to identify factors that distinguished this missional endeavor and then to determine how to measure outcomes. The missional aspect was considered earlier in the paper as reaching out into the community, whether through Life Groups or Rise University Preparatory or as the result of RCC activities. Success for RCC is simply to reach out to people and show them Christ's love. Success for Dayspring featured paying workers a living wage, to support the local neighborhood through the Neighbor Fund and equipping the underserved youth to have bigger and bolder dreams. Following Danny's lead and the other subjects' comments, we identified a kingdom-based orientation for a qualitative assessment of success and effectiveness as they mention relational righteousness and relational connections. Guided by Danny's and others' comments, we note that there are three dimensions in how and what Redeemer Church and Dayspring Technologies seek to do: they generate a sense of belonging or relational connectedness, develop reflected love or relational righteousness, and recognize blessings or relational stewardship of resources. Figure 4 signifies the goal and the three outcomes of Redeemer and Dayspring Technologies.

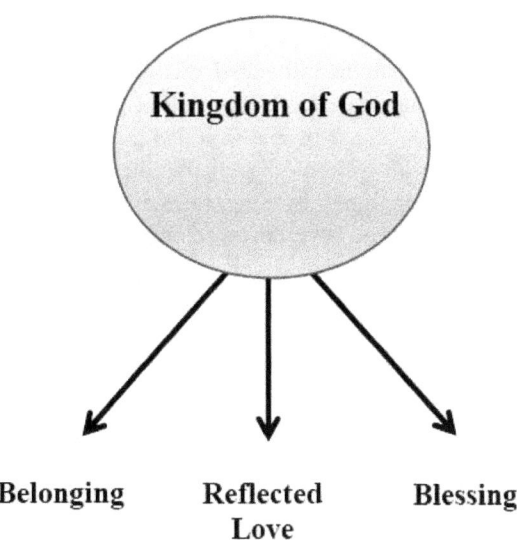

Figure 4. The Goal and Outcomes of the Redeemer and Dayspring Technologies

Three themes emerge: belonging, reflected love, and blessings. Belonging, a fundamental psychological need, is frequently the starting point for people's entrance into a sense of inclusion in the group. Welcoming others to fulfill the Great Commission requires God's people to have a relationship building orientation; however, it is no guarantee that others will respond as we wish them to. It is important to understand that belonging is a process, where the degree of interest in becoming a part along with actual participation is key. Therefore, it is incumbent on the church and/or business to provide Kingdom ministries that neighborhood people define as helpful and desirable and in which they can become involved; as neighbors are able to play helping others forward, they begin to develop a sense of belonging.

Next in the process of building a spiritual community, reflected love occurs where the love shown to others begins to be reflected back. In essence, people are being divinely loved into the Kingdom. One testimony of this occurring

> This neighborhood is primarily African-American historically, but it's changing as the whole Bay Area is changing with technology, money, because all of the—Silicon Valley, all of this is part of that. To live in the city as you know is very expensive. More and more people are being priced out and especially the African-American community who came here originally after

World War I and the beginning of World War II. This area, the Bayview-Hunters Point used to be shipbuilding. They would make warships to send out to the Pacific. A lot of African-Americans from Louisiana and the South, they came here to look for jobs. When the war ended, racism didn't end but they were isolated and segregated in this portion of the city and there were no jobs. All those people who had good jobs no longer had jobs and no one would hire them. Then you get the disintegration of a community when folks are not able to work, and slowly. Then, you have a drug epidemic that comes in and then you have the criminalization of drug. As a predominant Asian-American church in this particular neighborhood, it requires a long investment of trust because this neighborhood has been—Lots of projects come in here like we're going to change the neighborhood. Yes, because it's a needy neighborhood, so we're going to come in and change. When they come and then they leave. People are really tired of that. A lot of broken promises. Yes. That's why it just takes a long time for folks to trust that you're not just going to take up and leave. If you understand the pain and the brokenness and the issues and if they've seen that people are seen. Even though we've been here for fifteen years or more than that. We wouldn't keep going if we didn't feel like doors were not open and there had been just real hospitable—It's like Luke 10. Luke 10, where you go and if she will open the door and he's standing, we stay with it. Then, if they don't, then we walk, we go to the next house. We've experienced hospitality and peace and that's why we stay. There's enough of that that we feel. We did a whole series where we kept on reading Luke 10 and then we practiced in the neighborhood. We go and we wouldn't take anything and then see how people invite us in. We went to the local gym and we didn't bring a basketball. It was cool because the guys who were playing there, they said, "You can play with us." You realize if you bring your own resources, then it actually separates you from people. I think in one's vulnerability. That was a pretty formative time and practicing that we did. I think a lot of times, Christian mission, it's like let me fill your need. It feels more like, "Come in." You, yourself are vulnerable too. Then, even to not just feel people's needs because there's something not dignifying about that. What are ways to walk alongside and to expect things from them as well? We had some neighbors from three doors up who we invited for dinner and we had a good time and they invited us for dinner. That's part of it. It's not like I'm just going to always invite them to my house. Yes, they invite us. We entered their home. There's something that happens there as we are hosted and I mean we're trying to practice this neighboring with our neighbors here.

As people participate in the community of believers they find loving acceptance that, in time, they begin to reciprocate. Reflected love is found in the transition from receiving love to becoming a source of love for others. Ideally, an ethos of helping each other is created within the community. In this way, as reflected love is expressed, it can establish the groundwork for reconciliation with God and others, and it fosters the occurrence of community transformation.

The last dimension is blessing, or the return that comes from the generation and stewardship of God-given resources. There is a synergy among these three factors where authentic and healthy relational connectedness requires all three of these elements in order to foster holy interaction. One subject reported:

> One thing that is exciting about the integration is reconciliation. When we came into the neighborhood, we didn't know where we are going to start, it wasn't a strategy like we need to go there every week. It doesn't work that way but by trying to be open, to get them talking to the pastor for the current vision then see what happens. We have the flourishing of businesses, who care about the local neighborhood. We have Redeemer Church, who take case of the poor. With the most African American churches in my neighborhood, the relationship between African Americans and Chinese Americans is not very good especially about the immigrant mentality. When we first started going into this neighborhood by integrating business and ministry, there's a couple of incidents where its potential didn't matter to them. To me that was a sign of reconciliation and blessing. Many African American churches came to Danny ordination. They just came out to show up. So to us having a partnership for community transformation with the other churches has been a blessing.

Each component alone is necessary but not sufficient to guarantee success. At times, one component will be more evident or emphasized, but the outcomes being sought require all three factors.

Thus, we find that success for ECP may be defined as both establishing a sustainable business and creating spiritual community, or the relationships established with other believers and Jesus. Even though there may be some tensions between these two factors, these can be synergistic. For instance, one employee of Dayspring Technologies said, "I think that definitely happens. But they actually fit together. For a church to share with a business, it's not as straightforward because we need different kinds of spaces. For the most part, we're here at different times a week . . . so sharing space does work." Ideally, within the spiritual community, spiritual transformation occurs so that loving relationships with God and others are established, and the transformed people themselves become agents of reconciliation. Furthermore, ECP effectiveness should be evaluated on the grounds of holistic transformation rather than simply measuring effectiveness in terms of economic development or just leading people to faith in Christ Jesus.

With our more developed understanding of success and effectiveness, we are now ready to suggest ways to operationalize the three dimensions: Belonging, Reflected Love, and Blessing as shown in Table 8 below.

Table 8. Operationalization of ECP Outcomes

Belonging	Reflected Love	Blessing
• Access to people by providing economic assistance (e.g., employment, small loans)	• Greater neighborliness occurring (e.g., an increase in the sense of responsibility and accountability)	• Relationships-based investing (e.g., relationship-based small business loans)
• Community people make prayer requests	• Make the community a better place (e.g., a decrease in socio-economic problems or immorality, demonstrated by lower incarceration rate, etc.)	• Value creation in a responsible relationship between the creation and clients (e.g., corporate social responsibility)
• Requests assistance of ECP (e.g., the woman who needed help packaging her food for the media)	• Vocational stewardship[12] by giving our vocational self to the society and God's mission (e.g., a talent donation, join a neighborhood project)	• Graduates of job-training program getting full-time work
• Attends different types of meetings	• Mutually giving/sharing	• Local teenagers going to community college
• Frequency of meetings	• Faithfulness, diligence, and integrity in business transactions	• People who have experienced reconciliation

12. Amy Sherman defines vocational stewardship as a faithful steward of God-given gifts wherever you are, not restricting it to those in formal ministry (Sherman, *Kingdom Calling*, 27).

Case Study of Redeemer Community Church and Dayspring Technologies   81

Belonging	Reflected Love	Blessing
• Church attendance/ participation in ECP's sponsored activities	• Peace, harmony, and justice through the transformed (when the righteous prosper, the community and society rejoices.)	• Stories shared by clients and staff People paying off debts so they can contribute more to the church

As a sense of belonging develops, volunteering and assisting with projects begin to occur. People may choose to respond to friendly overtures. So, belonging tries to capture a sense of inclusiveness generated by the church and the business towards the residents of the community as evidenced by local residents getting jobs in Dayspring Technologies or increased participation in church-run programs. It is contact that starts the process of reaching people so that in time spiritual reconciliation occurs. The greater the number of different contacts, whether making a prayer request or church attendance, the greater the belongingness. This is not an exhaustive list of possible ways people can "belong."

Reflected love happens as people begin to respond to the loving overtures made toward them, typically as trust is established. Within the neighborhood, reflected love is like "playing kindness forward," because as a person receives assistance from the church plant, they show kindness to someone else in need. One facet of reflected love is to note how ECP revenues are used to help the lives of others within and outside the community. For example, as noted above, Dayspring Technologies takes 10 percent of the company's profit and intentionally sets it aside to support the community people, such as the Neighbor Fund. Some of the workers and members of Dayspring Technologies/ Redeemer Community Church help the Neighbor Fund voluntarily. It is the faithfulness and diligence exhibited on the part of workers that is their loving response. Reflected love can occur as people return for additional services, as residents request other types of assistance for the good of the neighborhood, and as there is evidence that neighbors are helping each other.

The last dimension, blessing, indicates accomplishments and advances realized as the result of having access to the entire ECP. The blessing indicator can be measured in part by things such as stories shared by clients and staff, graduates of job-training program getting full-time work, local teenagers going to community college, and the experience of reconciliation among different people. This is mirrored in one employee's comment of Dayspring Technologies:

> It was during the 2008 recession when obviously a lot of companies weren't doing well, losing a lot of work, Dayspring had also lost a lot of work and rather than laying people off, the whole staff decided that they wanted to all have reductions in their salaries so that everyone could still work.

It is through these qualitative stories, the level of socio-economic and education participation, and faith in Jesus that one may track the spiritual transformation and blessing in people's lives. The specific variables may depend on the type of business established and the various ministries of the church. Ascertaining the number of unemployed who had access to job training and employment coaching, number of jobs created, amount of revenue generated, how money was used, and how resources were stewarded are illustrations of possible variables. What implicitly flows through these indicators and the variables used to measure them is the importance of relationships. The variables for each dimension are not tabulated to see if a specific score or number is reached, but they provide a systematic way of assessing what is occurring in both the church and the business and changes that are occurring in the frequency of different events.

This brings us to the last topic we want to discuss, whether the measurements help Redeemer Church and Dayspring Technologies achieve their initial objectives. Danny's responses on this point were limited, but scores provide a way of seeing if various programs, whether in the church or the business, have returns and what the returns are relative to past years. For example, Redeemer Community Church stopped meeting on Wednesday night because the new people did not come. The reason why they did not come was they could not find a place to park because they share space with Dayspring Technologies. So they started experimenting with smaller groups in the middle of the week. They were finding that before the new people became members, they get involved. They were connecting with the church members. In this way, tracking of outcomes fosters assessment of different ministries. It helps to determine how much use is being made of different services and whether ministry programs need to be improved or replaced. As a community ages, child care needs may be replaced by needs for tutoring students or organized teen activities to keep young people away from gangs and drugs.

Another use of scores is to see if there is a progression from belonging to reflected love and then to the identification of blessings. Another concern is to ascertain whether the people who are involved in activities associated with "belonging" advance to demonstrate "reflected love"? At this juncture, there is need to quantify these activities to see if what we are hypothesizing about the operation of ECP is an accurate description of their actual experience. If the process associated with ECP, for example, works for five years and then ceases to produce additional "blessings," it is essential to know this. We must not be afraid to scrutinize what we are doing to advance the Kingdom of God.

The danger with creating quantifiable results is that people get obsessed with the numbers and fail to keep the statistics firmly attached to what is happening within the ministries. Quantification is a tool to aid management, but it can be misused by people who want quick answers and who fail to understand the real focus of ECP. Numbers may also be useful in identifying areas of weakness in ECP endeavors that are struggling or not fully developed. Narrative can serve as a compliment to numbers. It is important that assessment efforts continue in order to understand and actualize the benefits.

RECOMMENDATIONS

What becomes evident from the preceding analysis of Dayspring-Redeemer ministry is the importance of relationships as a building block in an ECP. The emphasis on relationships is true whether the activity is economic, social, or evangelistic; people want to be seen as a person who is valued in their own right. A redeemed approach sees the person as having inherent value and thus worthy of inclusion.

The concern for the development of relationship also brings our attention to the social/developmental aspects of an ECP ministry. Fledgling attempts are evident with the provision of job training. Yet, more programs could be provided in terms of child care, after school activities, English classes, etc. to support the neighborhood.[13] As other ECPs are analyzed in chapters 5 and 6, more attention needs to be devoted to this aspect of ministry as a holistic transformation is desired.

Another fundamental concept evident at Dayspring-Redeemer is the use of teamwork or work sharing. Either the people hired already possessed this orientation or learned it at Dayspring Tech, its presence is salient. When teamwork is found within the ministry, it is easier to have it carry over into

---

13. Since I did research on Redeemer Church and Dayspring Technologies in 2016, they added a new social/development program called Rise University Preparatory. This is a new middle school for the Bayview neighborhood started in 2018. When I visited Redeemer Church and Dayspring Technologies in 2019, they were teaching forty students. One of the founders of Rise University Preparatory noted, "We had long lamented over the inequalities in our city, and we were excited about working together with God's love and strength towards His vision for this place. The result was Rise University Prep!" See Redeemer Community Church, "Gospel Partners."

community activities. The carryover effect was manifested in the operation of the Neighbor Fund where present borrowers help to select those who would receive loans and then provide nurturing support. It will be important to see the degree of teamwork manifested in other ECP studies as the ministries at Selma and Lynch are evaluated.

It is important to note what is missing from this discussion that might be added to the analysis of the other two ECPs. As the goal and outcomes were discussed and then outlined in Table 7, views of other administrators, church members, and Dayspring Tech workers would reveal the degree of solidarity across participants in terms of goals, outcomes, and possible metrics. As Danny fills both the position of pastor of Redeemer Church and of CEO of Dayspring Tech, workers, congregants, and neighbors will of necessity interact with others involved in the ministry. The importance of the leader's orientation should be heard as this person helps to determine the company's culture and sets the expectations of management.

The provision that Yin notes of looking for emerging categories as one progresses through analysis of a multiple-case study are pertinent. The above discussion begins the process of understanding the nuances of a holistic transformational ministry. It will be important to track whether the same processes and orientations of Dayspring Tech are found in the other ministries as well as recognize any new approaches that emerge. Also, adding to the base of people interviewed will enhance the view that develops of the ministry and its facets.

SECTION SUMMARY

A current example of a fruitful entrepreneurial church planting (ECP) model is Redeemer Community Church and Dayspring Technologies. Careful examination of this enterprise was done to identify salient characteristics of effectiveness, and three emergent dimensions were identified—Belonging, Reflected Love, and Blessings. Common to all three was a relational aspect. The relational view of ECP to address the three commissions offers a corrective to the traditional tension between business (economics) and ministry (evangelism/discipleship). These three themes identified from qualitative study of one ECP need to be tested more thoroughly as will occur in chapters 5 and 6. However on a practical note, this case study provides substantiation that Kingdom-based business is economically viable. The other case studies will reveal whether the model is spiritual and has possibilities for developmental programs.

For practitioners of ECP, the study of Redeemer Church and Dayspring Technologies reveals the possibility of developing measures of success—not just simple quantifiable metrics but also ways to assess holistic transformation through narrative. This is particularly important as ECPs can pursue a variety of paths to achieve the ultimate goal of Kingdom-based business done as church planting. To further our understanding of the Great Commission requires time-consuming case studies. Instead, relational cooperation opens up the opportunity for neighborhood contextualization in terms of ECP ministry.

Those who use ECP need to look beyond business outcomes or aspects of running a church to outcomes of Kingdom transformation. In the process of Kingdom transformation as the precursor to the New Creation, there should eventually be large scale growth beyond the individual. The scope of attention must be broaded to include the community and society with its structural operations. We need to introduce and maintain Kingdom culture within our own sphere of influence as participants of *missio Dei*. It is additionally incumbent on us to show others the operation of Kingdom culture in our communities.

What follows in the next chapter is another case study that demonstrates the church as an agent of transformation in society.

5

Case Study of Blue Jean Church and Arsenal Place Accelerator

INTRODUCTION[1]

THE SECOND CASE STUDY is an ECP based in Selma, Alabama: Blue Jean Church (BJC)/ Arsenal Place Accelerator (APA).[2] BJC in partnership with APA is addressing racial tensions and poverty by using multifaceted capital in its holistic outreach to the community; their public witness includes business incubation, drug rehabilitation, job training, and community fellowship opportunities. By embracing a model of church life that sees "church" occurring beyond the four structural walls, BJC and APA seeped out into the marketplace, the neighborhood and the public space. In this way, BJC and APA provide a unique opportunity to study the possibilities of social transformation in American religious life. Furthermore, they reveal an ecclesiology of public life that assumes the witness of worshipping communities is all-encompassing, stretching beyond traditional notions of Sunday worship to offer a voice and a witness into broader social issues[3] in the context of multicultural societies. This is a study of a congregation that encourages social entrepreneurial ventures. What sets these activities apart is that they will serve as a significant entry point to the theoretical groundwork and theological consideration of the church as an agent of transformation in society. In order to examine the practical and theo-

---

1. A part of this case study material is adapted from my article, "Living Out Being a Public Church," 360–73.

2. Henceforth, BJC will be used in place of Blue Jean Church and APA will be used in place of Arsenal Place Accelerator.

3. Hull, "Come Back, Christianity," 86–88.

retical underpinnings of the social ministry of an ECP effort,[4] this chapter will begin with a brief exploration into the history and current praxis of BJC. There will be a brief description of data collection and discussion of research findings. Finally, this will be followed up by an evaluation comments by participants and recommendations.

BACKGROUND INFORMATION[5]

In the 1960s during the Civil Rights movement, Selma, Alabama was named the "Queen City of the Black Belt."[6] It has remained, however, a struggling city of about 21,000 residents. It was, and is, a city beset by poverty, with roughly 42 percent of its residents living at or below the poverty line.[7] As to crime, it is number 84 on the list of the top 100 least-safe cities in the US. Also, Selma is riddled by homelessness and has been described as one of the poorest cities in Alabama.[8] Selma is predominantly an African-American city with 79.8 percent of the residents self-reporting as African-American; 17 percent self-report as being white. The implication of the racial divide becomes more evident with white household income being almost triple that of African-American households.[9] The African-American median household income is $18,333 while the white median income is three times this amount, $54,580.

It was in this setting that a group of believers from the First Presbyterian Church of Selma met with several Selma community leaders in 2007. Not satisfied with the effectiveness of existing church outreach activities, they decided to strike out boldly and change the way "we did church" to attract those who did not know Jesus and had been marginalized by society. Consequently, they sought to serve people in poverty and those struggling

---

4. Ron Sider helps us to understand that action on the social front involves relief, development, and structural change. The timing and the depth of assistance is what distinguishes these three types of activist possibilities. The response in relief is immediate and the goal is survival of those in need; post-earthquake support might include food, clothing and shelter. Development is help through a long-term lens. It provides tools, skills and knowledge so people can become self-sufficient. Lastly, when it is recognized that a group of people are systematically disadvantaged, structural change may be the answer. Structural change is a macro-level form of assistance that typically operates in legal, economic or political arenas (Sider, *Rich Christians in an Age of Hunger*, 139–40).

5. This case study material is adapted from my book chapter in Moon et al., *Case Studies in Social Entrepreneurship*, 44–50.

6. McDonald et al., *Visions of the Black Belt*, 36.

7. Madhani, "Selma Anniversary Puts Spotlight on Deep Poverty."

8. Campo-Flores, "Selma, Fifty Years After 'Bloody Sunday.'"

9. Jacobson, "Is Today's Poverty Rate in Selma, AL."

with addictions. Aware that the targeted groups often feel shame about their lifestyle and tend to shy away from more traditional church services, this group from First Presbyterian wanted to provide a place where people were accepted as they are. Given the poverty—about 42 percent of people reporting incomes at or below $19,000 (see Chart 1) and an unemployment rate of about 10 percent in 2007—many individuals felt left behind. So Blue Jean Church (BJC) was born in 2007 in the basement of the First Presbyterian Church of Selma. Although congregants from the church had a hand in BJC's creation, the church itself was not involved in BJC.

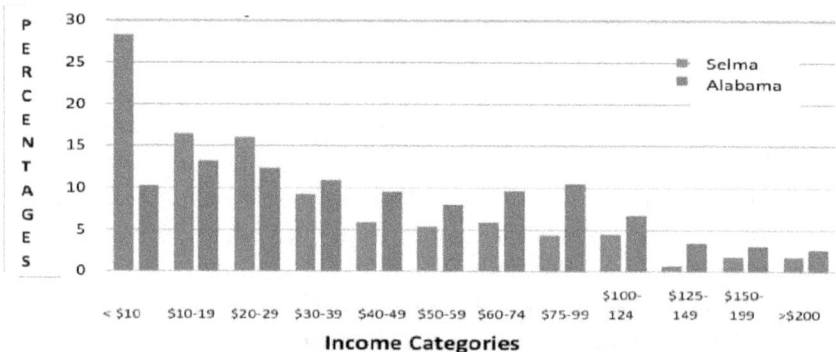

Chart 1. Percentage Income Distribution: 2013 Comparison of Selma with the State of Alabama

One of the unique features of BJC is that it never had the goal of becoming a mega church and thus it was indifferent to church attendance figures and membership rolls. The institutional aspects of the church are of secondary importance to BJC. It wanted to be a "sweet fragrance" (2 Cor 2:14) in the community, sharing its vision to be Christ to those in need: spiritually, economically and socially. With services held early on Sunday morning, at 9 a.m., individuals from any church could and did attend, with many then attending their home church worship service after the gathering. A diverse group began to meet in the basement of the Presbyterian Church. Considering the goal of the founding fathers to reach out, the church was in an ideal location to meet the disenfranchised because the surrounding blocks featured crumbling houses, empty lots and shuttered storefronts. At a typical service, both women and men from all stations of life in Selma equally fill the pews. Demographically, 25 percent were from an affluent suburban area of Selma, another 25 percent were from a less affluent suburban area, and the final 50 percent were from the inner-city people who live nearby.[10] As word spread about BJC, the numbers increased and the church moved to its own facility, an even more ideal location at 431 Church Street; a move funded by donations.[11]

Those who formed BJC did not limit their concern, however, to the worshipping community. Aware of the need for connectedness or the value of gathering, the leadership emphasized community fellowship within the church to foster the formation of friendships and partnerships across ethnic and socio-economic lines. In a city with distinct racial and economic divisions, the promotion of fellowship was essential to achieve a sense of equality and mutual respect. Community fellowship groups met both on Wednesday evenings and Saturday mornings to provide a time for people to gather, eat a bit or have a cup of coffee, discuss what is happening in their lives, and then have a time of prayer where they can voice their concerns and issues. The power of shared prayer was not overlooked as a bonding force among people and it helped to teach the value of appreciating one's blessings.

Plugging another gap was the creation of a family crisis program. With 80.3 percent of single-parent homes facing economic disadvantages and 28.9 percent of households with incomes at or below $10,000, families experience a whole variety of problems.[12] This program provides counseling to those who lack access to existing programs run by the city and county. BJC funds this program, and thus reaches out a caring hand to those both inside and outside the church.

As the church looked outside the community, the leaders of BJC wanted to support the economic, social, and spiritual transformation of Selma. Yet, BJC realized that no one church is would be able to develop a comprehensive plan to address all the community's needs. The initial idea had two major components: BJC established in 2007 and the Children's Policy Council (CPC).[13] The CPC was a pre-existing county entity with a connection to the Juvenile Court of Dallas County. Guidance for the CPC came from a founding member of BJC, Judge Bob Armstrong, who chaired the Council.[14] Given the fortuitous position of Judge Armstrong, he saw the opportunity to build a bridge between BJC and this pre-existing program.[15] The judge saw the possibilities of BJC becoming affiliated with the council. Thus, BJC's partnership

10. Shaw Dane, interview with the author, June 13, 2016.

11. The church moved their venue (1209 Selma Avenue, Selma, AL, 36703) again after the research was conducted.

12. United States Census Bureau, "QuickFacts: Selma, Alabama"; AFI, *Alabama Fatherhood Directory*.

13. Henceforth, the CPC will be used in place of the Children's Policy Council.

14. Bergeron, "Accelerator's Business Picking Up."

15. "Children's Policy Council Makes a Difference."

with the CPC connected them to teen pregnancy prevention programs, a Juvenile Redirection Program, a Juvenile Drug Court,[16] "a Peer Helper Program where students assist peers with tutoring, mediation and leadership, career fairs and parenting classes."[17]

While Armstrong was already a fixture of the Presbyterian Church and an enthusiastic leader in the emergence of BJC, as a judge, he was in a key position to make a difference. From his position as the Juvenile Judge, he saw the underbelly of Selma—children taken from their families, adolescents involved with drugs and alcohol, chronic truancy, juveniles who were arrested, etc. One ministry BJC provides is solidarity and representation in court. For example, someone from BJC often stands with a family as their children are brought before a judge. This practice keeps the family connected to the church and reduces social isolation. Another program is Teen Challenge, with ties to both the juvenile court system and BJC; it works with youth released from drug and alcohol rehabilitation programs. Apparently, these programs are serving as possible agents for social transformation, as Chart 2 below demonstrates a downward trend in incarcerations. The other cities included in the Table are cities with approximately the same population of Selma to facilitate the comparison of rates.

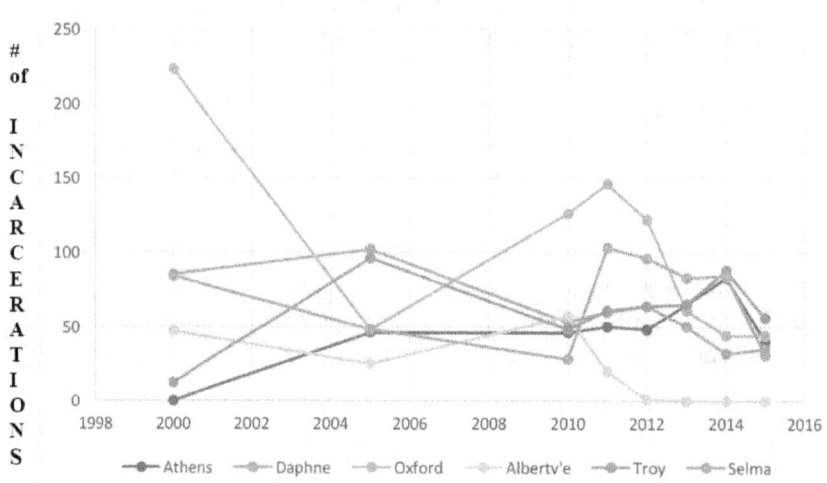

Chart 2. Juvenile Incarcerations, Selected Counties in Alabama, 2000 to 2015

16. Alabama Department of Early Childhood Education, "Children's Policy Council."

17. CPC of Alabama, "What Is a CPC."

Table 9. A Percent Change for Selected Counties
in Alabama, 2000 to 2015

County	Change 2000 to 2015
Dallas (Selma)	-22.6%
Limestone (Athens)	+28.2%
Baldwin (Daphne)	+29.6%
Shelby (Pelham)	+34.1%
Talladega (Oxford)	-13.1%
Marshall (Albertville)	+11.0%
Jefferson (MT Brook)	-7.7%
Pike (Troy)	-0.5%

Table 9 reveals that the incarceration rate was on a steady decline starting in 2011 in Dallas county and that its figure in 2015 compared well to the other counties. The drop in figures, when compared to other counties, would suggest that the intervention programs in place at Selma for troubled teens are having a significant effect. Table 9 shows the percentage change in 2015 relative to the juvenile incarceration figures in 2000, where negative values indicate a drop in the incarceration rates. Of the four counties showing a decline in juvenile incarceration rates, Dallas County/Selma has the largest percentage drop of incarceration rates at 22.6 percent. Though these figures do not provide indisputable proof that changes occurring in Selma are caused by BJC and its related partners, positive change is undeniably happening when compared to other areas of Alabama. This premise is strengthened in light of BJC's connection to the CPC.

Another intervention that the judge and the CPC have implemented in partnership with BJC is the provision of a school for troubled teens. As children are removed from the mainstream school system for a variety of reasons, they need a school where they are understood and their problems can be addressed. Judge Armstrong orders teenagers who appear before him to Hope Academy, a court-mandated alternative school in partnership with Selma City Schools, the District Court, and the CPC.[18] Hope Academy offers one-on-one job training, job placement skills, and therapy and counseling to sixty students. It enables students to aspire to a productive future. This program offers the possibility of a GED and/or high school graduation, thus, helping students at Hope Academy get a job. One example of Hope Academy's entrepreneurial empowerment is evident through a graduate who opened three car service shops, employing six workers in Selma. Various of BJC members are involved in all of these educational endeavors on a volunteer basis.

The third component of the original plan was economic. It took the group a while to determine what programs would be the most useful to spark economic revitalization in the neighborhood. BJC and Judge Armstrong decided on a business incubator, known as Arsenal Place Accelerator (APA) to revitalize the community. As an initiative of BJC (see Diagram 2), APA started in 2014. APA provides mentoring and support to novice entrepreneurs as they start their businesses and also offers affordable office space. The debut of APA was positively covered in local newspapers despite the fact that only one company was located there. But APA grew quickly from one to six start-ups, with more fledgling businesses projected.[19] Though this is encouraging, there are some qualifications that must be pointed out. For example, most of these businesses were started by people who wanted to move into a new career by transferring from one job into another. All but one of the businesses were started by white people. The business that was the first occupant of APA, G Momma's Cookies, is the only business that has employees. One of the positive attributes about the cookie business is that ten employees, as of July 2016, are earning a living wage with health insurance. The presence of a business accelerator, however, has the potential for creating more jobs, as noted by Sheryl Smedley, the Selma-Dallas County Chamber of Commerce Executive Director.[20]

Revival Coffee, another APA incubated business, positively illustrates the spirit of what APA is trying to achieve; this is a small batch coffee roasting business that was started in 2014 by Ryan Bergeron, a businessman interested in coffee roasting. Although Ryan and Revival Coffee have received a lot of attention from the media, it is still a single employee company. What demonstrates the interconnectedness of this business and the community

18. Deshazo, "Hope Academy Recognized at BOE Meeeting."

19. Bergeron, "Accelerator's Business Picking Up." Changes continue to occur after the research was conducted.

20. Bergeron, "Accelerator's Business Picking Up."

was the decision by the owner to donate 10 percent of the profits from the sale of different types of coffee to Selma service programs. He contributes to Teen Challenge Center, which boasts an 86 percent success rate as it works with those addicted to alcohol and drugs. He also supports Selma Life Ministries, a county-run pregnancy resource center, and Crisis Aid International, which targets human trafficking.

Collectively, what emerges is an outreach ministry that is broader than just the church-plant, BJC. Diagram 2 shows how each program (BJC, APA, CPC) is interconnected.

Diagram 2. Network of Affiliations of BJC, APA, and CPC

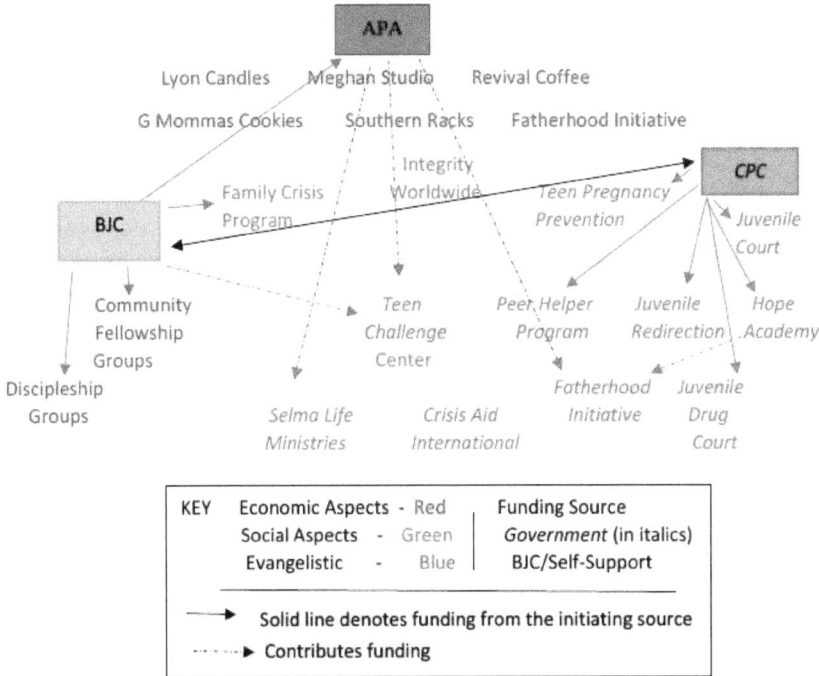

The dashed lines reflect the maturing of some of the programs as they now contribute to new ministries. Red denotes activities associated with the economic sector, blue represent evangelistic ministries, and green stands for social programs. The arrow from BJC to CPC implies participation by BJC in any of the CPC programs as needed. While CPC only gives rise to socially oriented activities, BJC supports both evangelistic and social programs.

This three-pronged approach addresses the spiritual sector through the church, the social sector through connections to various programs associated with the CPC, and the economic sector through an expanding APA. It is not simply a one-for-one approach where each component pushes toward its logical outcome, but it is a fabric of interconnectedness that addresses poverty, crime and homelessness in Selma. While there are a variety of other initiatives and ministries currently being undertaken in connection to BJC, APA, and the CPC, these three institutions represent the largest, most organized, and cooperative efforts in this case study. My analysis of holistic transformation could have highlighted other efforts, but for purposes of brevity and clarity, this study limited itself to investigating this three-pronged approach.

In short, the three-prong approach can be seen on different levels. Firstly, it operates on a personal or individual level. For example, it might take the form of members of a community fellowship group interacting within the church (BJC), the judge addressing a teenager who stands before him, or a pregnant teen receiving counseling. In all of these scenarios, one-to-one personal interaction occurs. Secondly, it operates on a group level. Several programs have been created to address problems that plague groups of people. Hope Academy provides schooling and training for youngsters who are not able to function in traditional schooling options. The Teen Challenge Center works with juveniles who are addicted to drugs or alcohol or both. Finally, the institutional level is illustrated by the operation of the CPC, a state-mandated organization manned by volunteers.

A unique feature of the triumvirate (BJC, APA, the CPC) is Judge Armstrong. Because of his position and resulting involvement, he was able to facilitate rapid connections between BJC and many of the local programs and inside innovators. These connections might have been made without Armstrong's leadership, but integration would have been much slower. His position aided him in identifying the areas that would have the greatest impact on the community. This in no way reduces the role of the Holy Spirit in achieving various outcomes; it simply identifies Judge Armstrong as a significant catalyst and change agent in the transformation process. The fact that few other individuals have been identified is indicative of the broad-based support from people affiliated with BJC. One question the dominance of Judge Armstrong raises is how leadership will be handled upon the conclusion of his involvement.

RESEARCH PROCEDURE AT BLUE JEAN CHURCH

While the historical background of BJC presents a vivid picture of holistic public transformation and renewal, it is necessary to examine the outcomes of planned efforts in order to evaluate the effectiveness of BJC. I interviewed twelve people involved with BJC in some capacity. I selected interviewees based on their position and knowledge of the broader outreach plan associated with BJC. I targeted those familiar with the church and its operation, as well as individuals involved with APA. To explore the more extended contacts the church had, I also spoke with three people from Integrity Worldwide, a non-profit organization that partners with BJC. Table 10 provides their specific demographic characteristics.

Table 10. Description of Subjects[21]

Organization	Sex	Race	Goals	Success (Definition)	Success (Metrics)
Blue Jean Church/ Founder	Male	White	Transformed lives & neighborhood	Life in Christ and community transformation	Based on relational connection
Blue Jean Church/ Worker	Male	Black	Holistic renewal	Relationships of mutual service	Based on empowerment
Blue Jean Church/ Board member	Female	Black	Neighborly love	Interdependent network with kingdom values	Based on collaboration
Blue Jean Church & Arsenal Place/ Board member	Male	White	Structural transformation	Community growth and empowered leaders	Based on integration of faith and work
Blue Jean Church & Arsenal Place/ Supervisor	Male	White	Transformed lives & neighborhood	Connected Neighbors and Neighborhoods	Based on relational connection
Arsenal Place/ Worker	Male	Black	Loving community	Neighborly love and partnerships	Based on changed lives and neighborhood cohesions
Arsenal Place/ Founder	Male	White	Holistic partnership & change	Small business success	Based on the financial viability and holistic transformation

21. To protect the identities of the respondents, I have changed their names.

Organization	Sex	Race	Goals	Success (Definition)	Success (Metrics)
Arsenal Place/ Supervisor	Male	White	Integrated sectors & flourishing	Changed lives and improved community	Based on the launching new kingdom-minded companies
Integrity Worldwide/ Community person	Male	White	Neighborly love & restoration	Mutual trust and community stewardship	Based on Spirit-led leadership
Integrity Worldwide/ Community person	Female	White	Spiritual & social connection	Relational restoration and collaboration	Based on connection to Jesus Christ
Integrity Worldwide/ Community person	Female	Black	Transformed lives & neighborhood	Improved neighborhood and connection to God	No specific metrics specified

All the respondents were between the ages of thirty and sixty. All were Americans or Canadians, with the exception of David who came from the Caribbean. It was unclear whether he identified himself as African American and whether others who interacted with him identified him as African American or Caribbean. Two shortcomings of the sample were the limited number of African Americans and women.

The interviewee questions were asked of each of the twelve participants. The questions dealt with the history, motivation and goals of the ECP, as well as theoretical and practical metrics of success. A final set of questions dealt with how to assess the performance of different church/business activities. The interviews were recorded and later transcribed to facilitate the tracking of major themes and ideas in the interviews. To guarantee standard practice for evaluative and accountability purposes, I followed a trifold paradigm: (1) identify goals; (2) state outcomes predicated on goal fulfillment; (3) offer explanations related to metrics of achievement. Below I discuss the results.

RESULTS

Identification of Goals

A systematic analysis of an enterprise starts with what that enterprise hopes to accomplish or what its goals are. Ideally, goals should serve as the driving forces for the determination of ensuing activities so as to work towards them. This approach holds true even when studying goals and outcomes of kingdom-based activities. To identify the goals of BJC and APA, let us consider the goals stated by the individuals solely associated with BJC. The first three rows of Table 5 in the Appendix D show what they said. Transformation of people's lives by Christ's love is one evident theme. The agency of the change is by loving the neighborhood, i.e., a relational approach. Another goal is changing the neighborhood to be a better place for everyone to live in, or the more specific idea of improvement through relational, economic, and spiritual renewal. David's statement comes the closest to an ideal phrasing of holistic community transformation. The other individuals basically echo these sentiments.

Next, we want to consider goal responses from the two people who have involvement with both the church and the Arsenal Place Accelerator. Their comments are in the last two rows of Table 1 in the Appendix D.

The notion of transformation resonates in what Daniel and Jonah say. The holistic goal of creating a Kingdom-like community is clear. Jonah has higher explicit expectations when he says that the restoration of community brings about the end of racism, extreme poverty, and unemployment, or in effect, reducing divisive forces that break down community and which occur on both the societal and community levels.

Using the three people who are outsiders to both BJC and APA (the last three people on my sample Table) as test cases to see if the goals have been communicated outside of the established circle, it is evident that those with Integrity Worldwide understand the vision that the others share. They may not credit spiritual forces or the operation of the Holy Spirit as playing a part in the transformation, but they understand the role of being a good neighbor and that jobs, education and interpersonal relationships are generated, as the community becomes united.

Definitions of Success

Goals are tied to outcomes, so next I want to consider BJC/APA's definitions of success as reported in Table 2 in the Appendix D. A glance at the different definitions of success reveals considerable variation in their respective perception of what constitutes success. Some of them are quite tangible and easily measurable: all with some affiliation to APA reflect an emphasis on stewardship, productivity, and creativity.

Others place an emphasis on the creation or restoration of relationships with other people: David, Mary, Daniel, Samuel, Israel, Ruth and Esther. Several themes emerge such as mutuality and reciprocity, being shaped by others through shared purpose, connectedness, trust, and mutual transformation, and sustainability. There appears to be consistency between their initial goals and definitions of success. All of these markers of success are associated with the social, interrelated reality of God. Thus, success in the social mission of the church might be determined by the extent to which the church reflects the mission of our relational God.

Metrics of Success

It is important to look beyond theoretical definitions of success to consider the practical ways people might use in determining success; these are referred to as operational definitions of success. Table 3 in the Appendix D reveals what people had to say about measuring success.

Most people clearly have ideas of what they want to see happen: making the love of Jesus incarnated, developing people, changed lives, etc. There are, however, not a lot of specifics in the metrics of success. Many of the statements include mention of relationships, especially among the five individuals with ties to BJC. Whether relationships formed by sharing a purpose for a summer project (Ruth) or people spending time with others at lunch or as a result of the ordinary flow of life (Joshua), relationships seem to be the key building block; advocates of neighborhood revitalization would agree on the importance of building interpersonal networks. At the same time, David, Jonah, and Abraham suggest that the formation of relationships will have the end result of raising people out of both spiritual and economic poverty. Ruth, Samuel and Joshua see spiritually changed lives as a conduit to changing elements within the community.

Beside these issues, another characteristic that emerges associated with their stated metrics of success is a holistic approach. References are made to spiritual growth, economic growth, and to community or social growth. This manifests itself in the statements of David, Jonah, Joshua, Abraham, and Samuel. Elements of holistic transformation are found in the statements made by Ruth and Israel.

Yet collectively, the comments reveal little understanding of what specifics need to occur within the broader community around BJC to produce success. It is interesting to note the response of Moses, a founder of BJC. His statements clearly indicate where he wants the activities of BJC, the Children's Policy Council and Arsenal Place to go, but he has little idea of how to connect people to the Lord, how to create a loving family community at BCJ and how to foster love that spreads out to the local neighborhood. It is very difficult to achieve an outcome when there is little awareness of what must be done to reach the goal. It needs to be acknowledged that if people possess a clearer idea of how to achieve an outcome, then they are able to articulate their plan.

The lack of awareness of the concrete steps needed to turn ideas and visions into reality is what slows the accomplishment of the laudable goals cited earlier. There were few specific suggestions of how to measure outcomes such as fathers' employment, and pay history with the court system. It is easy to develop a general sense of what is happening in a multi-faceted ministry like BJC promotes, but they, themselves, are currently not positioned to document its progress. The attendance figures reported earlier are a source of information but of little interest to a kingdom-focused ministry that has no interest in church growth. However, if a program is to be a good steward of its resources (money, time, personnel) it needs to know how it is progressing to guide plans for the future development of the ministry. Despite this lack of interest in specification among the interviewees, three common themes can be noted across the groups: (1) becoming a good neighbor, (2) demonstrating neighborly love, and (3) building a flourishing neighborhood together. Whether relationships are formed by sharing a purpose for a summer project (Ruth) or people spending time with others at lunch or as a result of the ordinary flow of life (Joshua), interpersonal relationships seem to be the key building block.

Application of Success Indicators to BJC, APA, and the Children's Policy Council

Despite the paucity of detail in the operational definitions of success, it is helpful to consider the developments people identified. Their assessment comments are in Table 4 in the Appendix D.

To simplify the extensive comments, content analysis of these remarks reveals three major themes. The first success indicator for BJC, APA, and the CPC is becoming a good neighbor. The spiritual dimension of the church helped to promote bonds among those attending the services. Additionally, the church was integrating the marginalized by means of attendance. This is reflected in Ruth's comment, "The other thing I get excited about is the revitalization of the community. As people of God we were not indifferent to people in need outside our spiritual community." There is a distinct carry-over from what is happening inside the church to activity outside the church.

Another change that is linked to "becoming a good neighbor" is the drop in juvenile incarcerations. With less detail, but also associated with the joint operation of BJC and the CPC, is the perception of Samuel: "Through a cooperative effort, crime and poverty have dropped significantly. Children at risk are succeeding. People are getting clean of alcohol and drugs, because of our Kingdom networks." Change is happening in the neighborhood and these people believe that the influence of BJC, APA, and the CPC, by promoting being a good neighbor, are responsible for the improvement.

The second success indicator for this case study is demonstrating neighborly love. Joshua reported, "I also see a big difference that APA is having on the economic development of our city." So APA's existence both provides economic hope for the future and is an economic presence previously missing in the neighborhood. Evidence of neighborly love can also be noted through the growing awareness neighbors have with regard to new possibilities and insights. Samuel's observation is consistent with the new perspective: "Arsenal Place Accelerator and Blue Jean continue to invest in the community and to walk toward a new reality in Selma." This sentiment is echoed by Ruth: "We got out in the marketplace and beyond the four walls and stood in solidarity with our neighbors to renew, rebuild, and restore Selma." Selma is no longer the hapless victim of larger social forces; rather, residents in Selma are beginning to feel they can control their own future.

The final success indicator is building a flourishing neighborhood together. Using the framework set by Jesus in Matthew 6:33, BJC, APA, and the CPC sought first the Kingdom of God and His righteousness by taking greater responsibility for their neighbors. The idea of "building a flourishing neighborhood together" is reflected in Moses' comment:

> God's manifest presence shows up every Sunday! Our worshipping community reconciles people to God and people to people by worshiping Jesus across ethnic boundaries such as black and white and socio-economic boundaries such as rich and poor. This enables people to form genuine friendship and partnerships for economic and social transformation of Selma. Such positive relationships help community members hold one another accountable and grow in their relationships with family members, neighbors, and God. We as a spiritual community try to work alongside our congregation and community members in relationships that lead to authentic community formation and holistic transformation.

The responsibility arises in the form of coming along-side rather than imposing a different way of doing things. Kingdom values, ethics, and culture have been generated through interaction with marginalized people outside the church. Both the early planners and those involved with the ministries of BJC and APA firmly believe that the ideal social relationships characteristic of heaven should be practiced in and through the community.

DISCUSSION

Ultimately, the study of BJC, APA, and the CPC was undertaken because it embodied a church-planting effort combined with a business model that sought to use economic, social, and spiritual capital in its holistic outreach to the community. This case study was especially interested in the process by which the BJC, APA, and the CPC program plotted their developmental course. So in this section, those steps were traced. Yet those affiliated with the broader Blue Jean Church ministries were unable to clearly define outcomes they wanted to achieve.

Content analysis of the remarks made by interviewees reviewed above revealed three aspects of the BJC collective: interpersonal ties within the church or physical proximity, neighborly love or relational proximity, and neighborly collaboration or Kingdom proximity. What needs to transpire for each of these components to occur requires specification. The previous section has proposed that the basic building block is interpersonal relationship. Let us first consider how the interpersonal ties were created as people became neighbors.

BJC was motivated initially by a concern for the spiritual welfare of its physically proximate neighbors.[22] The intentional choice was to move into the neighborhood and live in the community with its significant socio-economic needs. Figure 5 shows the increase in parishioners living within one mile of the church.

---

22. Sean Benesh states that too much church planting literature has been focused on churches in low-density cities predicated upon the use of the automobile. However, millions of people are flocking into cities. Those cities are becoming pedestrian-oriented. Thus, Benesh asserts that church planting in cities needs to focus on walkable churches (Benesh, *Multi-Nucleated Church*, 68; Moynagh, *Church In Life*, 128).

Figure 5. Percentage of Parishioners Who Live within 1 Mile of BJC

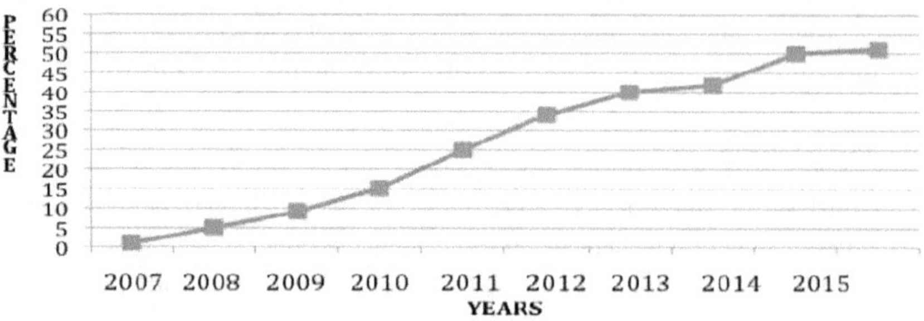

[Line graph showing percentage rising from near 0 in 2007 to about 50 in 2015, with values approximately: 2007: 2, 2008: 5, 2009: 10, 2010: 15, 2011: 25, 2012: 35, 2013: 40, 2014: 50, 2015: 50]

Living in the community (number of people in church who live within one mile of the church building or number of relocating people) provided the church people with an opportunity to reveal God's Kingdom, to proclaim the Gospel, and to be His agents within the community to minister to Selma. Rather than focusing on building a beautiful edifice and adding to its membership rolls, the concern of BJC was to equip the people of the church to be good neighbors, reflecting a Kingdom orientation. A preliminary step to becoming good neighbors involves an understanding of physical proximity;[23] this entails establishing one-on-one connections where people are reaching across barriers of social class and race and giving him/herself to their neighbor.[24]

The vision is that, as neighbors are redeemed and empowered by the Spirit, the individual can then meaningfully contribute to and participate in the renewal, transformation, and development of the community. Here the "good neighbor" is a boundary-crosser who seeks to develop *perichoretic* mutual relationships[25] or someone who promotes the sense of gathering. A good neighbor lives out their faith in relationship with other neighbors.[26] Thus, people are saved and transformed by a Community, the

---

23. Instead of physical proximity, John Perkins uses the term "relocation" for community development (relocation being the first step in order to produce reconciliation and then redistribution) (Perkins, *Restoring At-Risk Communities*, 21–22).

24. For a discussion of the main functions of the Church in secular society, see Heelas, *Spiritual Revolution*, 141–42.

25. The term *perichoresis* came into theological use through Gregory Nazianzent to attenuate the doctrine of the Father's monarchy. Within *perichoresis* (mutual indwelling/act of divine self-giving), God created us to participate in the divine life so that we might find our being-in-communion in the relationships with God, with others, and creation (Torrance, *Trinitarian Faith*, 234).

26. Phan, "Crossing the Borders," 16–17.

perichoretically-entangled *missio Dei* of the triune God in the world, for community or transformed human relationships.[27]

With the emphasis on being a good neighbor, where relationships based in equality and respect are formed, BJC is attentive to their needs, because the problems of one are owned as a problem of the community of believers. This reflects a movement from physical proximity to deepening relational proximity. Taking spiritual responsibility for the neighborhood, BJC faces problems and struggles by walking together with neighbors for the sake of the Kingdom. Reconciliation with God yields transformed relationships with others. In particular, by sharing with neighbors the incarnate presence of Jesus and the resources of BJC, new agents of transformation are born along with people who learn to be good neighbors.

From the beginning, BJC did not want to see itself as a spiritual beacon only. God's love and works of love had to be central elements. In the operation of relational proximity, both action and ability are needed, as illustrated by the parable of the Good Samaritan (Luke 10:30–37). Movement or action needs to be toward those in need where we enter a situation with broken elements, such as racial discrimination. We seek to share in the suffering of the other, and we share resources with those in need.[28] The parable also tells us that the Good Samaritan bound up the wounds of the injured traveler; he demonstrated his ability to help. BJC similarly possesses both the resources and knowledge of how to use resources to assist the neighborhood.

One of the most pressing needs of many small towns in Alabama is economic uplift. While it took several years to bring APA into operation, there was awareness from the beginning that helping people start companies that would then be able to hire workers was a form of economic assistance with short- and long-term payoffs for the community. Jürgen Moltmann calls this *economic symbiosis*.[29] He stresses that the Church is called to discover economic symbiosis by accepting economic responsibility, and that "such symbioses, in both limited and wider contexts, are to be seen as corresponding to and anticipating the kingdom of God in history."[30] The response of people to APA was not determined by the jobs it had created. Rather it is seen as a

---

27. Meeks, *Trinity, Community, and Power*, 113–14.

28. Here movement refers to boundary-breaking activity as a movement of Jesus becoming a neighbor to us. The insights into neighborly love in reference to economic capacity were gleaned from notes on Tom Nelson's speech at the Faith at Work summit in 2014.

29. Moltmann defines "economic symbiosis" as sharing economic wealth and materials for the balance of life in the socio-economic realm. See Moltmann, *Church in the Power of the Spirit*, 168–76.

30. Moltmann, *Church in the Power of the Spirit*, 176.

symbol of hope. And feeding that hope has been the role of the local newspaper that touts the progress of Revival Coffee and G Momma cookies. The presence of APA can spur local entrepreneurs to start their own businesses. An example of the "can-do" spirit is provided by one of the graduates from Hope Academy; this young man opened three car service garages with a total of six employees. Hopefully APA will be able to foster economic development capitalizing on productive and interdependent relationships. Thus, physical and relational proximity are operating jointly.

Many times church leaders feel the need to provide all the services that an area needs; that sense of obligation can be crippling. What lends strength to the activity of BJC was its collaboration with the Dallas County District Court and Juvenile Court, as well as other community social service programs already in operation and funded by the county. Local partnerships create a network of services reinforcing Kingdom proximity. When the scope of an outreach ministry of BJC is broadened to include the social dimension, we are then moving toward the idea of "society-as-Kingdom-proximity." The Fatherhood Initiative is an example of mutual collaboration as it draws on APA, the Selma Career Center, and Hope Academy. This initiative was a program sponsored by the Dallas County Workforce Investment Act. It allowed members of BJC to establish a program where fathers who have been ordered by the state to pay child support or who are not living up to their familial responsibilities are taught and coached on ways to be better fathers.[31]

The collaborative approach is a valuable alternative to the individualistic model used by many outreach ministries. So this could be a possible metric to track such as the number of vital partnerships. Since Selma is a city where race and social class divisions continue to fester due to structured historical and sociological trends, collaborative ongoing activities have been used to bring people from different backgrounds together. Ideally, people from different backgrounds working on joint projects would like to be most effective at breaking down divisions. People begin to discover that long-held stereotypes are inaccurate depictions of a group. This is reflected in Moses' comment:

> Our worshipping community reconciles people to God and people to people by worshiping Jesus across ethnic boundaries such as black and white and socio-economic boundaries such as rich and poor. This enables people to form genuine friendship and partnerships for economic and social transformation of Selma. Such positive relationships help community members

---

31. AFI, *Alabama Fatherhood Directory*.

Case Study of Blue Jean Church and Arsenal Place Accelerator 105

hold one another accountable and grow in their relationships with family members, neighbors, and God.

This is most likely true regarding the perceptions that both African-Americans and whites have about each other. Thus, collaboration may reduce the tendency for people to see themselves as "messiahs" bringing Christ to the neighborhood; collaboration encourages people to see themselves as recipients of gifts of the Kingdom as the neighborhood works together blessed by God's Spirit. One participant reported:

> Transformation started with leadership. Wise, Spirit-filled, father figures like Judge Bob ignite a desire to make a difference in Selma. He formed a leadership team and networks of transformation. Then he shared the influence and resources that he had in the Dallas County with the leadership team. These networks influenced each other and the whole neighborhood.

Thus, what sets BJC and APA apart is that they do not see the community merely as a network of ties or connections, but as mutual Kingdom proximity.[32]

Society-at-large is a place of Kingdom proximity because it is the location of divine activities of justice, shalom, protection and assistance to the disadvantaged, and interaction with neighbors based on *perichoresis*.[33] That is, society-at-large is God's redemptive venue and the Apostle John tells of a new city God is building for us (see Rev 21).[34] Several of the interviewees associated their activities with transformation of human society. For instance, the goals of BJC, APA, and some portions of the CPC are not achieved until the poor, the brokenhearted, the captives, and prisoners are reconciled to God and others so that they may rebuild, restore, and renew cities and societies ruined by sin and socially constructed barriers. This eschatological perception of society-as-Kingdom proximity helped BJC, APA, and the CPC get to Kingdom outcomes.

In sum, it becomes clear that what characterizes BJC, APA, and the CPC has to do with the interplay between physical proximity, relational proximity, and Kingdom proximity. Such approach illuminates the "public" nature of the Church by "not simply a description of the social function of the Church in a pluralist democracy, but a call to action, to Christians to embody Christ's rule"[35] in public realms. Consequently, BJC attempts to

---

32. Moynagh, *Church for Every Context*, 104.
33. See chapter 5, footnote 25 on page 102.
34. Swanson and Williams, *To Transform a City*, 78–80.
35. Paeth, "Jürgen Moltmann's Public Theology," 232.

overcome the modern privatization by rebuilding connections between the church and the public and between "the world in the kingdom of God and the kingdom of God in the world."[36]

RECOMMENDATIONS

First of all, I applaud the tremendous positive changes that have occurred in Selma. Yet there are limits on the assessment when no pre-established standards exist. Earlier in this paper, the areas of community life left unaddressed by the existing plan were pointed out. If public ecclesiology is to advance, an objective standard to guide development is needed so that new marginal people are not created in the process of holistic care. For example, as Robert Lupton points out, well-meaning attempts sometimes resulted in harming the poor by leading to an unhealthy dependency.[37]

Additionally, it was found that there are not a lot of specifics in the metrics of success. However, evaluation reveals the importance of relationship building. In the past when evaluation centered on profitability or the number of congregants, the importance of bonding was overlooked. When pursuing holistic transformation, the importance of relationships is front and center. Associated with friendship is accountability. As we want the other to thrive, accountability helps the person to grow. Too often assessment has used profitability or number of conversions as a substitute for the transformation that occurs both in the church and in the neighborhood when people individually and collectively walk with the Lord. Therefore, we need assessment that captures that transformational dynamic. We may gauge holistic transformation using the indicators emerged from interviewee data such as number of vital partnerships and number of people in church who live within one mile of church building.

Finally, one more caveat to be considered is the process used in program creation. While the group of leaders from the Presbyterian church met and decided on a general direction, it would have been helpful if the ideas of families in the neighborhood had been drawn upon. Incorporation of local people would have helped to give the neighborhood residents some sense of

---

36. Moltmann, *God for a Secular Society*, 251.

37. Lupton, *Toxic Charity*, 50. In this groundbreaking guide, veteran urban activist Robert D. Lupton reveals the disturbing truth about charity: all too much of it has become toxic, devastating to the very people it's meant to help. In his four decades of urban ministry, Lupton has experienced firsthand how our good intentions can have unintended, dire consequences. Our free food and clothing distribution encourages ever-growing handout lines, diminishing the dignity of the poor while increasing their dependency. We converge on inner-city neighborhoods to plant flowers and pick up trash, battering the pride of residents who have the capacity (and responsibility).

ownership of what would happen in their neighborhood as their ideas were heard. Secondly, as local people spoke, they could have indicated what were priority issues to them; thus, whatever plan emerged would have reflected local concerns. While the areas identified by the leaders are those commonly recognized as good starting points for neighborhood revitalization, the program has the appearance of being planned for the neighborhood, rather than with the neighborhood. So when Esther said, "Their collaborative efforts have united Selma," the question becomes, "Who is *their*?" When white people are the planners and the recipients are blacks, care needs to be taken to promote a sense of equality and respect between those formulating the ideas and those expected to participate. It is evident that the planners sought to assist the neighborhood; what is important is to discover how local residents perceive the offer.

In an incidental conversation I had with a local African-American man, I asked how local African-Americans felt about the program. He indicated that there was fair acceptance of the program. Local people were happy to see the activity generated by BJC and the various outreach programs that had been developed. Follow-up conversations are needed to explore more thoroughly the perceptions of African-Americans about BJC programs and the lack of inclusion of blacks, especially in leadership positions. Furthermore, empowerment of African-American residents is needed for the vitality of the program and the propagation of this approach in other cities in Alabama.

SECTION SUMMARY

The researcher examined a current example of ECP, BJC and APA in partnership with the Juvenile Court of Dallas County of Alabama. Careful examination of this church/business endeavor was undertaken to identify their own definitions of the social action of ECP activities, the approaches of measuring social action, and the results of these measurable social activities. It became evident that specific goals and measures had not been identified. Yet, from their comments, three emergent dimensions were found—Becoming a Good Neighbor (physical proximity), Neighborly Love (relational proximity), and Neighborly Collaboration (Kingdom proximity). More specifically, physical proximity can be gauged by the number of people living within one mile of church building; relational proximity may be measured by the number of businesses formed or number of jobs formed or number of students taught to obtain GED; and Kingdom proximity is being evaluated by number of vital partnerships. Common to all three was a neighborly relationship, which echoes the elements of the Kingdom of God on earth. The *perichoretic* view of ECP offers an alternative to the dichotomous approach of business metrics, which tends to focus on profits and mission metrics of spiritual fruit/ impact; it notes the presence of physical, relational, and Kingdom proximities. These three dimensions identified from this qualitative study need to be tested more thoroughly in order to validate the usefulness of this three-dimensional *perichoretic* matrix.

One major contribution the BJC/APA ministry makes is its attention to relational proximity. The conscious and successful attempts to interact with the neighborhood provides a model other ECP ministries could learn from. The identification of other area services and the creation of ties to them were facilitated by Judge Armstrong and a pre-existing Kingdom-orientation in many of the neighborhood programs that may not be found in other locales. Furthermore, the study of Blue Jean Church and Arsenal Place reveals the possibility of measuring both qualitative and quantitative ECP outcomes in all three arenas: spiritual, economic, and social. We should raise the level of assessment in order to not be content with common assessment standards, such as counting souls saved or detecting profits. That is, these metrics should be supplemented. What distinguishes these metrics is to reap spiritual fruit, perform better as an organization, and develop social development. I will discuss later on in chapter 7 how the multiple metrics help protect against financial profit trumping the other metrics. Attention to activities on the individual, community, and institutional levels is needed. To push the use of the ECP model ahead, more careful consideration of how to operationalize the three commissions is needed since their theological and theoretical foundations are already well established. The advancement of the Great Commission (discipleship/reconciliation), the Creation Commission (stewardship), and the Great Commandment (transformation) requires mission strategies and outcome measures that are effective.

In sum, this study highlights the difficulties of articulating goals, outcomes and measurement indicators. This research underscores that there are no universal standards for practitioners of ECP to measure mission endeavors. Instead, proximities of relationships, both in Community and in a community, is a significant standard for a ECP enterprise to operate and measure against. Here Community (capital C) refers to the perichoretically-entangled *missio Dei* of the Triune God in the world, and community (small c) refers to transformed human relationships. Practitioners with a heart for neighborly proximity create opportunities for ECP to achieve the eschatological not-yet gaze of social mission of the church. The focus on neighborly movements in *perichoretic* relationships permits the use of various paths to narrow the gap between the Kingdom of God and a not-yet-redeemed world.

The vision of those who use ECP programs should be on the *missio Dei* where interaction between the church and the neighborhood occur. This is because the mission of the church is to engage in the *missio Dei* as two-way traffic of inter-cultural interactions between the church and the neighborhood and between whole-life discipleship (the Great Commission and the Great Commandment) and a call to cultivate the world (the Creation Commission). In the process of presenting the entire Gospel, there should eventually be the integration of faith, work, and *oikonomia*. This integration will enhance the quality of ministry in global churches to reflect a holistic picture of God's working in the world: ministries that feature Christian communities living out the entire Gospel in their neighboring communities, the larger society, and the world.

What follows in the next chapter is another case study of ECP that offers a grassroots understanding of success based on holistic transformation.

6

Case Study of Meridzo Ministries

INTRODUCTION[1]

OUR NEXT CASE STUDY is Meridzo Ministries (MM) based in Lynch, Kentucky.[2] This case study emphasizes spiritual renewal, relational development, and social impact in the heart of the Appalachian Mountains. The discussion in this chapter advances a possible grassroots definition of success rooted in relational transformation. Insights from case study research will then be applied to Clemens Sedmak's kinship model in order to posit three proxy indicators based upon interviewee data.

HISTORICAL OVERVIEW OF MERIDZO MINISTRIES

In the heart of the Appalachian Mountains lies the city of Lynch, Kentucky, located at the intersection of Virginia, Tennessee, and Kentucky. In the 1940s, the United States Steel Corp hired over four thousand workers from thirty-eight countries to work in the coalmines.[3] The coal mining industry helped to build a strong American working class in Lynch. However, after the coal industry's demise in 1960s, a large proportion of the skilled populace moved away, leaving a multitude of poor, illiterate, and broken people.[4] Economic deterioration in the area bred hopelessness and dependency that served to lock the citizens of Lynch in perpetual destitution. The chronic inability to find and keep jobs resulted in a poverty rate of 31

---

1. A part of this case study material is adapted from my article, "Transformative Metrics for Holistic Ministry," 121–39.
2. From here, I will use MM for Meridzo Ministries.
3. Sentinel Group, "Putting Feet on Jesus in Lynch, Kentucky."
4. Schmidt, "Decline of the Town That Coal Built."

percent in 1960. Also lacking were successful role models in the community. This disorder of their community had also taken a moral and spiritual toll on residents.[5] Lynch, which once boomed with over ten thousand residents in the 1940s, dwindled to about seven hundred people.[6] In light of this desperation, the downtrodden in Lynch, Kentucky began to cry out for God to hear their pleas.

In 1998, Lonnie and Belinda Riley visited Lynch, Kentucky to resolve issues related to Belinda's mother's estate. While there, the couple witnessed the deep poverty and hopelessness. After returning to their home in Mississippi, God showed Lonnie a verse upon which his entire ministry in Lynch would be based, Isaiah 41:17–20.[7]

These verses reminded them of the poor and needy in Lynch, but also the assurance that God was equal to the situation.[8] Lonnie and Belinda were convinced that God was calling them to minster to the spiritual thirsty of Lynch, even though it would mean leaving a well-paying, secure job as a pastor in Mississippi. The Rileys responded and moved to Lynch, despite no promise of a job or any income.[9]

In 1999, they arrived in Lynch and launched Meridzo Ministries.[10] This initiative began by the Rileys getting acquainted with the town's people. Four months later Lonnie and Belinda, along with two hundred fifty others, participated in a powerful city park prayer meeting that set the course for later ministerial fruitfulness. Lonnie encouraged the people to ask for God's forgiveness for their misplaced trust in both the coal industry and in the government rather than in God. In a display of raw and cathartic emotion, people wept and prayed for two and a half hours.[11] Lon-

---

5. Appalachian Regional Commission, "Appalachia Then and Now."

6. Pulliam, "Gas Station Fuels Spiritual Life."

7. "The poor and needy search for water, but there is none; their tongues are parched with thirst. But I the Lord will answer them; I, the God of Israel, will not forsake them. I will make rivers flow on barren heights, and springs within the valleys. I will turn the desert into pools of water, and the parched ground into springs. I will put in the desert the cedar and the acacia, the myrtle and the olive. I will set junipers in the wasteland, the fir and the cypress together, so that people may see and know, may consider and understand, that the hand of the Lord has done this, that the Holy One of Israel has created it" (Isa 41:17–20 NIV).

8. Riley et al., *Miracle in the Mountains*, xv.

9. Riley et al., *Miracle in the Mountains*, 20–21.

10. The name of Meridzo was derived from a form of a Greek verb meaning "to care or to share" (Riley et al., *Miracle in the Mountains*, 78).

11. For Lonnie, success is defined as "let God be God" (Riley et al., *Miracle in the Mountains*, 70).

nie recognized later that this prayer meeting in the city park marked the beginning of the transformation of Lynch.[12]

Afterwards, they did not receive any new word from God for six months. It appeared to them that God was inactive.[13] Faithful to God's leading, Lonnie and Belinda continued to serve the needs of the community through simple acts of kindness: hedge trimming and cookie give-aways.[14] After they found out that some families did not have enough to eat, they launched a food bank, "Bread of Life." The food bank qualified to receive surplus food from other state sources in 2000. After the food bank, Lonnie and Belinda were able to obtain several buildings to permit the introduction of different businesses and ministries.

As Meridzo Ministries increased in influence, criticism and setbacks began to test the Rileys' commitment to Lynch. Some locals thought that Meridzo Ministries was trying to buy up the town in a power play. Lonnie realized that the good intentions of Meridzo Ministries could be interpreted as a grab for property and fiscal gain. Confirmation of Lonnie's fear were realized when the mayor began to distribute a video that depicted Meridzo Ministries in a negative light in the hope of turning public opinion against the Rileys. The mayor eventually called for a city council meeting where Lonnie learned the mayor wanted to tax all new missionaries coming to the town, and every new project.

Lonnie then contacted a constitutional law firm in Washington DC, and three lawyers quickly came to Lynch to address the planned taxing ordinances. After a special meeting with the mayor and the lawyers, the local officials agreed to never bring up the ordinance again, and the planned legislation was dropped. Lonnie refused to utter a negative comment against the mayor and God's ministries triumphed.[15] Eventually, the mayor was pressured into leaving Lynch after evidence of embezzlement was discovered.[16] It was through persecution and endurance that Lonnie and Belinda gained a foothold in Lynch. Following these initial setbacks, the Rileys' fortitude resulted in the launching of 22 distinct ministries in Lynch.[17] Seeking to empower other local groups, some of the ministries have been handed over to local churches and other missionaries.

12. Sentinel Group, "Putting Feet on Jesus in Lynch, Kentucky."
13. Riley et al., *Miracle in the Mountains*, 24.
14. Riley et al., *Miracle in the Mountains*, 23–36.
15. This anecdote comes from a personal interview with Lonnie Riley, the founder of Meridzo Miniseries.
16. DellaMea, "Lynch, KY."
17. Riley et al., *Miracle in the Mountains*, 76.

DESCRIPTION OF MERIDZO MINISTRIES

Meridzo Ministries is divided into two branches: non-profit and for-profit.[18] The non-profit branch offers many outlets for proclaiming the gospel such as a functioning local church and Heaven's Door Chapel. Also, included are two facilities used to host children's camps. The for-profit branch contributes to community development by creating businesses such as Lamp House Coffee Shop, Black Mountain Exchange gas station, Faithfully Fit fitness center, and Agribusiness Center. The Agribusiness Center is notable for its development of new industries and job opportunities. The Center discovered that the shower rooms originally built for coal miners provided the perfect environment to grow shiitake mushrooms, and potentially other vegetables. Along with the for-profit ministry, Lonnie and his team helped establish a lumber company that both provides employment and sells lumber at a reduced price for home repairs. A candle factory and a sewing company were also established as sources of employment. Overall, the for-profit branch reflects a commitment to community development.[19]

Another important aspect of Meridzo Ministries is volunteer facilitation. Since 1999, "over thirty thousand volunteers from thirty-five states and four countries have come to Lynch to repair homes, clean up parks, and build playground equipment, hold dental and medical clinics, evangelize, and cover the city in prayer."[20] The volunteer work mutually reinforces communal relationships, as volunteers work shoulder to shoulder with local residents. This created opportunities for the residents and the volunteers themselves to be mutually transformed. The poor were not seen as recipients of charitable acts, but instead they emerged as agents of transformation themselves. Thus, the collaboration serves as a teaching aid to both the local residents and the volunteers. Regarding the steady stream of volunteers, Lonnie said, "We did not have a preconceived strategy on how to win the people of eastern Kentucky, but God did."[21] The volunteers endeavor to make possible more one-on-one contact. Even though they do not always share their faith when they do physical work, there is a lot of personal witness occurring. This is reflected in one subject's comment:

> People tell us a lot here at the counter. They don't know what they would do without Meridzo ministries because it is such a huge blessing. They said that they would not have clothes for their children and for their neighbors, their grandkids, if we

18. Pulliam, "Gas Station Fuels Spiritual Life."
19. Riley et al., *Miracle in the Mountains*, 105.
20. Riley et al., *Miracle in the Mountains*, xiii, 51.
21. Weeks, "Unemployment, Poverty."

were not here. They say, "I hope you know how much Meridzo Ministries is a blessing to this community. Also through this ministry our lives are being transformed by volunteers. We are mutually growing in the Lord. Through prayer why God healed these or changed someone's life.

In this way, people in the community feel Meridzo Ministries is a huge blessing to them.

RENEWAL ASSOCIATED WITH MERIDZO MINISTRIES

Over the 18 years of their ministry, Lonnie and Belinda have seen a change in Lynch. One aspect of transformation occurring in Lynch is spiritual renewal. For example, "over 1,500 people in the area have given their lives to Jesus, and 40 percent of the people in Lynch are now believing Christians."[22] Additionally, five new churches have been started in Harlan county.[23] As a result, spiritually, the climate is different in that a renewed sense of hope has permeated the once desperate Cumberland county.

Another significant change is the pride in their community that residents manifest. Evidence of this community pride is that residents now take care of their property. Belinda said, "We have a lot of blighted properties belonging to people who have just moved away and not taken care of their abandoned real estate, but yes, we have seen a change."[24] Besides pride of place, a resident recognized Meridzo Ministries as a key resource for the town as well as others outside Lynch.[25]

The ministry sees its mission as helping people both economically and physically (through job creation and welfare services) and spiritually (through evangelism and discipleship). In this way, Meridzo Ministries demonstrates a good example of how people can be transformed *by Community for community*. Here *Community* (capital "C") refers to the perichoretically-entangled *missio Dei*[26] of the Triune God in the world, and *community* (lower-case) refers to human relationships (community-building) transformed by covenant.[27] Overcoming obstacles on their way, Meridzo Ministries has shown grace in the face of resistance, endeavored to make local communities healthier by addressing the actual issues local

---

22. Sentinel Group, "Putting Feet on Jesus in Lynch, Kentucky."
23. Riley, "Testimony."
24. Schmidt, "Decline of the Town That Coal Built."
25. Many people and ministries outside Lynch reached out to Lonnie for partnership.
26. Torrance, *Trinitarian Faith*, 234.
27. Scripture demonstrates that human beings are created, saved, and transformed by Community for a community (Hahn, *Father Who Keeps His Promises*, 240).

people were facing and creating relational networks of mutual support and accountability. This relational ministry has taught people about hope in God that results in hope to people.

RESEARCH PROCEDURE AT MERIDZO MINISTRIES

As ministries are established, it is important to consider the outcomes and not just their intentions. One of the issues incorporated within the discussion of ECPs is a query facing many churches and outreach ministries today: How can we measure the success and effectiveness of ECP? Due to the absence of an existing method for evaluating ECP's effectiveness, I chose to use the case study approach.[28] Insights into Meridzo Ministries' accomplishments and effectiveness were gathered from fourteen subjects; interviewees were selected based on their position and knowledge of Meridzo Ministries. I sought people familiar with the church and its operation, as well as individuals involved with the for-profit branch. Three Lynch residents and one person from Freedom Center, a non-profit organization, were also included among the subjects. I used the information from these interviews and a few incidental conversations to provide insight into Meridzo Ministries' effectiveness. Each participant was interviewed in a semi-structured format lasting between one and a half to two hours. Table 11 lists the specific demographic characteristics of the subjects (see Table 11 on the next page).

Table 11. Description of Subjects

Organization	Sex	Race	Relationship to Context[29]	Goals	Success (Metrics)
Meridzo Ministries/ Founder	Male	White	Outsider	Holistic revitalization	Based on relational connectivity
Meridzo Ministries/ Founder	Female	White	Local	Transformed lives & neighborhood	Based on community building
Meridzo Ministries/ staff	Female	White	Outsider	Holistic renewal	Based on community building

---

28. Eisenhardt, "Building Theories from Case Study Research," 532–50.

29. "Relationship to Context" shows whether my subjects were raised in the town or from outside.

Organization	Sex	Race	Relationship to Context[29]	Goals	Success (Metrics)
Meridzo Ministries/ staff	Female	White	Outsider	Love for God & neighbor	Based on changed lives, neighborhood cohesions, and identity transformation
Meridzo Ministries/ staff	Female	White	Outsider	Holistic partnership & change	Based on changed lives, neighborhood cohesions, and identity transformation
Meridzo Ministries/ staff	Female	White	Outsider	Transformed lives & families	Based on relational connectivity
Meridzo Ministries/ staff	Male	White	Outsider	Transformed community	Based on relational connectivity
Meridzo Ministries/ staff	Male	White	Local	Love for God & neighbor	Based on changed lives, neighborhood cohesions, and identity transformation
Meridzo Ministries/Staff	Male	White	Outsider	Manifestation of the coming Kingdom God	Based on community building & the financial viability
Meridzo Ministries/Staff	Male	White	Outsider	Spiritual, social, structural change	Based on relational connectivity
Freedom Center/ Staff	Female	White	Local	Love for God & neighbor	Based on stories of transformed lives and relational connectivity
Lynch/Community person	Male	White	Local	Holistic transformation	Based on changed lives, neighborhood cohesions, and identity transformation

Organization	Sex	Race	Relationship to Context[29]	Goals	Success (Metrics)
Lynch/Community person	Male	White	Local	Kingdom-like community	Based on changed lives, neighborhood cohesions, and identity transformation
Lynch/Community person	Male	White	Local	Love for God & neighbor	Based on community building

Demographic analysis of the respondents reveals both the strengths of this study and gaps for future statistical review. The respondents were all Americans between the ages of twenty-eight and sixty. Ethnically, all of the respondents were Caucasian. The fact that no African Americans are involved in the activities of Meridzo Ministries possibly indicates a lack of inclusion.[30] Future studies should seek to broaden the ethnic scope of this study by analyzing the responses of African American participants as they constitute 20.9 percent of the population in Lynch. While diversity is present in terms of gender and age, the dominant Caucasian cultural bias cannot be overlooked. It should be noted, though, that Lynch is 79.60 percent White;[31] in this way, the respondent sample is fairly representative of the dominant culture, but minority voices should be sought for further illumination.

All respondents were asked the same questions during the interview process. The questions addressed five primary areas related to Meridzo Ministries: (1) history, (2) motivation and goals, (3) theoretical metrics for evaluating success, (4) operational definitions of success in practical terms, and (5) performance assessment. Questions were asked in a logical and chronological structure, beginning with Meridzo Ministries as a startup on through the development of its various programs over the years. The interviews were recorded and then later transcribed to facilitate the processing of major themes and ideas.

Whether studying a community of faith associated with Kingdom-based activities or any organization, one must first identify the goals or vision of the organization. Goals reflect the underlying reason for existence. These goals provide insight into the why or strategy of what an organization

---

30. Nevertheless, Meridzo Ministries is partnering with an African American pastor for a city transformation project.

31. Sperling, "Lynch, Kentucky."

does (activity) and how it does it (methodology) and thus serve as driving the outcomes of an organization.

As a Kingdom-based effort, goals, or vision, are driven by God's call. These goals and visions usually describe what Christian congregations feel called to and is their *modus operandi* for their mission in the world. Consequently, it is important to hear what their goals are. The following discussion is based on the responses each subject provided.

DATA RESULTS OF MERIDZO MINISTRIES (MM)

Identification of Goals

As we explore what people involved with MM have to say about its goals, we will be considering their responses to the question asked during the interview. Table 5 in the Appendix D reports the statements the respondents made about the goals of Meridzo Ministries. The first ten respondents are staff of MM; the other four are community people.

Two major themes that emerge from those fully invested in MM are: holistic ministry and the integration of faith with life's vocation and God's *oikonomia*. Holistic ministry, as Ron Sider has written, is the sharing of the gospel by both "word and deed."[32] One participant reported:

> The real reason behind this ministry is to share Jesus and help people. We are not here to make a profit. Whatever profits that the store makes, they will help fund other parts of the ministry. Our specific purpose is share and talk with and be a witness to this community. We also build a relationship and making friends by providing a convenience in the service to the community by having this place here.

In this way, MM strives to do holistic ministry in several programs started by MM such as the gas station including the grocery store, fitness center and the teen center.[33] As MM shares the gospel and participates in acts of mercy and justice, they are bearing witness to both the extrinsic value of the Creation Commission (the work of the Son) in their for-profit branch such as Lamp House Coffee Shop and the intrinsic value of the Great Commission (the work of the Son) in their particular ministry. This culminates with a deeper communal appreciation for the-in breaking New Creation (the eschatological work of the Spirit), such as Lynch's 100th Anniversary Celebration[34] in 2017.

---

32. Sider, *Churches That Make a Difference*, 64.
33. Sider, *Churches That Make a Difference*, 60.
34. Stevens, *Other Six Days*, 120–23.

In this way, MM has rejuvenated Lynch by addressing joblessness and issues of spiritual brokenness in view of loving relationships.

The second theme, the integration of faith with life's vocation and God's *oikonomia*[35] where people live together in obedience to the Great Commandment within the context of the Creation Commission and the Great Commission[36] is reflected in Ruth's statement: "Meridzo Ministries seeks to restore the community that has been destroyed by extreme poverty and unemployment through living the faith-life and 'creating lakes in which we can fish.'" It shows that MM connects God's *oikonomia* in and through their ministry (life of vocation) to their faith. Belinda and Ruth echo these sentiments.

Next, let us consider goal responses from the four people who are outsiders to Meridzo Ministries. Their statements may serve as test cases to see if the goals have been communicated outside of the established circle. For one thing, the concept of "good works and Good news" (holistic ministry) resonates in what the four people (Sarah, Israel, Luke and David) said. The holistic goal of "love God and love our neighbor" through genuine spiritual transformation and good stewardship is there. Luke has higher explicit expectations when he says that such Kingdom relationship brings about the end of extreme poverty, unemployment, and hopelessness. For another, it is evident that the person involved with Freedom Center understands the vision that Meridzo staff share. Furthermore, Sarah observes, "The mission and purpose of Meridzo Ministries are . . . to give expression in helping people by generating jobs and share the Good news by creating relational networks of assistance." In this way, it is through good works and Good news that MM endeavors to advance foretastes of the Kingdom God. In short, the outsider perspectives verified the authenticity of the two dominant themes that emerged across the insider perspectives, mainly holistic ministry and *oikonomia*.

Definitions of Success

Now that the goals of Meridzo Ministries have been presented, let us move toward a consideration of a theoretical definition of success or what should be observed if the goals are realized. The responses of the fourteen subjects are in Table 6 in Appendix D. Closer inspection of the various definitions given by the interviewees reveals a significant similarity in their respective

---

35. *Oikonomia* refers to God's plan for God's whole household of creation. In this way, God wanted human beings to unwrap the gift of creation and bless the world with their own gifts. See Sunde, "All Is Gift."

36. Self, *Flourishing Churches and Communities*, 71.

perceptions of categorical success. For instance, six individuals define success as following the will of God or relying on God. While these intangible definitions of success are not useful when seeking outcomes that can be tracked or counted, six interviewees suggested that people need to be aligned with God for the ministry to be a success.

Interestingly, this theocentric definition of success (following the will of God) is found in statements made by six other participants if one parses similar linguistic definitions: "love God and our neighbor"; "seeing children serve the Lord"; "peoples' lives are transformed"; "community glorying God together"; "seeing God at work in the community"; and "people and community being affected for Christ." These definitions reveal that there is concern among subjects to define success, and as Pastor Shawn Lovejoy argues, our definition of success should match God's definition of success.[37]

Additionally, this information posits the importance of covenantal relationships in descriptions of success. Two participants place an emphasis on the creation and restoration of relationships within a family, a larger neighboring community, and God. These relationships can be characterized by what Scott Hahn terms covenantal relationships, which are distinguished from economic or contractual relationships in their form of exchange. "While a contract involves the exchange of property in the form of goods and services ("That is mine and this is yours"), a covenant calls for the exchange of persons ("I am yours and you are mine"), creating a shared bond of interpersonal communion."[38] Thus, contract-based relationships identify people as customers, employees and clients,[39] while covenant-based relationships view them as spouses, parents, children, and siblings.[40] The Bible offers a vision of this sacred kinship that will lead us toward a life of communal flourishing, that is, *oikonomia*. One way in which this manifested is through a reframing of vocational identity. Rather than seeing some jobs as particularly spiritual and sideling a majority of God's people, biblical stewardship, centered in Christian community, advocates the need for every vocation (gas station, fitness center, coffee shop) to fulfill God's mission. In this way, covenantal relationships move us away from quantified concepts (numbers, activity, approval, or fame)[41] in determining success.

---

37. Lovejoy, *Measure of Our Success*, 179–80.
38. Hahn, *Father Who Keeps His Promises*, 75.
39. Bell, *Economy of Desire*, 103–9.
40. Hahn, *Father Who Keeps His Promises*, 26–27.
41. Lovejoy, *Measure of Our Success*, xvi–xvii.

Metrics of Success

One of the concerns of this research is to investigate an operational definition of success that might drive the outcomes of ECP. It is essential to look beyond the theoretical definitions of success to consider how interviewees measure success in practice and what they really want to see happen in their communities. Table 7 in Appendix D reveals the practical ways in which Meridzo Ministry personnel articulate their operational metric of success. This data will contribute to a working definition in that it transcends theory by observing actual assessments.

Subjects clearly have ideas in determining operational definitions of success, though Table 7 in Appendix D reveals a wide spectrum of possible metrics. Some of the prominent definitions include: creating economic and spiritual networks of mutual support, transformational development, right relationship with God, vibrant community, stories of changed lives, sharing economic resources, as well as emotional and spiritual relational opportunities. Intriguingly, most of the statements of the ten individuals mention God's presence and provision. Whether God's reign was reflected by a decline in bar attendance (Hanna), in praising God for an award given by the local Chamber of Commerce (Ruth), or in the development of intergenerational mentoring (Lonnie), the concept of the in-breaking Kingdom of God seems to be the foundational building block for metrics of success at Meridzo Ministries. The concept of the Kingdom is partially manifested through communal wholeness and restoration. This is exemplified in Lonnie' desire to know what God is doing in people's lives and in the community. In short, the metrics of success at Meridzo Ministries are closely related to Kingdom principles, which involves an increasing awareness of God's presence and provision through mutual interrelatedness,[42] but also community recognition of what God is doing through Meridzo Ministries.

Collectively, the fourteen comments on operational definitions of success reveal more tangible, practical, and deeper understanding of fruitfulness than the comments on theoretical definitions of success. Interestingly, the responses of Lonnie and Belinda, founders of Meridzo Ministries, reveal a clear picture of how to help the unemployed learn to practice good stewardship, how to recover and cultivate communion with God, and how to foster a community that reflects the Trinity in Lynch.

Accordingly, it becomes clear that few understood what a metric was, but they recognized the change brought about by the agency of the Holy Spirit. They also realized that success is not determined by the quantity of whatever transpired. While the goals and ways to achieve outcomes may

---

42. See Grenz, *Social God and the Relational Self*, 23–57.

be satisfactory to them anecdotally, there are a lot of soft definitions and outcomes, lacking reliability and validity. Each respondent provided specific suggestions on how to measure outcomes which in actual practice would make comparison difficult. Due to a lack of record keeping on the part of Meridzo Ministries, evaluative analysis might be based on qualitative statements rather than on quantitative data.

Application of Success Indicators to Meridzo

So far, we have focused our attention on a grassroots understanding of success as articulated by Meridzo Ministry respondents. These emergent strands now position us to examine possible application of the success indicators. Practical achievements across the various respondents are offered in Table 8 in Appendix D.

To simplify the extensive comments of Table 5 in Appendix D, content analysis identifies three major themes emerging from their statements. These three themes include: (a) connection, (b) participation, and (c) identity transformation. Let us examine each of the three themes.

CONNECTION LEADING TO COMMUNION FORMATION

Our first theme for analysis is connection. Thirty-six percent of the participants from fourteen subjects state that MM was birthed out of, what Donald Miller has described as relational connectivity with God and neighbor and contributed to relational connection.[43] By "building incarnational relationship with people in the surrounding culture,"[44] MM has formed bonds of spiritual kinship with neighbors. This relational connectivity involved multiple layers of deepening intimacy leading to *communion formation*. For instance, MM instituted various practices in order to make contact and engage people in both their business arrangements and church initiatives. Expressions of relational connectivity include: (a) involvement in the life of the community through acts of service such as hedge trimming, cookie give-aways, attending community prayer meetings, and connecting people to communities of faith, and (b) creation of employment opportunities through job initiatives (Solomon's Porch Retreat Center and Merizdo Agribusiness Center).

This holistic ministry of MM helped create links connecting people to people, people to God, and community to God. In other words, MM contributed to building networks (connection) for spiritual renewal (communion

---

43. Miller, *Spirit and Power*, 277.
44. Halter and Smay, *Tangible Kingdom*, 127.

formation). Several comments prioritize connection leading to communion formation. For instance, Gideon suggests that Meridzo "care(s) for the people and bring(s) hope back to them. We try to remind people that God loves them and that God has not forgotten them." David observes, "It is through loving relational interaction with God and others that Meridzo Ministries manifests foretastes of the Kingdom God." Jonah said:

> The Rileys . . . made friends with the local people and sought to respond to needs and situations as they arose. From the contacts they made with Lynch townsfolk, they not only helped others in basic ways but they also deepened their awareness of systematic problems in the area, such as food scarcity.

These comments show that Lonnie, Belinda, and Meridzo staff have attempted to connect themselves and their neighbors to "true Community such as the Triune God and Christian communities."[45] This spiritual connectivity (communion formation) prompted a new experience of hope and economic revitalization (community building), and it also led to a growing desire to enjoy and live life as spiritual kin (*oikonomia*).[46]

Participation leading to Community Building

The second theme that emerges from interviewee data is participation. Twenty-eight percent of the fourteen respondents indicate that MM helped to rebuild the neighborhood in Lynch (community building). This was accomplished through interaction and participation with neighbors. For example, Lonnie and the Meridzo staff sought to transform Lynch by equipping people to be economically self-sufficient by running businesses such as a gas station, a fitness center, and a coffee shop. Locations such as the coffee shop or the gas station became centers for community formation in that local people were able to connect with one another and create a sense of belonging.

Several comments manifest this mutual interrelatedness within a larger neighboring community. One respondent said, "Meridzo staff try to show people how to love on other people like Christ loves us. That way they know what the love of Christ looks like when you take somebody who has not done what you've asked." Additionally, Mary commented, "MM is truly transformative in that it went from spiritual support into community." These comments show that MM has provided an environment where community finds its strength in mutual love. As mentioned above, Scott Hahn terms these relationships *covenantal relationships*. Thus, it was through participation

---

45. Lee, "Assessing the 'Success' of Business as Mission," 61.
46. Newbigin, *Gospel in a Pluralist Society*, 154.

that MM has offered a vision of this sacred kinship that could lead people toward a life of communal flourishing.

One example of the interrelatedness is provided by Black Mountain Exchange, a gas station started by MM; this venue is also an example of Third Space. Given the nature of the business it is public, open to anyone who wants to come in, and relational, especially for regular customers. The people who work here welcome the community and endeavors to build relationships. The contextual element is represented by providing space where friends and neighbors can intermingle over a common event, filling their gas tank, eating pizza or buying food. Black Mountain Exchange started as a convenience store that sold fresh pizza, soft drinks, candy, bread, milk and other staples. As many residents were without cars, the establishment of the store eliminated the need to shop in Cumberland making life easier for many.

As time went on, MM discovered that it was very difficult for local people to get gas and diesel; Black Mountain Exchange started selling gas last April. To help the locals, MM try to keep their gas prices at least ten cents less than other area gas stations, taking into account the local economy. The motivation to help others through business by putting human well-being about profit maximization appeals to the local people. These business practices manifest the Kingdom orientation and facilitates the blossoming of relations. The end result is entrepreneurial success and relational fruitfulness for the Black Mountain Exchange.

In this way, MM sought to build relationships of trust that went beyond mere assistance; the goal was mutual friendship and community formation. In particular, the businesses (the coffee shop, gas station, and the agribusiness center) contributed to vigor and a sense of community in Lynch. There is also the inclusion of a spiritual dimension in these exchanges as staff pray with customers about their concerns, provide free gospel tracts and Bibles, and provide assistance when possible. Testimonies of the kindness of the staff culminate into a shared narrative of transformation that transcends its economic function.

Additionally, it is business like the Black Mountain Exchange that help the local people stretch their dollars. While making a small contribution, the poverty rate of Lynch has dropped from 24.4 percent to 17.8 percent over the last five years. Just as the Exchange was opened to address a need, the creation of new businesses can also be one way to reduce poverty in the area. The solution of a gas station and convenience store also illustrated how residents could meet and organize to solve problems for the common good of their community.

IDENTITY TRANSFORMATION LEADING TO OIKONOMIA (GOD'S HOUSEHOLD RULE)

A final theme from my data is identity transformation. Thirty-six percent of the interviewees from fourteen respondents say that MM sought to cultivate what Eddie Gibbs and Ryan Bolger call an atmosphere in which local people could identify themselves as both a part of a kingdom community and local community.[47] One indicator of identity transformation can be noted in a comment made by Abraham, an employee at a local gas station owned by MM; he states, "If it's lunch time we sit there and have lunch. I like the people that come here. They are not merely customers or neighbors but brothers and sisters." Lonnie similarly reported joy in "seeing residents take part in ministries that were freely chosen and nourishing for the benefactor." These statements reveal an identity transformation that points toward sacred kinship within the family of God (*oikonomia*). As mentioned above, even though some in the community did not join in MM, a few Lynch residents began to see each other as "brother and sister" and saw the community as "my" community. David reported, "It is exciting to me to see how the neighborhood is changing and coming together. Meridzo is a key player in this." Such experience of "being with" has fostered neighborhood revitalization.

These filial ties were not connected by blood-based relations (John 1:13) but by covenant-based relationships. This in turn not only created a space for Kingdom family-type relationships to develop, but it also diffused responsibility to neighbors in the community. This is mirrored in Israel's comment:

> I get excited when the community works together. After we built relationships with people, it gave us the opportunity as a marketplace missionary, to share, to build Kingdom relationships. We create and secure the markets. We're using the resources that are here and the people that are already in place to do that. We train and equip those operators so that they have the best opportunity for success. Everybody wants them to succeed, provide for them.

By giving the residents an opportunity to care for the poorer people, they experienced "a sense of love and being loved," which was noted by Joshua. In this way, residents entered into a new awareness and experience of being neighbors and friends rather than a mere collective of local strangers. *Oikonomia* thus entailed a deepening relationality and sense of mutual belonging rooted in the kingdom of God.

---

47. Gibbs and Bolger, *Emerging Churches*, 95–115.

In short, a brief analysis of interviewee data connects the three emergent streams (connection, participation, identity transformation) to their desired results (communion formation, community building, *oikonomia*). Specifically, some of the respondents noted the emphasis on relational wholeness focused initially on spiritual awakening that overflows into reconciliation with one's neighbors. Other subjects commented on transformative networks for community revitalization leading to community building. Other interviewees mentioned neighborhood solidarity as important resulting in an intensifying experience of mutual indwelling. Each theme offers a pathway for three desired results leading to *Community-for-a-community*. As described in the section of renewal associated with Meridzo Ministries, *Community* (capital "C") refers to the perichoretically-entangled *missio Dei* of the Triune God in the world, and *community* (lower-case) refers to human relationships (community-building) transformed by covenant. These three linking themes and their results reveal that human beings are created, saved, and transformed by *Community-for-a-community*.

Grassroots Definition of Success Rooted in Meridzo Ministries

The three linking themes, three desired results, and the outcome of MM suggest that if a church is about a network of Kingdom relationships, we may measure success based on relational health and increased holistic connectivity. In light of the data collected from the interviews and my analysis, several interpretive questions arise regarding a metric of success: What percentage of local people have any proximity to MM? How many people does MM staff know on a first-name basis? How accessible is MM staff to local residents? How many people in the community would regard MM as a friend or brother or sister? While I affirm that it is possible to measure success based on levels of connectedness, statistical questions help in evaluating these qualitative commitments.

As we begin to think more concretely about how to evaluate success, once again we are limited to a single focus—a relation-centered metric. Previous evaluations of ECP have been similarly limited, whether by use of a business metric and its emphasis on profits or a spiritual metric revolving around spiritual fruit. However, despite MM's singular attention on relationships, it does capture the holistic nature of the gospel message, which epitomizes ECP's attention to changed interpersonal relationships, conscious attempts to interact with the neighborhood, and community transformation. Some respondents have even made the leap to talking about success based on holistic transformation encapsulated in Kingdom relationships ("love God and neighbor"). Meridzo Ministries helps to embody the transformational dynamic lacking in previous attempt to evaluate outcomes of ECPs.

RECOMMENDATION

One caveat to the preceding discussions on goals, activities, and evaluative metrics of Meridzo Ministries is their use of "responsive planning." This approach prioritizes direct guidance from God over human planning. It also focuses on God flowing into the human heart resulting in increased benevolence. So responsive planning rejects a typical model in which goals, activities, and measuring tools are envisioned first before doing a ministry. This planning suggests that God's purposes are worked out through the person who receives revelation. However, the concept of responsive planning might at times place too much emphasis on the role of the "illuminated" person. What about God's direct action in the world? Though the voice of the Spirit can of course be heard in moments of spiritual intimacy, the Spirit also hovers over the face of the earth as a life-giving presence. In this way, the notion of Creator Spirit opens our spiritual senses to the creative pneumatological work all around us. Meridzo's emphasis on revelation, though valid, may at times neglect the already present voice of the Spirit in the community.

Along with responsive planning, it would have been more effective for them to include local people in the neighborhood, especially African-American families. Incorporation of minority voices would have helped to give minority members some sense of belonging and ownership of what was taking place in their neighborhood. If African-Americans joined the missions of Meridzo Ministries, it could have broken down racial barriers and helped to interweave the interests of Meridzo Ministries and local people.

Furthermore, while responsive plans are recognized as suitable starting points for neighborhood transformation, the programs have the appearance of being responded for and by Caucasians, rather than for and with the whole multiethnic neighborhood. When Gideon says, "A big part in bringing hope is letting people know God has not forgotten Lynch," the question becomes "Who is *them*? Do African-Americans or residents of other races feel the same way?" When white people are prime movers in response to the movement of God and the recipients are blacks, it is important to note that a missionary's relationship to neighbors is one in which both persons are broken; both of them need the Gospel of reconciliation and transformation. So a missionary's perspective should be less about how they are going to alleviate the material and non-material poverty in recipients' lives, through an unconscious god complex, and more about how they can collaborate with recipients to restore relationship to self, to others, to the rest of creation, and to God.[48]

It is evident that Meridzo Ministries sought to assist the neighborhood; what is also important is how local residents including African-Americans perceive their ministry. I hope to explore more thoroughly the perceptions of African-Americans and the lack of blacks in administrative positions in future conversations. Empowerment of black residents is needed for the vitality of Meridzo Ministries.

MERIDZO MINISTRIES' HOLISTIC TRANSFORMATION

Given the prevailing theme of MM respondents on relationships, it opens the door to discuss how holistic transformation can be achieved in an ECP. Specifically, the case study of Meridzo Ministries illustrates that Meridzo Ministries was birthed out of and moving toward relational connectivity with God and neighbor. That is, the starting point and end point of Meridzo Ministries was the Great Commandment (love for God and neighbor). At the heart of the Great Commandment is the Spirit-driven vision for *oikonomia* (embodied love and mutuality empowered by the Spirit). This serves as an invitation to experience more deeply spiritual kinship within the family of God. So the Meridzo staff see themselves and others as objects and subjects of God's mission. Figure 6 reflects Meridzo Ministries' three praxes used for holistic transformation.

---

48. Corbett and Fikkert, *When Helping Hurts*, 75.

Figure 6. Three Holistic Praxes of Meridzo Ministries

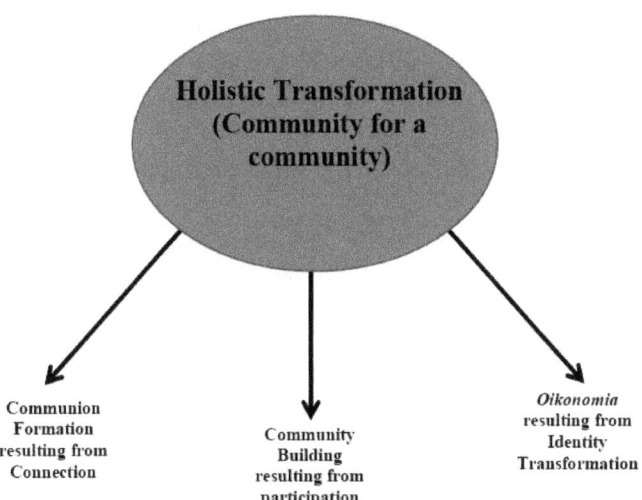

Meridzo Ministries' Three Praxes

According to interviewee data and shown above, three transformative outlets occurred in MM:

1. Communion formation (resulting from connection),
2. Community building (resulting from participation), and
3. *Oikonomia* (resulting from identity transformation).

The goals of these three outlets were rooted in relational transition. In particular, the relational transitions for each of the above three areas were:

1. Communion formation: From orphanhood to spiritual family,
2. Community building: From contract relationship into a covenant relationship, and
3. *Oikonomia:* From mere proximity to neighborly intimacy.[49]

The above terminology (communion formation, community building, *oikonomia*) embraces various relational connections with God and others through proximate depth.

---

49. Kisskalt, "Mission as Convivence," 12.

130   Faith in the Marketplace

Interestingly, the above three linking themes of MM are suggestive of Austrian theologian Clemens Sedmak's kinship model.[50] Based on his work within the context of Catholic social teaching, Sedmak presents four distinct kinship types: (1) Blood-based kinship, (2) Milk-based kinship, (3) Water-based kinship, and (4) Wine-based kinship. While I have been using the term *spiritual kinship* within the context of *oikonomia*, Sedmak's quadrilateral broadens kinship to include various relational experiences, both natural and spiritual. See Table 12.

Table 12. Clemens Sedmak's Kinship Model

Sedmak's Kinship Element	Meaning
Blood	Belonging through birth or to spiritual initiation
Milk	Belonging through communal family life or to spiritual formation and whole-life discipleship through true Community such as the Triune God and Christian communities
Water	Belonging based on compassion and transactional service (giving water to the thirsty)
Wine	Belonging through companionship or celebration (the wedding of Cana)

The main idea of these kinship types is that even though human beings have broken relationships with God and other people, we as bearers of the image of God are yet connected in some way to divine and human communities. The claim is then made that restoration of broken relationships is made possible through kinship translation. That is, there can be a transformation from one relationship to the next, such as water → blood (service to spiritual initiation or family), as shown in Table 13.

---

50. Sedmak's kinship model may serve as a bridge in repurposing the emergent themes from MM and framing a grassroots evaluative model. Sedmak, in his presentation at the fifty-ninth annual Midwest Missions Studies Fellowship, provided a helpful framework for expanding our conversation on the relational types.

Table 13. Transformation between Levels

Transformation between levels	Meaning
Water → Blood	Service to spiritual initiation or family
Blood → Milk	Spiritual initiation to whole-life discipleship
Milk → Wine	Whole-life discipleship to companionship

Table 14 below shows a possible application of Sedmak's concepts in connection to the three linking themes, three key results, and outcome of MM.

Table 14. Application of Clemens Sedmak's Kinship Model

Category of Missional Praxis	Key result	Feature of Missional Praxis
1. Connection	Communion formation	Water → Blood
2. Participation	Community building	Blood → Milk
3. Identity Transformation	*Oikonomia*	Milk → Wine

As the table above shows, the process of translation or transformation involves various experiences of spillover, both natural and spiritual, because the metaphor in play deals with liquids. For example, as one interviewee indicates, "Our specific purpose is share and talk with and be a witness to this community . . . build a relationship and making friends by providing a convenience in the service to the community by having this place here." Someone may be simultaneously water-based (compassion service) but also moving toward blood-based kinship (spiritual initiation).[51] As this transition is occurring, there is also the possibility for

---

51. Sedmak's understanding of water-based kinship involves acts of compassion. Using the example of giving water to a thirsty stranger, this act of kindness becomes a possible starting point for relational transference. For example, water-based kinship (acts of compassion) may transfer into blood-based kinship (which can be understood as entrance into the family of God). See Sedmak, "Mission as Kinship on the Margins."

a transforming into milk (spiritual formation and whole-life discipleship). This is reflected in one subject's comment:

> We're providing jobs to people that otherwise might not have jobs. We had one of the girls, that was one of our first employees, was a little, sixteen-year-old girl. She came in with no job skills or anything. Now she is in Lexington, Kentucky managing two retail stories, because of the experience she got here. The training she worked here opened doors for her there. But more importantly, she wasn't in church and she came to us. We host thousands of people mission teams every year coming to do work in the community, come to the coffee shop. She came to me and said, "I want to know more about mission," She's not in church, but she said, "I see how these people are helping in my community. I might want to help someone in their community someday." She was affected by the missions even though she wasn't in church, but she saw what was going on in Meridzo Ministries. It moved her.

Additionally, Sedmak's paradigm is more soluble than hierarchical. For instance, as we invite a stranger in need into the Kingdom of God, water-kinship (compassionate service) is transformed into blood-kinship (child of God); blood-kinship (spiritual initiation) can also be translated into milk-kinship (spiritual formation and whole-life discipleship). Another manifestation of this fluid translation occurs in the process of turning water (compassionate service) into wine (belonging through celebration). This might take the form of transcending pity into a loving celebratory community as one participant notes, "It is exciting to see the community come together in purpose." Thus, the transformation of water into wine facilitates encountering the stranger with openness. In communal celebrations, socio-economic and racial barriers are loosened to experience mutuality.

A key concept to expressing this transformation of relationships is *perichoresis* (mutual indwelling). God created us to participate in the divine life so that we might find our being-in-communion in the relationships with God, others, and creation. Simply put, it is a sense of *Community-for-a-community*: "I am because you are."[52] These *perichoretic* relationships are developed by relational boundary-crossing, or Sedmak's liquid transformation, which enlarges the circle of belonging. By crossing boundaries and differences, one can transform a one-way relationship (water-based kinship) into a two-way relationship (wine-based kinship). Sedmak called

---

52. This phrase is derived from the term *Ubuntu*. It embraces the idea that humans cannot exist in isolation. See Robb, "Ubuntu."

these relational changes "kinship moments" or "kinship experiences." He argued that these four kinship structures (water, blood, milk, wine) could shed new light on the concept of mission in ways that could potentially alter missional praxis.

In sum, based upon our analysis of this case study in Lynch, we discover that economic thriving and community transformation are both the consequence of relational well-being rather than a precondition of relational flourishing. Additionally, Sedmak's categories provide a useful paradigm for understanding and evaluating transformative movements in ECP ministries such as Meridzo Ministries. These findings suggest that the focus of ECP practitioners should not be initially on planting churches, producing wealth, or dealing with poverty issues, but on working to achieve spaces and structures that can contribute to bringing about right spiritual and neighborly relationships. Relationships, both spiritual and neighborly, may occur along with planting churches or producing wealth. It is through loving God and our neighbor (the Great Commandment) that it will become possible to advance "foretastes" of the Kingdom God and to bring shalom and justice to our communities, societies, and nations.

SECTION SUMMARY

In light of this case study from Lynch, Kentucky, we wrestled with the question of how to measure the success and effectiveness of Entrepreneurial Church Planting. Christians have postulated a variety of possible metrics in order to evaluate ECP achievements. Some Christians maintain that in order to experience personal development and the common good, we should pay attention to the transformation of the heart (the Great Commission), which then naturally leads to social transformation on the individual level.[53] Others argue that we should follow "creation ethics" (the Creation Commission) based on the norms laid down by God for all humanity, which will result in economic flourishing.[54] While both "personal salvation" or "stewardship" approaches offer a variety of helpful principles, they may at times fall into the trap of contributing to either a highly individualistic Christianity or full-fledged secularism. Whether the need be for the good news of Jesus Christ (the Great Commission) and/or for bread and a place to work (the Creation Commission), both approaches presume that Christians have resources and the poor have needs. What is missing from both of these approaches is a focus on biblical relationships (*Community-for-a community*).

---

53. Evangelicals and Progressive Pentecostalism often focus on this view.
54. Preece, "Vocation in Historical-Theological Perspective."

A current example of holistic transformation was examined in the case study on Meridzo Ministries. Rather than beginning with theoretical metrics of success, this study sought to inductively discover emergent themes in a grassroots ECP ministry. Careful examination of this fruitful ECP was done to identify possible evaluative indicators for assessing missional effectiveness; three dimensions identified included: (1) communion formation, (2) community building, and (3) *oikonomia*. Common to all three were both horizontal and vertical relational dimensions. These characteristics suggest that the mission of the church is intended to be integral to perichoretic indwelling (the divine life—Community) and for interpersonal transformation (a community). Individualistic or materialistic cultures tend to think about and measure actualization and transformation only in terms of *me* rather than *we*. But we are made for community ("love for God and neighbor") as we participate in God's mission by fulfilling the Great Commission and the Creation Commission. This study has demonstrated that *Community-for-a-community* is a significant outcome for ECP practitioners to measure, and that a real measure of ECP's success and effectiveness is based on relational transition. This can be seen in identity shifts—from orphanhood to spiritual family (communion formation), from contract relationship into a covenant relationship (community building), and from mere proximity to neighborly intimacy (*oikonomia*). The results of this study indicate that it is within the framework of *Community-for-a-community* that an ECP program is enabled to maintain unity between the Great Commission and the Creation Commission.[55]

It is important to note that what we measure determines our goals, activities, and consequences. Thus, we need to develop new strategies to move our communities, societies, and nations towards relational flourishing with God and others. One possible strategy suggested in this chapter was the combination of grassroots insights with Clemens Sedmak's kinship model. Because Meridzo Ministries emphasized a narrative of holistic transformation through identity transference, this case study naturally lent itself to models focused on relational movements such as Sedmack's. Such a relational strategy will eventually facilitate spiritual transformation as well as challenge intransigent social boundaries and increase kingdom-based civic participation.

Now that we have examined the last case study, what follows in the next chapter is cross-case analysis of the data findings of all three case studies. By comparing the data findings of each ECP, we will consider helpful components of the ministry to assess missional effectiveness.

---

55. Self, *Flourishing Churches and Communities*, 71.

7

Model of Holistic Transformation

INTRODUCTION

A "Bonsai Tree" is a tree that is intentionally grown to be tiny through artificial means.[1] If you take the seed and plant it under normal conditions, it will grow to be around fifty feet high. If the seed is placed in a different environment, however, say a small, shallow in-home pot, it might grow to a height of only two feet. There is nothing inherently different about the seed; what changes is that the pot is smaller and therefore the roots get pot-bound. In this way, the pot determines the growth and shape of the tree.

This insight from the bonsai tree applies to church planting as well.[2] The type of container or situation in which a ministry is planted determines its form and goal as it grows to maturity. We note that for some church planters, ministry is contained in the private realm, emphasizing personal spirituality and family life;[3] for others, the central focus of ministry is social justice or development.[4] In these two pots, the church is merely viewed as an instrument for God's universal mission in or for the

---

1. Hemphill, *Bonsai Theory of Church Growth*, 9–15. Jay W. Moon also used this illustration at the North Central Regional Conference of the Evangelical Missiology Society in Deerfield, IL, on March 19, 2016. I borrow this illustration from them both.

2. Long and Moon, *Entrepreneurial Church Planting*, 5.

3. For these church planters, the main goal is to create countercultural communities of faith amidst an essentially secular society. As a result, individual conversion and evangelism become the main focus of the mission. Successful potting in this paradigm results in the multiplication of congregations, living out an alternative lifestyle based on gospel values (Brown, *Death of Christian Britain*, 175–92).

4. Such Christians advocate common goals such as economic flourishing of the society. Fruitfulness in this pot means progress in the economic realm.

world, and the world is seen as a mere target of missions. But might there be a pot that is large enough to include both evangelization and development? The church cannot be solely instrumental, since it has a "being" as the image of the Triune God that precedes its "participation" in God's mission in the world. How, then, might the church combine its God-given identity while acting in a secular world which either marginalizes or instrumentalizes the Christian community?

One innovative path forward in a post-Christian world is Entrepreneurial Church Planting (ECP)[5] which focuses on the church's being (love for God and others). This model demonstrates a relational ministry centered on holistic networks of stewardship (economic development) and whole-life discipleship (evangelism) through an emphasis on social/relational development. Globally, the ECP movement has been an emerging phenomenon with examples appearing in Asia, Africa, Latin America, North America, and Europe over the last decade.[6] Although various case studies showing the performance of ECP have been presented,[7] there is far less research on identifying what constitutes ECP effectiveness, or even how to measure its effectiveness. To address the issues of determining when success has been achieved or church growth along with economic and social development were well-established, I did three case studies of ECPs to examine the unique characteristics or trends that distinguish ECPs and what outcomes they attained. Chapters 4–6 presented these three missional praxes of ECPs, providing the data for the analysis, especially interview information. From a thorough study of these trends, I hoped to identify what factors in ECP operation result in economic sustainability, evangelism, and social development in order to develop metrics (implicit or explicit) that ECP practitioners could employ to evaluate their performance relative to a Holistic Transformation Model.

ANALYSIS OF THE MINISTRIES OF THREE ECPS

What emerges from a detailed consideration of these three ECPs is a basic and continuing commitment to the Great Commandment (love of God and others) that remains paramount in collaboration with the growth of business

---

5. Entrepreneurial church planting (ECP) is an umbrella term describing the birth and growth of the new expressions of churches by using entrepreneurial approaches. It goes under various designations of "fresh expressions of church," "dinner church," "liquid church," "tentmaking," and "business as mission."

6. Moynagh, *Church In Life*, 2; Lee, "Eschatological Framework," 95–109.

7. Joo, "Entrepreneurial Church Planting (ECP)"; Long and Moon, *Entrepreneurial Church Planting*; Lee, "Holistic Framework for Measurement of Entrepreneurial Church Planting"; Moynagh, *Church for Every Context*; Moynagh, *Church In Life*.

enterprises and/or social development activities and/or evangelistic outreach. It is important to realize that the form of evangelistic outreach can be forthright as suggested by an emphasis on preaching and street evangelism or it can be softer as occurs with Bible study and discipling; evangelism happens but the form can vary. The focus on the Great Commandment is a distinctive differing from other church planning approaches and other Tentmaking and BAM approaches. Granted, evangelistic outreach and economic development activities are found in predominately entrepreneurial ministries, but the centrality of commitment to social development is less pervasive. In sum, common to each ECP is the operation of holistic transformation. Given their commitment to operating their ministry to achieve holistic transformation, we need to consider what they accomplished in terms of economic sustainability, evangelism, and social development.

With regards to economic sustainability, one factor that makes discussion of these ministries in terms of economic viability more enlightening is that they have been in operation for over ten years. It would then appear that the initial selection of the type of business to establish seemed to have been appropriate for the locale, the conception of how to run the business was good, and the response to the business has been sufficient to maintain it. However, this description is most applicable to Dayspring Technologies. From its inception, the Blue Jean Church has relied on grants or support from governmental agencies to fund its ministry. Meridzo Ministries is a mixture of being a faith-based mission with support coming from outside the ministry and having income from some of their businesses. These two ministries do not have the same concern as Dayspring about being financially self-sustaining. Without the need to support themselves, they may have a different operational dynamic. Despite these differences, common to each ministry was its desire to address the economic plight of the neighborhood; yet the approach for rejuvenating their respective areas differed.

The most noteworthy economic enterprise of the three ministries was Dayspring Technology. Redeemer Church wanted to partner with a sister entity and also provide business opportunities for the area. Yet what distinguishes it, is its commitment to biblical principles: reduce the presence of administrative hierarchy, have greater equity in pay and include employees in evaluating requests for business loans. Similar practices were implemented to create better relationships with clients of Dayspring Technologies, such as not accepting orders if it were not feasible to fulfill them in a timely fashion. To the company, establishing and following biblical principles were more important than increasing their bottom line. Evidence that this operating orientation works is a continued growth in the bottom line and their ability to add to their workforce.

Selma, Alabama certainly is in need of an economic boost which the Blue Jean Church is providing. It is proud of the business accelerator,[8] Arsenal Place Accelerator, that they helped to establish. Yet it has not generated any new businesses, but it has provided support to five existing businesses. The other disappointment is that the businesses have provided few new jobs or on-the-job training. G Mommas Cookies has expanded its business and Revival Coffee Company is now sold at a growing number of eateries. What is commendable is that the businesses have continued to stay in business. The creation of the Accelerator is a contribution to the overall economy of Selma as there is now an infrastructure to nurture new businesses. The potential for growth is definitely present with the existence of the accelerator.

Lynch, Kentucky shares some similarity with Selma as both are depressed economically. Yet, Meridzo Ministries started in a place characterized by economic despair with the departure of mining. Few other economic opportunities existed in Lynch because of the long-established dependency on the mines. Into this economic vacuum, Meridzo Ministries brought hope as new businesses slowly became established when buildings and money became available. The situation in Lynch showcases the tremendous impact that employment has in terms of self-esteem, income, friendship, help in structuring one's life, etc. Several respondents mentioned the presence of hope as there was now economic activity occurring and other community services began to be provided. While more jobs are needed, I consider their business efforts as positive for what they have achieved and the businesses established have good prospects for growing.

The other main focus of many ECPs is evangelism. Again, the sites vary considerably in terms of their evangelistic endeavors. Even though church is part of its name, the Blue Jean Church provides little overt proclamation of the Gospel. However, consistent with a holistic transformation orientation, spiritual outreach occurs in activities that initiate people into whole-life discipleship. Similarly, the deeds of its workers and their lifestyle bear witness to a personal spiritual transformation.[9] Various groups meet at the church which reflects the concern church members have for struggling individuals and simultaneously help to create a safe worship place where judgment is left at the door. Obvious evangelistic activities are minimal at Dayspring Technologies. Yet, the principles that govern the operation of the business actively demonstrate Christian ideals, the owners and directors are known to be Christians and even the workers, clients, and suppliers have all noticed

---

8. An accelerator is different than an incubator. The accelerator is supposed to take existing small startups and accelerate their growth.

9. Jones, *Evangelistic Love of God & Neighbor*, 18.

the different approach Dayspring has that bears silent witness to spiritual transformation. Many of these evangelistic efforts represent the softer side of spreading the Good News. With unchurched people, this softer approach may be less threatening and more inviting.

Where Meridzo Ministry shines is in the area of evangelism. Given the strong belief and practice of loving God and then loving their neighbors that is held by the Rileys and by many of their workers, this ministry is the epitome of evangelism—loving others to God. The approach the Rileys use in loving others to God was particularly apt for a community soured on life and with little hope that the future would be brighter. People who have been down on their fortune for an extended period of time may be more open to a gospel that brings hope. It is evident in the comments that workers made in the various ministries that loving God and then loving others permeates all that is done.

Social development can overlap with evangelism since many of the programs and activities associated with addressing the social environment in which people live can also occur as an outgrowth of evangelistic activism. Programs to reach teens and provide after school activities frequently are offered by both evangelistic and social outreach. So this assessment is not so much focused on the source within the ministry that provides social outreach, but whether or not it happens.

One advantage that the Blue Jean Church has is that it operates in a neighborhood blessed with pre-existing groups and organizations with programs to benefit the neighborhood. To their credit, the church did not seek to seize control of these programs, but merely wanted to enhance their operation. Consequently, the church became involved with the juvenile court system, the family crisis center, a school that serves high school drop-outs, etc. A good example of the neighborhood connection was when, together with a local teen center, they established a place for adolescents to gather, keeping them from loitering in public places and reducing the likelihood of encounters with the law. They knew that a teen without a record has a better chance of finishing school and finding employment. When teenagers did run afoul of the law, individuals from the church would stand with the family in juvenile court. Their presence in court demonstrated concern for the teen, and showed the court that the teen had a support system. Upon release from the detention center, the judge would recommend that the teen attend a weekly meeting at the church, complete with a meal where various church members came to mingle and evidence support for those released. With this networking, the church is credited with a keen sense of support for the community. Dayspring, in comparison, does little to establish or develop such social ministries to address problems within the community. However, the directors of Dayspring are open to community proposals for activities or programs such as the "Neighbor Fund."

Meridzo Ministries has risen to the challenge and established various groups and programs to support the people of Lynch. The Family Crisis Center is a good example. When a town loses its long-time employer, many processes are set into motion that can be ameliorated by the Family Crisis Center. As a result, its higher assessment in the area of social development is occasioned by how other social programs have been established or have been in partnership with Meridzo.

In sum, Table 15 summarizes the elements of these three ECPs in terms of the Holistic Transformational Model.

Table 15. Application of the Holistic Transformation Model

Ministry	Primary Elements	Subordinated Elements
Redeemer Church	Business Evangelism	Modest amount of Social Development
Blue Jean Church	Social Development Modest Business	Modest amount of Evangelism
Meridzo Ministries	Business Evangelism Social Development	---

From this brief analysis, while each ministry is commendable, operating with the holistic transformation model is difficult. What might help ministries to take corrective action as well as grow their ministry is to have a mechanism for evaluating their present status. Additionally, identifying the overall missional goal, effectiveness, and metrics of ECP might help ECP ministries grow by noting opportunities for development.

CROSS-CASE ANALYSIS

With the conventional practices and fundamental principles of the ECPs established, it is time to examine these organizations in terms of what they have achieved relative to their goals. In the analytical process of doing cross-case analysis and reviewing themes that emerged as described in chapters 4–6, I was able to identify the key characteristics of the goals, outcomes, and metrics of the three ministries.

GOALS

Table 16 below shows the key characteristics of the goals of the three ECPs. Despite different verbiage, we find three major factors among the reported goals of the three ECPs: improved relationships (cited by all three ECPS), redeemed business practices (Redeemer Church and somewhat by Blue Jean Church), and neighborhood/community rejuvenation (Blue Jean Church and Meridzo Ministries).

Table 16. Research Findings of the Goals of Three American ECPs

Study Site	Goals
Redeemer Church & Dayspring Tech	Relational reconciliation, Relational expression of love for God and others, Transformed business practices
Blue Jean Church & Accelerator	Becoming a good neighbor, Demonstrating neighborly love, Building a flourishing neighborhood together
Meridzo Ministries	Holistic relational healing (communion formation), Transformative networks (community building), Mutual relational flourishing for the whole town (*oikonomia*)

The size of the communities is one factor that influences how the goals are stated. Lynch, with about 900 residents, emphasizes community whereas Blue Jean Church in Selma, AL with a population of over 37,000 addresses the resurrection of a neighborhood. Redeemer Church also focuses on having a local impact as a specific goal in the Bayview/Hunters Point area of San Francisco with a population of 884,000.[10] Common themes for goals among all three ECP's were as follows:

1. Emphasis on Business Reconciliation: For example, Redeemer Church's goal is to run a business using redeemed business practices, such as the idea of 2:1 employer-employee salary structure where employers' salaries cannot be more than double the salary of the highest paid worker. In a way consistent with redeemed business practices, Redeemer's goal is socio-economic reconciliation. One manifestation of this orientation is the implementation of the Neighborhood

10. United States Census Bureau, "QuickFacts: San Francisco, California."

Fund policy at Redeemer Church. This small business loan approach is a relationship-based investing model, where the loans apply the principle of socio-economic reconciliation as a way of bearing witness to the reconciling power of Christ. Similarly, Blue Jean Church and the Arsenal Place Accelerator's focus is on being a good neighbor—lifting the neighborhood economically, socially, and spiritually. Business acceleration is simply one expression, among others, of the church's goal for community transformation. In the case of Meridzo Ministries, with businesses coming after the establishment of the Meridzo Ministries, there are no specific references to business practices in their stated goals, even though they eventually started more than twenty-two businesses.[11]

2. Attention to Relationships: The second theme common to all is the attention to relationships, directly stated by Meridzo and Redeemer Church and indirectly referred to by Blue Jean Church and Accelerator. What all three either knew from the beginning or discovered in the process of establishing the ministries is the importance of biblical relationships—love for God and others. The stated goal of relational reconciliation or the repair of broken relationships and relational expressions of love for God and others by Redeemer Church respondents is echoed by participants associated with Meridzo Ministries, as they mentioned holistic relational healing as a goal. An indirect reference to relational priority was given by respondents from Blue Jean Church when interviewees discussed the importance of becoming a good neighbor. Being a good neighbor can be learned, but it also suggests that as our relationship with God becomes closer, our relationship with others improves. This supposition is supported by the statement that demonstrating neighborly love is also a goal; our positive attitudes toward others needs to be followed by caring behavior toward our neighbors.

3. Focus on Neighborhood Rejuvenation: Concern for enriching or building a vibrant neighborhood or town is the third theme. Meridzo Ministries notes the method for achieving this: the creation of transformative networks. Working from newly established and restored relationships, they are reaching out to others around Lynch to help and support them. In Meridzo Ministries, there is little reference to "them" and "us" as the emphasis is on "we." In the case of the Blue Jean Church and Arsenal Place Accelerator, transformative networks or the "we"

---

11. Meridzo Ministries did not start off by engaging the business sector but they found that it was so effective. As a result, they kept adding more businesses.

orientation means that the resources of the ministry are used to restore the neighborhood. The concept of neighborhood rejuvenation is also at the heart of Redeemer and Dayspring Technologies and influenced the site they selected for their ministry. For instance, they saw success in much broader terms than just profit. They asked themselves what the right level of profit should be for the business, how their organization should treat people through the business and ministry, and how they could impact the community. This is termed the "Economics of Mutuality." To use Steve Garber's words, this is the greater economy, the Kingdom of God, based on a covenantal cosmos which has a sense of responsibility to people and the creation.[12]

OUTCOMES

As we turn from goals to consider desired outcomes, we see a variety of stated outcomes of three ECPs in Table 17 below.

Table 17. Research Findings of the Outcomes of Three American ECPs

Study Site	Outcomes
Redeemer Church and Dayspring Tech	Faithfulness, Seeing the lost redeemed and transformed
Blue Jean Church and Accelerator	Mutuality and reciprocity, Being shaped by others Connectedness, Trust, Mutual transformation, *Oikonomia* or "the art of living together"
Meridzo Ministries	Biblical stewardship, Spiritual renewal, Covenant relationships

Analytically, we can identify two basic categories of desired outcomes: (1) spiritual renewal and trust in the Lord and (2) relatedness. What is interesting is that there is a common business outcome as one of the three bottom lines of financial/social/spiritual capital among the three ministries. Among them, the two ministries which emphasized relationships in their goals (Redeemer Church and Meridzo Ministries) have as stated outcomes

12. Garber, *Visions of Vocation*, 132–35.

the manifestations that God-based and God-guided relationships produce blessings such as economic vitality or enhanced human capital by recognizing God's faithfulness, spiritual renewal, and salvation. It is interesting to note that these two ministries make a special point of acknowledging the blessings they have received. Additionally, I observed the logical progression from their goals to what they expect to accomplish.

Blue Jean Church, with less explicitly stated goals involving the operation of the Holy Spirit (see Table 16), indicates outcomes that would provide the means for achieving the goals that are relationship based: mutuality and reciprocity, being shaped by others, mutual transformation, and *oikonomia* (the art of living together). These outcomes have the potential to meet the goals, but they are also capable of fulfilling many other possible goals outside the ones mentioned specifically by the respondents of Blue Jean Church. What seems to be missing among the outcome statements is reference to specific practices associated with the creation of jobs, recreational programs to absorb the energy of adolescents, and the operation of a school program to enable more students to earn high school diplomas. This may reflect their reliance upon grants or government support to fund their ministry, which would differentiate them from the others. Many of their ministries are developed to resolve problems in Selma and yet would not be included if there were an outcomes assessment based on their stated metrics as illustrated in Table 18 below.

Taken together, there appears to be lack of fit between the statements of what constitutes goals and ways to measure the success, especially for the Redeemer Church and the Blue Jean Church. That is, the metrics lack adequate specificity. In a practical sense the respondents were not able to suggest ways to actually measure the outcomes. If ministries are not able to operationalize adequately their outcomes, assessment of holistic transformation is jeopardized.

In sum, the prevailing culture of the three ECPs is one where the love for God and others dominates. In other words, the emphasis which enables the orientation toward love for God and others to be manifested is a concern to form relationships with individuals. Obviously, this is an idealistic statement, but it represents what they are achieving. Additionally, it appears that the nature of the ministry influences the goals and outcomes. Furthermore, for the three ECPs, the process is more valued than the concrete accomplishments. Consequently, consideration of Tables 18 and 19 above showed that the presence of interpersonal relationships is a common thread in each ministry.

METRICS

Now that we have examined goals and outcomes, we can consider the metrics of three ECPs in Table 18 below.

Table 18. Research Findings of the Metrics of Three American ECPs

Study Site	Metrics
Redeemer Church and Dayspring Tech	Relational connections: between *mission Dei* and human participation,
	between company and the environment,
	between business and clients
Blue Jean Church and Accelerator	Formation of relationships,
	Spiritually changed lives.
Meridzo Ministries	Transformative networks,
	Economic development,
	Greater awareness of Lynch by outsiders,
	Neighborhood solidarity

From the data, we can identify one significant category of desired metrics: holistic connectivity with God and others. Relational connectivity involves multiple layers of deepening intimacy, leading first to having acquaintances and then later perhaps to either friendship, community formation or *oikonomia*. In doing so, each ECP created a system within itself so that the leaders were not only givers of time or resources, but also recipients who could learn and benefit from others. Interview results indicate that their orientation was that those forming the ministry saw their neighbors as images of God. For example, one respondent notes that the ministry "care(s) for the people and bring(s) hope back to them. We try to remind people that God loves them and that God has not forgotten them." In this way, those forming the ministry not only saw themselves as people to minister to others but also to be ministered to. As a result, it became a goal of the ministry to discover how best to love and serve local groups within the community. In the process, the ministries shared the Gospel and contributed to building a sense of community made possible by receptive relationships; the process was truly interactive. The ministries further encouraged people to explore whole-life discipleship, experience communal life with Jesus, and participate in God's mission.

Another component of many metrics is change—as a way to indicate accomplishments. Yet, if ministries are not able to make initial measurements, change in a process or a condition cannot be precisely determined. The metric mentioned by participants of the Blue Jean church, for example, is spiritually changed lives which requires a starting point and some other point in time to permit comparison. Meridzo Ministries subjects noted a metric for economic development but provided no suggestion for specific measurement, particularly needed as inherent in the concept of development is the passage of time. Indirectly, what these responses suggest is the need for leaders to have clearly stated initial goals and the ability to construct metrics to measure the outcomes.

FOUR FOUNDATIONAL PRINCIPLES IN MAKING ECP EFFECTIVE

These research findings reveal that a focus on biblical relationships (the Great Commandment: love of God and others) in the ECPs helps guide goals, activities, and metrical analysis regarding mission endeavors. Also, but not evident from these observations, is that many aspects of the ministry operate under the umbrella provided by the church as illustrated in Diagram 4 in chapter 8. This focus also serves to maintain balance between evangelism, business activities, and social development. Thus, it can be concluded that what contributes to the effectiveness of ECP is the reliance on biblical relationships. While most of my respondents were not able to provide measurable approaches to metrics, as in Table 18, their responses were tied to relation-centered fruitfulness. Since the goal of multiple ECPs was described as a network of Kingdom relationships, the ministries implicitly saw success based on relational health and increased holistic connectivity with neighbors. That is, we can know that the success of the three ECPs is defined as holistic connectivity with God and neighbors.

Based on these various considerations, it is possible to identify four foundational principles that make an ECP effective.[13] These key themes are (1) personhood, (2) in-between-ness, (3) entrepreneurship, and (4) *oikonomia*.

Personhood

To begin with, "personhood" emerged as the most important theme from the interviewee data. From the data, we can see that the ECPs' goals (see Table

---

13. The theological identity usually determines the process and the performance of a community of faith (Nel, "Congregational Analysis," 432).

16) are "relational reconciliation," "becoming a good neighbor," and "holistic relational healing." Also, in the ECP's outcomes, relational terms were mentioned, such as "seeing the lost redeemed," "reciprocity," and "covenant relationships." Furthermore, considering the metrics of three ECPs in Table 18 above, similar relational concepts were echoed such as "relational connections," "neighborhood solidarity," and "the formation of relationships." In this way, the goals, definitions, and metrics of the three ministries indicate that the ontology of personhood (love for God and neighbor) is essential to all three ECPs' goal, activities, and metrics.[14] More specifically, interview results show that most respondents believe that when God creates human beings in His own image—He creates persons capable of being part of mutual loving relationships. That is, the essence of being a human person necessitates relationship and cannot be reduced to an individual level. Without proper relation to the "other," a human remains an "individual," but cannot be a "person." Too often, many Christians and missionaries have treated unbelievers or people of other faiths as objects, as holes that needed to be filled, rather than as persons with their own God-given agency.

However, the theme of "personhood" challenges church planters to seek genuine human encounters by setting a priority on engaging the neighbor as a person. For instance, the ministries studied did not emphasize programming at the start. Rather, the founders and early supporters first moved into the neighborhoods and related to their neighbors. As a result, each ECP was accepted by its community and gave help to their neighbors. It was in these relationships that it became possible for the three ECPs to earn trust.

Moreover, personhood—the coexistence of otherness and communion—is exemplified in holistic ministries of the three ECPs. In the Trinity, the three are one, but are unique as they each have a different purpose. In like manner, the three ECPs have attempted to be holistic as they are a business, a church in separateness, and a dispenser of social programs, but experience unity in terms of space, resources, and vision. This separation-in-unity approach allows no dualisms between the spiritual and the physical, and it leads these three ECPs to be a fruitful spiritually and economically integrated community of the faithful.

---

14. Ontology is the study about the essence of things. It derives from the Greek *on* (being) and *logia* (written or spoken discourse). Personhood refers to relatedness. Thus, ontology of personhood, according to John Zizioulas, being is communion (Zizioulas, *Being as Communion*, 102).

In-between-ness

Another major concept undergirding the three ECP ministries concerns the in-between-ness of the Son's work, which connects people with God and the Christian community within the local community. In-between-ness represents evangelism. In Tables 18–20, subjects mention "connection," "redeemed," or "spiritually changed lives." These themes, common to all three ECPs, promote the work that Christ came to do. Interview results reveal that the most fundamental human need is for communion with God and others through the people of faith. Thus, each ECP endeavored to help people (re)connect with God and others as Jesus came to reconnect people to God and regain a sense of being a person and further the community of faith. This relational transformation eventually determines all other relationships.

Thus, the three ECPs tried to create situations and relationships to restore God-relations. Specifically, the relationships were fostered through regular contact, frequent interaction, and accessibility over time. An anecdote from one of the ECPs highlights this idea:

> One day while Lonnie was out in Lynch, a man from across the street yelled, "Preacher, come here!" The man then went on to exclaim, "I have been living in this town for seventy-two years, and since I have known you, you are the first man I have ever seen that put feet on Jesus." Lonnie responded, "Sir, I am humbled that you would say that. I believe God has had many people here over the course of these years to put hands and feet on Jesus, but I am glad God has chosen this time to reveal that to you. And you can come to know this Jesus just like I do." That man gave his life to Jesus right on that street corner.[15]

This respondent sought to connect Lonnie to Jesus and was an example of the embodied narrative of Christian workers throughout the years in Lynch. In this instance, the subject "saw" Jesus through Lonnie's everyday behavior without direct interaction. The man's exclamation revealed his openness and readiness to respond to the good news and accept it. Similarly, the main priority of the other two ECPs was also helping people find and enjoin relationships with God and the body of Christ from what transpired in the neighborhood or in daily activities such as grocery shopping, as well as in ECP's business arrangements and church initiatives. In this way, by utilizing the ordinary communal relationships and context within which Christians live and work as spaces for mission, in-between-ness stresses both the relational character of God's inner life and God's movement in the world.

---

15. Sentinel Group, "Putting Feet on Jesus in Lynch, Kentucky."

Entrepreneurship

The third main theme is entrepreneurship. If we return briefly to what Volland had to say about an entrepreneur[16]—as a visionary who challenges the status quo by energetically creating something of kingdom value[17]—we have the orientation necessary to discuss entrepreneurship. This term reflects the Father's work, with God talking the initiative, to create the world out of emptiness to provide a place for the beings that God created. However, this act had risk attached for the people God created and had the freedom to choose whether to follow the Lord or not. Thus, creation was the greatest entrepreneurial endeavor of all time. While entrepreneurship is commonly associated with business activities in the form of exchanges, it can equally be applied to transformed business practices, such as "transformed business practices," "biblical stewardship," "transformative networks," and "economic development." These terms (found in Tables 18–20) symbolizing the Father's materialistic and non-materialistic work in creation can be applied to economic activities of the ECPs. The three ECPs showed that entrepreneurship served as a springboard for the formation of a community of persons[18] (company) that could satisfy people's basic needs through work and contribute to the well-being (especially the economic and social well-being) of communities. For example, in the case of the Blue Jean Church, a pastor and a county judge launched a business incubator to help people start their own businesses. Meridzo Ministries sought to transform Lynch by equipping people to be economically self-sufficient as they work at businesses created to meet community needs and provide employment at a gas station, a fitness center, and a coffee shop. In this way, each ECP saw its particular duty to organize human labor and form a "spirituality of work" that could help all people come closer to God through work. Thus, community residents participated in the Father's continuing creation and deepened their friendship with Christ.

Furthermore, entrepreneurship reveals an ecclesiology of public life in the context of various neighborhoods. In *A Passion for God's Reign: Theology, Christian Learning and the Christian Self*, Jürgen Moltmann and Nicholas Wolterstorff make the claim that Christians must find the "public" nature of

---

16. See the section on Key Terms in chapter 1.

17. Volland, *Minister as Entrepreneur*, 3.

18. Here "community of persons" refers to a company. "Community of persons" actually gets closest to the full realization of what a company and corporation can be. The etymology of the words "company" and "companions" (*cum*, with; *panis*, bread) suggests "breaking bread together." The etymology of the word "corporation" (*corpus*, body) suggests a group of people "united in one body" (Casarella, *Jesus Christ*, 268).

the faith in this age of crisis.[19] For each ECP, this has meant creatively engaging with new ecclesiological models that can bear witness to the gospel through socio-economic-evangelistic engagement. The three ECPs have tried to embody the gospel in the public square with their emphasis on the workplace, marketplace, and community. For them, entrepreneurial activity is not merely a means of sustainability; it also involves contributing to human dignity and helping to form a community of persons.

Oikonomia

The last concept undergirding the three ECP ministries concerns *oikonomia*, (sharing, mutuality, taking care of God's household), both an orientation and an activity. In Tables 18–20, there is recognition of joint fellowship with others such as "building a flourishing neighborhood together," "mutual relational flourishing for the whole town," "the art of living together," and "increased publicity, and neighborhood solidarity." This orientation is related to *oikonomia*, which mirrors the eschatological, in-breaking work of the Spirit through living the Great Commandment. All subjects noted that their community of faith was not characterized as an end in itself, but its goal was rather to point beyond itself to the Kingdom of God. This focus should be descriptive of all followers of Christ and therefore, should be found in missions as well. So they built the church as a means of sharing the gospel, equipping the saints and witnessing to God's reign in the world. Furthermore, their commitment to advancing "foretastes" of the Kingdom of God to their community bound them together as part of the family of God. Consequently, the three ECPs think that in God's *oikonomia*, every person was created to be a mutual gift-giver, blesser, and sharer, crafted in God's Triune image. In this way, the concept of *oikonomia* enriches the being of person and the church as a community of mutual participation in God's own life and the life of the world.

If so, how specifically did each ECP participate in God's *oikonomia* toward the individual as well as the group? In the case of Meridzo Ministries, Lonnie Riley and the Meridzo staff started with actions prompted by the Spirit in the neighborhood. The Rileys refer to their model of ministry as responsive planning[20] or listening to the voice of the Spirit or where they minister as the Spirit directs. It is the guiding principle of everything Meridzo Ministries does to participate in God's *oikonomia*. Margaret Poloma and Matthew T. Lee describe this principle as "a model that embodies

---

19. Moltmann et al., *Passion for God's Reign*.
20. Riley et al., *Miracle in the Mountains*, 66.

the interactive ritual chains between Spirit and humans."[21] Central to this model is that revelation gives rise to theocentric, Christocentric, and pneumacentric actions that synergistically combines the will of God for a community with people already involved in a loving relational connection. Rather than entering into a community with a preconceived plan and time schedule, responsive planning for God's *oikonomia* invites missional practitioners to center their planning on direct guidance from God, leaving their schedules open to divine surprises as they realize no one specific program fits all situations. Thus, responsive planning honors God's timing and sequencing of events and offers an alternative approach; goals emerge through relational connections (both divine and interpersonal), and in this way, every relational encounter is an opportunity to encounter and experience the will of God. Responding to God's direction, the Rileys and their staff sought to help the poor, the orphan, and the widow—the neglected of the earth who are both loved and called by God to join God's mission. In short, Meridzo's response to the Triune God occurs as a result of their relationship with the Spirit and neighbor.

Extending this practice, Meridzo invites local people to seek the common good (love for God and neighbor) on the basis of respecting the differences of others and contributing to one another in representation of the new humanity in Christ and the Triune God. This was illustrated, as local people witnessed the many volunteers who came to Lynch to hold dental or medical clinics or open new businesses to benefit Lynch; many were inspired to join the movement of neighborly restoration. Consequently, Meridzo Ministries not only participate in the *missio Dei* of the Triune God, but it also encouraged people to share in the mutual indwelling life of the Triune God.

Likewise, the relationship between the other ECPs (Redeemer Church and Blue Jean) and their neighbors was predicated on open sharing and mutuality as described in chapters 4 and 5, respectively. These practices provided a reflection of the Trinitarian fellowship of equals whose mission everyone seeks to join. In sum, *oikonomia* is primarily the work of facilitating and cultivating environments in which God's people and their neighbors can come together in shared life to discover their participation in God's mission.[22]

Thus far, we have examined when effectivness in ECP has been achieved. These four themes suggest the need to (1) form churches that see their neighbors as persons, (2) to connect individuals to God and to encourage integration of the Christian community with the local community,

---

21. Miller, *Spirit and Power*, 277.
22. James, *Church Planting in Post-Christian Soil*, 151.

(3) form a community of persons, and (4) make spaces for seeking the common good (love for God and neighbor) together. Figure 7 presents the four themes in a visual way.

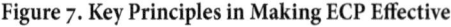
Figure 7. Key Principles in Making ECP Effective

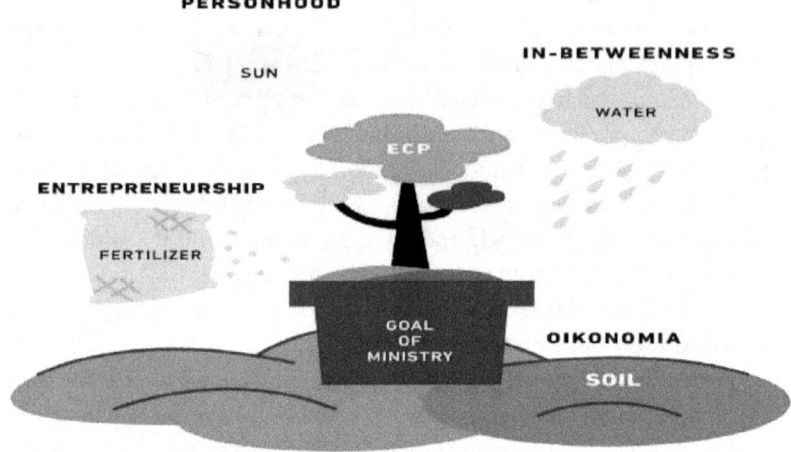

To return to our bonsai analogy, the pot stands for the goal of ministry (holistic transformation). The tree symbolizes an ECP. The four themes represent growth factors for the ECP to flourish. In order for the bonsai tree to grow within a specific context and produce fruit, the ECP needs to have personhood, as the bonsai tree needs sunshine on a daily basis. Also, the ECP needs in-between-ness as the tree needs water on a daily basis. Furthermore, the ECP needs *oikonomia* as the tree needs the soil in which it takes root communally. Finally, entrepreneurship is needed as it can serve the ECP to grow and to support the community as the tree needs fertilizer to help it grow.

Theologically, these four principles are important, because they provide different starting and ending points for churches and enrich the representational works of the three persons of the Trinity; in this framework, the first theme, personhood, represents the relationships between God, world, and church. This factor is foundational for any mission activity, but especially for ECP activities as the world is included. The other three topics listed above show the work of the three persons of the Trinity; in-between-ness intersects with the work of the Son's Great Commission, entrepreneurship reflects the work of God the Father in the Creation

Commission, and *oikonomia* mirrors the work of the Spirit in the Great Commandment. Together these four factors reveal the emphasis on relational participation in the *missio Dei*, which is rooted in the context of the doctrine of the Trinity and provides the boundaries within which ECP activities and metrics operate.[23]

Typically measuring new expressions of churches is conceived as transactional: evaluating its ministry by quantifiable elements of reconciliation or economic development. As a result, many ministries have so emphasized the church's activities, regardless of whether its mission is economic development or evangelism that they have forgotten the church's ethos (love God and other). However, these four concepts do suggest that church planting must start and end with the relational dynamic found in the Trinity. It is the Triune God who initiates and finishes mission. Consequently, with a focus on the Trinity, we should approach the neighborhood incarnationally, viewing ministry as a response to the Holy Spirit's initiatives, and evaluating our ministry relationally.

In sum, these four factors serve as identity markers for holistic ministry success and positive agents for both individuals and communities on the path to becoming what God wants them to be. These four themes will help Christian leaders develop expectations of where the church should initiate its focus and then later how it should gauge its ministry. When all four of these themes co-exist, pathways and principles will occur to support genuine spiritual transformation, community development, and *oikonomia*.

ECP PERFORMANCE INDICATORS

Now that we have examined the key growth factors of ECPs (personhood, in-between-ness, entrepreneurship, and *oikonomia*), we are positioned to offer a conceptual framework for measurement of ECP ministries. Remembering our earlier bonsai analogy, if the tree merely has sunlight and does not have water, soil or fertilizer, it may wither and die. If the plant has too much water and not enough sunlight, or not enough soil for it to be nourished and to drain, etc., then the poor plant will not develop. Thus, all four factors are needed, but they are needed in proper amounts each day to cultivate an environment that maximizes fruitfulness in its location.

Such is the case for an ECP. For any ECP to flourish, the four elements are required to be present and in functional proportions as follows.

---

23. Some of the themes have been implied in the work of Mark Lau Branson and Nicholas Warnes, thus their work deserves additional consideration. See Branson, *Starting Missional Churches*, 36–45.

Table 19. ECP Performance Assessment Factors

ECP Growth Factors		Tree analogy
Personhood (Church's missional existence)	In-between-ness (evangelical)	Change in amount of water
	Entrepreneurship (economic)	Change in amount of fertilizer
	Oikonomia (social)	Change in amount of soil

As Table 19 shows, personhood is separated from the other growth factors as it is the generating cause of the three growth factors of ECP.[24] As a result, extending out from personhood are three types of relationships: in-between-ness, entrepreneurship, and *oikonomia*. In reality, the three growth factors represent relational spaces—evangelistic, economic, and social—within which God's mission can occur.

To assess the growth factors, these three dimensions must be measurable, i.e., they need to be operationalized. Since these three themes provide a framework for missional and theological assessment of the economic-social-evangelical models, I want to develop simple corresponding metrics to guide the assessment of ECP outcomes. With the use of this framework, ECP practitioners can attempt a structured evaluation on the difference they can make and are making.

However, since it is difficult to measure the three factors (in-between-ness, entrepreneurship, and *oikonomia*) directly, I created indicators to measure any change that might occur to assess ECP outcomes. Here an indicator can tap the amount of change from one level to the next. And levels refer to four stages: (1) compassionate service, (2) spiritual initiation, (3) whole-life discipleship, and (4) belonging through celebration, as described in chapter 6. In the bonsai tree, we do not just measure how much water the tree gets once. Rather, we are more concerned about how much continued intake occurs on a regular basis. The same is true of change in the amount of fertilizer and soil. You do not merely think about fertilizer one time: rather, you consider how much and when you add fertilizer to the tree. Also, you want to know about the change in the amount of soil and guarding against erosion.

---

24. Here personhood symbolizes the Trinitarian life (the relationships between the Father, the Son, and the Spirit) and the missional relationship between God, world, and church. Its manifestation is relationality with God and neighbor, more specifically, words, deeds and lifestyles exhibiting the love for God and neighbor in various circumstances.

To keep the tree alive, you have to look at the change in these essential elements. Similarly, in an ECP, we need to pay attention to indicators across stages of growth in order to monitor holistic transformation. People usually skip right over indicators of change to proxy indicators or metrics. This is because most people use static indicators like the number of baptisms or disciples as opposed to variables, where the researcher can detect the amount of change. However, if the change in in-between-ness, entrepreneurship, and *oikonomia* areas is measured, then people have a handle on where they need to spend their time and attention. Thus, indicators of change would assist church planters in moving away from static numbers to dynamic relationships. In other words, I advocate measuring the change in numbers instead of simply counting the number of people in programs. Below are several indicators that I found in my interview data.

Table 20. ECP's Indicators of Change

ECP Growth Factors	Tree analogy	Indicator(s) of Change
In-between-ness	Change in amount of water	Change in the number of relational connections to ECP Change in the number of transformative stories
Entrepreneurship	Change in amount of fertilizer	Change in the amount of vocational stewardship
Oikonomia	Change in amount of soil	Change in the number of volunteers and changed lives for the common good

Let's take an example of an indicator in each of the three ECP growth areas.

1. In-between-ness: In order to monitor the growth in in-between-ness, ECP practitioners need to pay attention to *the change in the number of relational connections to ECP or change in the number of transformative stories between them and their neighbors*. What this example suggests is that instead of solely focusing on a static number of evangelistic activities, like *the number of people in church attendance* or *the number of people in Bible study*, at one point in time, we consider the movement from compassionate service to spiritual initiation that indicates relational growth in evangelism, or a move from a static indicator to

dynamic relationships. However, indicators of change of in-between-ness are open-ended rather than static metrics. For example, if you see *the indicators of change of in-between-ness to* going down significantly (some fluctuation is expected), that is a negative change in terms of relational connection and belonging through an ECP. Large dips in the number of relational connections suggest that you are losing your relational capacity; increases are indicative of positive growth. If it stays the same, then you may be treading water. In this way, ECP practitioners can measure the growth in in-between-ness by the change in the number of contacts someone affiliated with ECP has with their neighbors or change in the number of transformative stories between them and their neighbors. In the same manner, the other growth factors can be measured by the indicators below. However, there is virtue in using several indicators simultaneously as more aspects of the activity are measured and are a closer approximation of reality.

2. Entrepreneurship: In order to gauge the growth in entrepreneurship, it is necessary for ECP practitioners to be concerned about *the change in the amount of vocational stewardship manifested*. As mentioned earlier in chapter 4, vocational stewardship refers to a faithful steward of God-given gifts wherever you are, not restricting it to those in formal ministry.[25] The change in the amount of vocational stewardship can be monitored, for example, by the change in the number of people who got off welfare and into a job or got a new job with a higher salary and better benefits. Meridzo Ministries uses this indicator of change. In the case of the Blue Jean Church and Redeemer Community Church, the change in the amount of vocational stewardship was gauged by the change in the number of individuals attending a job fair or the change in the number of businesses formed or number of jobs formed. In this way, the indicator of change of entrepreneurship may help to show where the important change occurs in economic development and whole-life discipleship. In practice, we use the indicator of change of entrepreneurship as follows: is *the change in the number of vocational stewardship* positive or negative? How big is it? If it is a big number or if it is positive, that is indicative of growth, especially if it continues for several months in entrepreneurship as the tree has grown. If it is static, an ECP is staying about the same. If it is negative, an ECP is declining; it is important to identify causes or conditions responsible for the decline. Accordingly, ECP practitioners have to make more of an effort towards *the change in vocational stewardship* as one needs to add more water to the tree because it is lacking water. In sum, what the indicator

---

25. Sherman, *Kingdom Calling*, 27.

of entrepreneurship does is that it gives you an indication of positive or negative change in terms of economic development or movement from spiritual initiation to whole-life discipleship. Once again, it is important to use an assortment of indicators.

3. *Oikonomia*: In order to measure the growth in *oikonomia*, ECP practitioners take notice of, for example, *the change in the number of volunteers and changed lives for the common good*. This is illustrated by Redeemer Community Church and Dayspring Technologies which measure this factor by the change in the number of vital partnerships. In the case of Meridzo Ministries, the indicator of change of *oikonomia* was gauged by neighborly intimacy through various events for the common good. In this way, the indicator of change of *oikonomia* will help to account for how and when ECP practitioners have a relational impact on the lives of the people who live around an ECP. If the change in this area can be assessed on a regular basis, then church planters may have a handle on where they need to spend their time and attention in social/relational development. As a result, the indicator of change of *oikonomia* will move entrepreneurial church planters from static numbers to dynamic social relationships and from whole-life discipleship to companionship for the common good. Even though the indicator of change of *oikonomia* does not tell the whole story of social development, this will help account for whether a person, family, or community is relationally changing in meaningful ways.

Collectively, the indicators of change can help to indicate the degree of balance between evangelistic activities, business development, and social development that contribute to holistic transformation. These indicators will be discussed further in chapter 8 in order to demonstrate how they can apply to ministry/business.

SECTION SUMMARY

In light of the need for a model of holistic transformation, we wrestled with the question of how to combine God-given church's identity (love for God and neighbor) and its mission in a world which neither marginalizes or instrumentalizes the Christian community. One expression of integrating the church's being and activity was Entrepreneurial Church Planting (ECP). In order to monitor the holistic transformation of ECPs in their local communities, this study has investigated goals, activities, and metrics for three ECP sites, *viz.*, Redeemer Community Church, Blue Jean Church, and Meridzo Ministries.

One of the more significant findings to emerge from this study was that the three ministries placed a huge value on relational development: love for God and neighbor. Given the repeated identification of this goal, it becomes a significant outcome for ECP practitioners to measure. This finding, while preliminary, suggests that a real measure of ECP's success and effectiveness needs to be based on transformation of evangelical, economic, and social relationships. These can take the form of gatherings, recognition of blessings as well as actions that promote reduction in racial and economic discrimination.

The second major finding to emerge from the cross-case analysis of the responses from those involved in the three ECPs was four foundational themes (personhood, in-between-ness, entrepreneurship, *oikonomia*). These themes represent the growth factors for an ECP to flourish in its context. Theologically, in relation to the trinity, personhood implies God's inner life and God's missional movement in the world; in-between-ness reflects the work of the Son's Great Commission; entrepreneurship mirrors the work of God the Father in the Creation Commission; and *oikonomia* intersects with the work of the Spirit in the Great Commandment.

Based on these findings, I developed a conceptual framework, which attempts to provide theoretical and theological concepts to be measured by which entrepreneurial church planters could measure their performances. In particular, in this framework, I suggested several indicators of change to guide the assessment of ECP outcomes. These indicators would assist church planters in moving away from the traditional numbers-based models to a relational framework and from static numbers to dynamic relationships.

Furthermore, the analysis of the three ECPs revealed that what is needed in post-Christian contexts today is a return to relationships. Currently, many churches have come to operate and evaluate ministries largely within secular imaginary, in which mission is a quantifiable human effort to accomplish the Creation or Great Commissions.[26] However, according to my interview data, we need to view the interdependent relationships between the persons of the Trinity as a suggested remedy for the church's reason for being. This relational Trinitarian perspective gives church planters a fresh theological framework from which to view the operation of churches and their evaluation.

What follows in the next chapter is to provide an overview of the research findings and analyze the implications of the study, achievements and limitations of the research, as well as offer recommendations for future research.

---

26. Barram, *Missional Economics*, 3.

8

Conclusion

INTRODUCTION

IN HIS MOST RECENT book, *The Lean Startup*, Eric Ries sought to discover why some startup companies succeed and others fail. His hunch was that most fail because they measure the wrong criteria as with many startup companies that focus on statistics about the millions of hits on their website or thousands of tweets per day. But these metrics are only useful in making companies feel recognized; they say nothing about their overall impact on the market or their long-term outlook.[1]

In the same manner, ECP practitioners have measured their business/church's success and effectiveness by business metrics with a focus on profits or quantitative mission metrics with an emphasis on spiritual fruit such as the number of baptisms. Even though these metrics help ECP practitioners get surface feedback about the current status of a ministry, such measures fail to assess transformational change in people or in neighborhoods. More importantly, they fail to capture the change that occurs with the holistic nature of the gospel message: changed interpersonal relationships, conscious attempts to interact with the neighborhood, and community transformation. What is needed is a fuller set of measures to evaluate the holistic dimensions of ECP activities.

In order to push beyond business-centered or spiritual-centered measures to monitoring holistic transformation, this research has studied three American ECPs (Redeemer Community Church, Blue Jean Church, and Meridzo Ministries) to explore the following research question: how are ECP practitioners currently measuring the performance and the effectiveness of

1. Dixon, "Eric Ries On 'Vanity Metrics.'"

church-planting efforts combined with business models in order to develop a holistic framework for metrics to aid in the assessment of ECP outcomes. As a result, chapters 4–6 presented the three missional praxes of ECPs which provided the data for the analysis. Chapter 7 then dealt with cross-case analysis of the data findings of all three case studies.

The present chapter gives an overview of major research findings of these three case studies and the resulting implications of the study. To put the analysis into perspective, achievements and limitations of the research will be discussed. The chapter concludes with recommendations for future research and final statements, including my personal reflection.

Research Findings

Three primary findings have emerged from careful study of the three sites: (1) a focus on relationality, (2) emphasis on growth and development rather than distinctive outcomes (although the ministries made little use of specific measures to track progress), and (3) a concern for holistic ministry to occasion holistic transformation.

To begin with, the most obvious finding that emerged from the analysis is that relationality creates opportunities for missional activities and promotes holistic outreach. Careful observation of the three ECPs revealed that they embraced evangelistic, economic, and social transformation by focusing on relationships. In building relationships with the marginalized as friends in various realms, ECP practitioners attempted to move closer to holistic community transformation. In many cases, missions with people on the margins often assumes that "our" task is to meet "their" needs spiritually or economically.[2]

However, a focus on relationships in the three ECPs offered an alternative to the commonly used measuring approach of counting baptisms, handouts or outreach activities. As chapters 4–6 demonstrate, providing free food as well as job training, the three ECPs actively reached out to their local communities, cultivated authentic relationships with their neighbors, employees, and customers, and served them in practical ways—such as vocational stewardship and church/non-profit partnerships. These forms of incarnational witnessing gradually brought economic, social, and evangelistic vitality to their communities to varying degrees.

There is no question that each site saw a distinct improvement in terms of social and evangelistic vitality. However, one domain for which growth is more debatable is the economic area. Economic growth is particularly a concern in both Selma and Lynch. Selma still grapples with

---

2. Heuertz and Pohl, *Friendship at the Margins*, 19.

remnants of institutionalized discrimination while Lynch is still engaged in restarting an economy devastated by the demise of the coal industry. When the ill-effects of an economic downturn reverberate throughout an entire area, resuscitation takes time. Redevelopment is definitely evident given the mere presence and operation of a business accelerator in Selma and the creation of several businesses in Lynch. While these business gestures are indicative of improvement, there is still a way to go in producing economic robustness. Both of these sites suggest that quick fixes are not the answer. However, foundational work is occurring in all three sites as there is a focus on schools, provision of job training, and the existence of various social service programs. An obvious theme throughout the activities associated with economic growth is a relational aspect. What become incumbent on each ministry is to help people "see" the blessings the communities experience. In this way, with a focus on holistic relational transformation, the three ECPs demonstrated a more foundational form of success and effectiveness of the church.

The common element that made the three ministries able to embrace all three realms in synergetic unity was a focus on loving relational interaction with God and others (the Great Commandment). They exemplified what loving relational interaction with God and others, powered by the Holy Spirit's call for God's people to apply the relational commission of love for God and others in their roles and responsibilities looks like. We note that the Holy Spirit is the prime transforming agent and what empowers believers with various gifts to continue the mission of Jesus Christ in the world. What results is a type of holistic synergy between the Holy Spirit's power and the pouring out of his gifts upon all flesh; the Spirit empowers believers for partnership with God and others toward global holistic transformation.[3] This synergy is also noted by Amos Yong who sees that the Holy Spirit (love for God and neighbor) serves as the mover between the Father (the Creation Commission) and the Son (the Great Commission).[4] Thus, a focus on the Great Commandment (relational transformation) enables the three ECPs to not become dualistic (the Creation Commission or Great Commission), but rather enables three sides of the tension to be valued interactively. Consequently, a focus on loving relational interaction with God and others (the Great Commandment) is considered to be the central source of the success and effectiveness of the three ECPs.

Another important finding was an emphasis on the gains rather than on specific outcomes. According to the interview data, the metrics cited by

---

3. Moynagh, *Church In Life*, 301.
4. Yong, *Spirit-Word-Community*, 106–9.

the three ECPs studied were grounded in the change of a process. For example, the goal of the three ECPs was not just church sustainability, but love for God and neighbor. This focus is consistent with the observations of Paul VI's ideas in *Ad Gentes,* for now "there is no possibility of expounding the Gospel directly and forthwith. Then, of course, missionaries can and must at least bear witness to Christ by charity and by works of mercy."[5] Schreiter states it as "not just to convert, but to bear witness to the Trinitarian life, to bear witness to the very life of God."[6] As a result, the outcome metrics of the three ministries were associated with changes which reflect relational transformations such as the change in number of relational connections to ECP, change in number of transformative stories, change in the number of vocational stewardship, and change in number of volunteers and changed lives for the common good. In chapter 7, I termed these "indicators of change," because they show maturation in their faith. These indicators revealed that process is more valued than the outcome. These relational ways of measuring ECP's *neighborly* movements will open our imagination for the measurement systems that extend beyond church sustainability where the focus is mainly on attendance and economic returns.

The last major finding was a concern for holistic ministry to occasion holistic transformation. Each case study provided an opportunity to compare conceptually existing dualistic systems of church planting to those of ECPs that includes both evangelization and economic development by means of relational vitality. Even though none of the research sites had leaders who were able to articulate a holistic worldview that unites evangelism and (economic and social) development in most instances, they provided anecdotal evidence of this worldview. For example, the three case studies challenged old divisions between a secular public domain and private belief as they sought changed lives and social relationships through the nonprofit branch of an ECP as well as material and economic transformation through the for-profit branch of an ECP. This worldview led to fruitful local community development. Additionally, although their monitoring holistic transformation efforts seemed more descriptive than concrete data, what they achieved showed that they resisted the tendency to make their own institutional stability or survival the primary end, an important point suggested by Newbigin.[7] They recognized that their primary end is participation in God's mission in the world holistically by loving God and neighbor

---

5. Second Vatican Council, *Ad Gentes* 6.

6. Scherer and Bevans, *Theological Foundations*, 99.

7. Newbigin noted that many churches are focused on their own survival. He argued that a church that is focused on keeping itself alive may be working against the very plans of God. See Newbigin, "What Is a Local Church Truly United," 14–29.

and their application. In this way, the three case studies clearly show that the church needs "to discern God's action in the world holistically and to participate in His mission" holistically.[8]

One area underdeveloped in all three ministries, especially in Selma or the Blue Jean Church, is an emphasis on training others to assume leadership roles in the ministry. While institutional stability should not be the goal, a concern for institutional growth should be present. It is notable that in each of the ministries the leadership continues unchanged; sometimes for growth leadership change can be useful. The topic of ECPs is still new and unresearched enough not to know when leadership change can occur without endangering the viability of the ministry. For ministries to continue with a holistic orientation, it is important that the leadership remain in touch with the larger community and maintain relevant programs.

IMPLICATIONS OF THE STUDY

We have seen that our approach to metrics in the church is often largely the result of Western management models or modern quantitative approaches influenced by the dominant culture rather than theological and/or missiological perspectives. However, this research has revealed that a true measure of an ECP's success and effectiveness needs to be based on transformation of evangelical, economic, and social relationships. In other words, the ministries need to frame their ending point in terms of the Triune God's work through the Father within all creation, through Christ within the reign of God, and through the Spirit within the coming Kingdom of God. The key to these metrics is the intersection between the immanent Trinity (the inner life of the Triune God) and economic Trinity (the Triune God's missional movement in the world). Alan Roxburgh and Scott Boren in their book *Introducing the Missional Church: What It is, Why It Matters, How to Become One* deftly illustrated the Triune God's relationship with the church and the world.[9] Even though Roxburgh and Boren remarkably demonstrated a different starting point for the church to become the missional church, they did not advance the conversation about an ending point of the church, such as assessment tools to tell you where you are. Advancement can be precisely determined with these measurement tools. Thus, there should be metrics applied to the missional church and a more theological and missiological standard by which to measure a church's effectiveness and success. Considering this, two implications are highlighted here: (1) missional assessment of ECP performance and (2) relevance of ECP to other missional issues.

8. Cardoza-Orlandi, *Mission*, 46–37.
9. Roxburgh et al., *Introducing the Missional Church*, 31–39.

Faith in the Marketplace

Missional Assessment of ECP Performance

This study has shown that beginning with a focus on the missional ministry as found in God's inner life understandably can result in several different ending points. For example, the three ECPs intentionally embraced the work of the three persons of the Trinity in the world and in the lives of people instead of being content to attract more people into the congregation. Additionally, the three ministries put an emphasis on discernment of the Holy Spirit through prayer, Scripture, and community involvement. Guided by the Spirit, work in the local community generated open-ended activities by each of the three ECPs. Here open-ended activities refer to being open to the guidance and direction of the Holy Spirit. Furthermore, each ECP provided distinct indicators of change appropriate for their site.

Based on these findings and referencing Table 20 (ECP's Indicators of Change) in chapter 7, I provide a conceptual framework by which the holistic transformation of an ECP can be measured. After that, I will demonstrate how it can be applied in practice.

To begin, the relational view of an ECP offers an alternative to the long-standing tension among business (economics), evangelism/church planting (ministry), and social development (transformation) found in the "Holistic Transformation Business" model depicted in chapter 2. Newbigin notes that salvation is received through mutual relationships among human beings.[10] In addition, Moynagh's work on the church helps to expand on our understanding of relationships by identifying four dimensions: (1) personal participation in the inner life of the Trinity or spiritual growth; then on a group level, (2) intimacy among the members of the local church; (3) willingness to align with the wider church; and (4) proclaiming the good news to others and discipling new believers, seeking to transform society, and safeguarding creation.[11]

---

10. God from the beginning chose human messengers who then shared the message with others (Newbigin, *Open Secret*, 70).

11. Moynagh suggests four dimensions (Up, In, Out, Of) and several indicators. Here UP represents participation in the inner life of the Trinity; IN stands for intimacy among members of the local church; OF symbolizes interdependence with the wider church; and OUT signifies proclaiming the good news, teaching, baptizing, and discipling new believers, serving the world, seeking to transform society, and striving to safeguard the creation. Even though he provides a comprehensive yardstick for four sets of relationships (with God, with the world, with the fellowship, and with the wider Christian family), since an ECP's context is often reduced to the marketplace and it always has to do with entrepreneurial approaches, this study is focused on developing a framework specifically tailored for measuring the ministry of an ECP. See Moynagh, *Being Church, Doing Life*, appendix.

Continuing conceptually, to develop a more fully existing framework as well as Moynagh's, I take personhood (relationality with God and neighbor) as the starting point. Once personhood is established, the next step in the progression can be involvement in one or more of the growth factors in an ECP (in-betweenness, entrepreneurship, or *oikonomia*) depending on what aspect of the ministry an individual has contact. As is suggested by Diagram 3 below, there are multiple contact points so that in time most people will connect with all three of the major factors in an ECP.

Diagram 3. Basic Diagram of the Operation of
Entrepreneurial Church Planting Four Factors

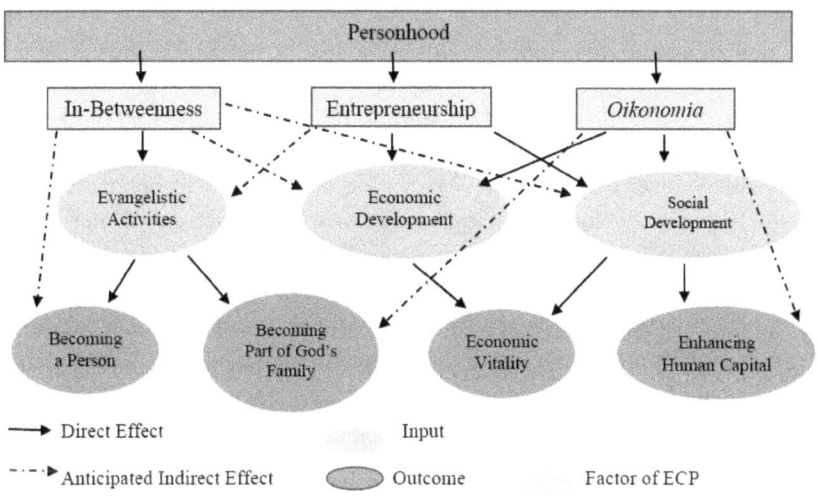

When an ECP is developing and growing, given a commitment to holistic transformation, the three factors become associated with missional praxes or the inputs as identified in Diagram 3. The logical extension of In-Between-ness is engagement in evangelistic activities which in time fosters an individual's movement toward helping people in need and becoming integrated into God's family (note the lines denoting anticipated direct effects in Diagram 3). In a similar way, Entrepreneurship fosters the growth of economic development—whether for marginalized people or as a mainstream economic venue for the community. Vocational stewardship occurs when people are faithful stewards of God-given gifts (whether it is baking cookies or being proficient with a computer) wherever you are, not restricting it to opportunities in formal ministry.[12] The third growth factor is *Oikonomia*

12. Sherman, *Kingdom Calling*, 27.

where the praxes are becoming neighborly to the poor and needy and then, more holistically, living together for the common good or the occurrence of different aspects of social development depending on the context. It is in the operation of *Oikonomia* that the personal resources of each individual are nurtured. In this context, people more fully become kingdom workers as Howard Snyder points out.[13]

With the conceptual discussion of the three growth factors (In-between-ness, Entrepreneurship, *Oikonomia*) outlined, let us explore corresponding operationalization of these factors:

1. In-between-ness: This involves an evangelistic connectedness. For example, In-between-ness can transpire in the neighborhood, in daily activities such as grocery shopping, as well as in both their business arrangements and church initiatives. In the case of Meridzo Ministries, expressions of in-between-ness with its neighbors include: (a) involvement in the life of the community through acts of service such as hedge trimming, cookie give-aways, and attending the community prayer meeting, and (b) creation of employment opportunities through job initiatives, e.g., Solomon's Porch Retreat Center and Merizdo Agribusiness Center. As for Blue Jean Church, they see their neighbors not as members of class or race, but as persons defined by otherness in relation. In this way, an ECP can instituted various practices and ministries to involve people on the personal level for an evangelistic connectedness.

2. Entrepreneurship: Salvation, though personal, is not limited to the individual experience; rather, it involves a life of whole-life discipleship within the context of a workplace. Thus, expressions of Entrepreneurship include vocational stewardship. Dayspring Technologies' focus on whole-life discipleship illustrates this well with their economic hope for the future by creating businesses. It was through this for-profit branch that the Dayspring staff was able to engage the hopeless and poor to equip, enable, and empower them toward faithful stewardship of their talents and faith. Entrepreneurship can be seen in the push for a sense of belonging and creative connective outlets such as the gas station, coffee shop, and fitness center of Meridzo Ministries. But it also can be seen as people become willing

---

13. Snyder, *Models of the Kingdom*, 153. Snyder pointedly remarks that we are not kingdom builders, but kingdom workers, because the kingdom of God is God-initiated, God-oriented, God-centered, God-fulfilled and God-glorified. Lesslie Newbigin also strongly asserts that mission is not our business, but God's.

to lend their musical talents, teaching skills in Bible Studies, and gifts of hospitality by inviting people into their home.

3. *Oikonomia*: This represents a profound experience of relational intimacy with God and neighbors. *Oikonomia* involves a communal identity shift; those who once were mere neighbors now recognize the possibility for mutual indwelling in God. Though "in-between-ness" serves to expand relational connection and belonging through an ECP, *oikonomia* is an awakening into a mystical family that embodies Eucharistic ties. This spiritual stirring includes a two-way movement; first, spiritual kin are united to each other, then they are sent into the world to invite others to the open table of God's self-giving love. This is reflected by Joshua's statement as reported in Table 8 in the Appendix D:

> God used the missionaries to restore and to re-instill hope. That is the thing that has really happened. People are starting to see that they are worthy of being loved. They're starting to see that other people care about them and love them and want to help them. That gives them the love of themselves, that gives them the love for their own community, that encourages them to want to better themselves both in the natural world and in the spiritual world. There's the spiritual side and the physical side. There's a restoration. God's even restored the ecosystem here. There's just been a whole restoration. God continues to build His Kingdom.

In this way, *Oikonomia* can result from a transformed heart for the city such as the city-wide prayer meeting.

From these inputs in an ECP, my research identified four common relational outcomes: becoming a good neighbor, becoming part of God's family, economic vitality, and enhancing human capital (see Diagram 3). "Becoming a good neighbor" signifies being in relationship with others, i.e., as individuals are spiritually transformed, they are innately relational and created in the image of the Trinity. In Zizioulas's words, it is "being in communion."[14] Thus, success in life looks like the *perichoretic* relationality (mutual indwelling with God, self, others, creation).[15] "Becoming part of God's family" refers to spiritual initiation and integration. Frequently, as a consequence of evangelistic endeavors, people are incorporated into the family of God, often via a local congregation. As their relationship

---

14. Zizioulas, *Being as Communion*, 102.
15. See Morris, *If Aristotle Ran General Motors*, 183–211.

with God and a community of faith matures, their understanding of the broader implications of being part of God's family may extend to support and action within social and economic domains.

Another outcome is "Economic vitality." As economic development continues, two common spin-offs are the creation of economic vitality and enhancing the human capital in the neighborhood and community. Economic vitality is not solely the economic value generated by the businesses established by the ECP, but the creation of jobs, the flow of money into local stores, food markets, and various service providers. Thus, participation in economic activities includes both spiritual and moral practices that are foundational for wealth creation.[16]

The last major outcome is "Enhancing human capital" which include a host of activities that nurture human skills and abilities, whether it is teaching people computer skills or showing them ways to improve their nutrition and physical well-being or helping people improve their resumés.[17] By standing in solidarity with the marginalized, ECP practitioners help change people's marred identities and help them put their narratives into perspective, alter moral behavior, and create new meaning, vision, and hope for the future. Thus, both "Economic Development" and "Social Development" as well as "*Oikonomia*"[18] would be significant input factors.

Finally, the ultimate outcome, *missio Dei* (see Diagram 3), is achieved as both the inputs and outputs influence the operation of the ECP. It is at this point where holistic transformation becomes evident. It is by engaging with the *missio Dei* that the economic, social, and evangelistic are combined and intermingled.

A summary of the fully developed conceptual framework for tracking evangelism, business effectiveness, and social development of ECP is reflected in Diagram 4 below.

---

16. Bornstein, *Spirit of Development*, 71.

17. Thurow, *Investment in Human Capital*.

18. In secular literature, *oikonomia* is more closely related to economic than social development. Yet, in transformation development, it is linked to spiritual and ethical judgments. In *oikonomia*, there is the idea that it is not to pursue economic goals for their own sake, but to advance the good life. This concept is compatible with engaging in *missio Dei* or seeking social impact. Thus, it can be seen that "enhancing human capital" or social impact is an outgrowth of *oikonoma*. See Leshem, "Retrospectives," 225–38.

Diagram 4. Operation of Entrepreneurial Church Planting

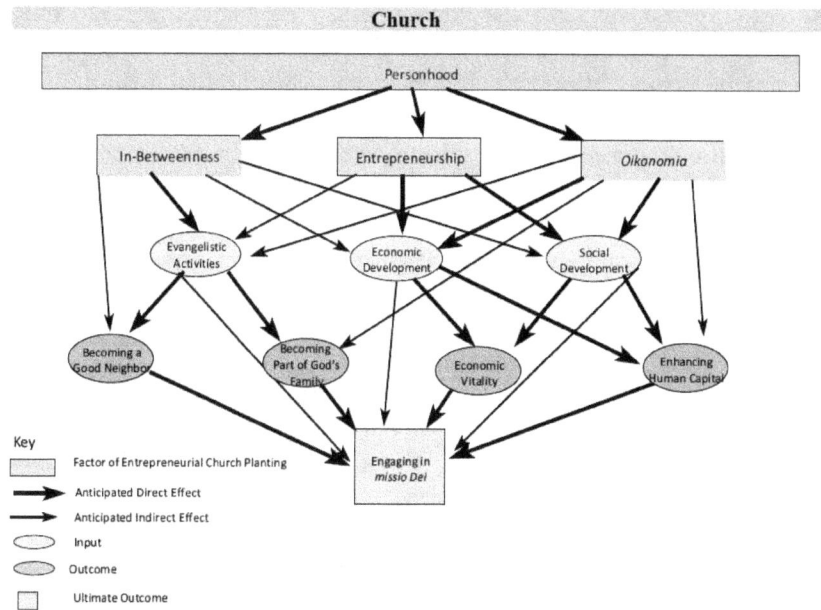

Diagram 4 is a presentation of ECP's performance process with the factors of ECP, both inputs and outcomes, direct and indirect effects as they all effect engaging in *mission Dei*. As mentioned before, the Church represents an image of the Trinity. This diagram is open, since one factor can contribute to several relational outcomes (becoming a good neighbor, becoming part of God's family, enhancing human capital, and economic vitality). For example, in-between-ness may lead to "becoming a good neighbor" and "becoming part of God's family" through evangelistic activities, but it can also occur as a result of social development or economic development. In this way, the operation of an ECP has several factors that give rise to still different activities.

Additionally, the four outcomes occur in three dimensions. These outcomes are consistent with the holistic transformation thought to occur with an ECP—spiritual cleaning of an individual with the occurrence of the fruits of the Holy Spirit, along with economic growth and the ministries which emerge to support people's spiritual and material growth.

Assessment of Outcomes of ECP

A critical part of any research study is to evaluate the outcomes. Outcome assessment is to determine whether outcome variables have been affected by any of the factors and/or inputs (see Diagram 4 above). More sophisticated analysis would be required to specifically link an outcome with a specific input, since multiple inputs are thought to affect each outcome. For basic outcome evaluation, comparing observations at some later point, perhaps done every six months, with baseline observations would provide feedback on any of the indicators and convey whether the status quo was being maintained, or whether some change had occurred, either positive or negative. Simple subtraction would provide change numbers. By collecting data on multiple indicators for each outcome, ECP leaders could have a good overview of what was happening as the result of ECP ministries and in what specific areas change was happening. In this way, for evaluation to occur one must have metrics for both inputs and outputs.

The operational discussion of the indicators of change or inputs is already dealt with in chapter 7. Table 21 below (an abbreviated version of Table 20 in chapter 7) shows sample indicators for each outcome. It is important to emphasize that the indicators in Table 21 are examples. In actual analysis, you would need to use multiple indicators for each of the ECP growth factors. The development of reliable indicators is a standard skill of research methodologists, such as sociologists.

In particular, the ministries of Blue Jean Church and Meridzo Ministry are sufficiently complex that proper evaluation requires assistance from people trained in program evaluation. If the area of evaluation of ECP grows, in time, appropriate measures may come to exist. Actual monitoring of outcomes would require detailed record keeping on a host of indicators. A fuller list of indicators is provided in Appendix E. Additionally, the change numerics would help assess movement from missional praxis to results and be a guide to where real transformation was occurring. Furthermore, indicators used would need to be appropriate to the ECP setting and the type of ministry activities.

Conclusion 171

Table 21. Indicators for Evaluating Outcomes[19]

Outcome	Indicator
Becoming a Good Neighbor	Number of contacts someone affiliated with ECP has with their neighbors
	How many neighbors can a person who is a part of ECP identify by name
Becoming Part of God's Family	Number of occasions when an individual part of ECP spent time with other Christians, also a part of ECP
Economic Vitality	Number of individuals attending a job fair
	Number of people who got off welfare and into a job
Enhancing Human Capital	Number of people who completed their GED
	Teen pregnancy rates
	Number of teens jailed or imprisoned
	Number of parents who helped out at their children's school

The other value of change numerics is to alert people to possible ECP activities and ministries that may occasion statistically significant change numbers (statistical procedures for evaluating changes in frequencies, percents, proportions, etc., are readily available). A research methodologist can help in developing indicators appropriate to the ministry's situation. In this way, ECP practitioners can have a better understanding of how much and when ECP activities should occur to further holistic transformation. It is important when the indicators are used to sort them into different categories and not treat all indicators of being of equal value in understanding the operation of the ministry. A useful distinction is to break indicators into those measuring the quality of relational connections, those associated with behaviors of new converts, indicators associated with more mature Christians, etc. One thing to remember is that data tend to imply a one-size-fits-all approach without navigating the context or multiple causation. Therefore, numbers alone are not the most helpful ways to assess goal achievement. The initial phase of evaluating an ECP's outcomes may involve the counting

---

19. The indicators listed are just a few of those that should be used to collect information. See Appendix E.

of resources and activities; full-fledged assessment, however, involves examination of various holistic processes.

If holistic transformation is truly the goal of an ECP, it is important the ECP practitioners examine change numerics by race, social, and gender across time. As the Kingdom of God does not make distinctions (1 Cor 12:13; Gal 3:28), it is important that ministries serve everyone equally. Also true, if an ECP wants to serve, evaluation of services is essential so if initial relationships and activities are not effective within four or five years, new initiatives can be started.

Relevance of ECP to Other Missional Issues

Now that we have developed metrics to aid in the assessment of ECP outcomes, we need to explore three correlations between ECP and other missional movements. This is especially important at a time when the understanding of what church is, is undergoing change and concomitantly different forms of church are found in various cultural settings. In specific, I want to consider the relationship between: (1) transactional service to holistic transformational development, (2) missional engagement in the marketplace, and (3) the church as *institution and organism*.[20]

1. The Movement from Transactional Service to Holistic Transformational Development. Evangelical missional praxis has now progressed from transactional service to holistic transformational development.[21] Transactional service, often taking the form of handouts delivered at the time of the request, is limited because it rarely involves ongoing, transformative interaction with the needy. Specifically, the relational dimension is limited to a one-way exchange because the delivery system is triggered when the resources of the individual are inadequate relative to the need.[22] Consequently, much transactional service fosters dependency by the poor. Holistic transformational development, on the other hand, is predicated upon relationships and capacities being offered before being requested and is associated with an openness conducive to on-going contact. Theologically, holistic trasnformational development grounds relationships in both the Great Commandment (person-to-God) and the Great Commission (person-to-person), i.e., someone who has been transformed then

---

20. A part of this material is adapted from my article in Lee, "Holistic Framework."

21. Cnaan and Boddie, *Invisible Caring Hand*, 10–11; Perkins, *Restoring At-Risk Communities*, 163–80; McKnight, *Careless Society*, x–xiii.

22. McKnight, "Why 'Servanthood' Is Bad," 2.

reaches out to someone in need. This shift in the initiating entity (extending aid before it is requested) further implies an understanding of poverty alleviation based upon the concept of biblical stewardship (person-to-creation); specifically, thinking patterns are transformed regarding humanity's right relationship with creation (Gen 1:26–28). Holistic transformational development helps us realize who we are as co-creators with God in our cultivation of the world in all of our activities.[23] In the same manner, the three ECPs illustrate this holistic transformation development very well by integrating whole-life discipleship (the Great Commission and the Great Commandment) with a call to cultivate the world (the Creation Commission).

2. Missional Engagement in the Marketplace. This study has shown that even though the three ECPs studied did not intentionally use John Perkins's three-fold strategy of community development (relocation, reconciliation and redistribution), their operation was very similar to Perkins's three R's; they relocated themselves and created a business. These missional movements resulted in progress towards racial and spiritual reconciliation. Interestingly, according to Perkins, the hardest component of his three R's to achieve in community development is redistribution. Each of the three ministries corroborated Perkins's assessment. For example, in Selma no real redistribution occurred as the businesses associated with the accelerator had few employees. More importantly, there were few suggestions that redistribution was a conscious goal. Similarly, in Lynch, businesses were started but at the time of this study they employed few people. Redistribution had started, but had effected little change. Nevertheless, we can see the potential for redistribution that hopefully would occur through ECPs. Such ministries are in a position to construct practices to promote redistribution rather than rely on the vagaries of the marketplace. If one disengages from the marketplace, it might be difficult to have influence in the areas where there is need. Given this, we should carefully consider the ramification of interaction with the capitalist reality while still maintaining a commitment to Kingdom expansion in the marketplace. The three ECPs definitely revealed that it takes a while for an ECP to grow to where it can have enough employees to help foster redistribution. Dayspring Tech with its commitment to the 2:1

---

23. Forster, "Theology That Works," 7–8 (a sixty-page manifesto on discipleship and economic work published by the Oikonomia Network). Stewardship comes from the same Greek word (*oikonomia*) as economics, which refers to "the care for our common home" or "the art of living together" (Snyder, *Liberating the Church*, 61).

ratio for managers to employee pay is one workable example. When the ECP pays a living wage (this is a good example of how an ECP can construct a useful practice for redistribution), it can facilitate movement towards redistribution as well as reconciliation.

3. The church as *institution and organism*: As the three ECPs have shown, an appropriate vision of evangelical-economic-social mission with the poor and the disenfranchised involves being a counter-cultural community as participants in God's mission, "because to be church means to share in the mission of Jesus, which is to preach, to serve, and to witness with his whole heart to the kingdom of God."[24] Here a countercultural community is a missional community called out but sent into the world to act for God's universal mission. So this missional community requires both gathering and dispersing, exclusion and embrace, and institution and organism.[25] Borrowing from nineteenth-century Dutch theologian and politician Abraham Kuyper, the church as an *institution* maintains its distance from society and retains its missional focus in calling people to itself and equipping them to be disciples of Jesus as shown in Ephesians 4.[26] Yet as reported in each of the three case studies, the institutional aspect of the church is not emphasized. Redeemer Community Church has not regularly recorded basic statistics, like church attendance. Similarly, the Blue Jean Church puts little pressure on the people who participate in various activities. Gathering occurs, but the impetus to attend needs to be within the individual; there is little evidence of external urging. Unchurched people do not have the established memories of church attendance. With a marketplace mentality, the unchurched see church as merely one option of where to spend Sunday morning.

On the other hand, the church as an *organism* does not hide its light or withhold its salt from the world; rather, informed by God's self-giving love and guided by scriptural precepts as opposed to societal norms, the Body of Christ goes out into the world[27] and seeks to transform the world by forming transformative social justice networks.[28] Accordingly, the church as *institution and organism* interdependently bears witness to the five marks of mission:

---

24. Bevans and Schroeder, *Constants in Context*, 306.

25. Stevens, *Liberating the Laity*, 22; Volf, "Vision of Embrace," 200–205; Stevens, *Other Six Days*, 211.

26. Graham, *Kuyper Center Review*, 78.

27. Graham, *Kuyper Center Review*, 79.

28. Keller, *Generous Justice*, 145–46.

(1) To proclaim the Good News of the Kingdom; (2) to teach, baptize, and nurture new believers; (3) to respond to human need by loving service; (4) to seek to transform unjust structures of society; and (5) to strive to safeguard the integrity of creation and sustain and renew the life of the earth.[29]

It is evident from the overview of programs associated with each ministry that concern for racial and economic inequality is coupled with action. However, it was difficult to ascertain in this study how much personal internalization occurs with regards to these issues. As topics on equality can challenge a person' values, holistic transformation does require conformity to biblical values. To use James Davison Hunter's words, the church is the "faithful presence within"[30] and it should aim to reflect holistic gospel transformation in its action. In this way, those who want to participate in the evangelical-economic-social mission of God need to become neighborly to the poor and needy in every aspect of life as God became a neighbor to us all.[31] If the church rediscovers this vision through creative expressions such as an ECP, the door will be opened wide to evangelism, reconciliation to God, self, others, and creation, and the flourishing of humanity.

ACHIEVEMENTS AND LIMITATIONS OF THE STUDY

I chose a case study approach as a methodology to explore the following research question: How are ECP practitioners currently measuring the performance and the effectiveness of church-planting efforts combined with business models. This question embraced three main aims which were: (1) to reveal the ECP's goals, (2) to identify theoretical definitions of success and effectiveness of ECPs, and (3) to detect operational definitions of success and effectiveness of ECPs. The research findings demonstrated that an ECP's goal was holistic transformation, that its theoretical definitions of success and effectivness were relational, and that its operational definitions of success and effectiveness were based on transformation of evangelical, economic, and social relationships. The case studies also provided the four boundaries within which ECP activities and evaluation operate (personhood, in-between-ness, entrepreneurship, and *oikonomia*). These four factors serve as identity markers for holistic ministry success and positive agents for both individuals and communities on the path to becoming what God wants them to be. Based on these findings, I constructed a

---

29. These Five Marks of Mission were adopted by the General Synod of the Church of England in 1996 (Walls and Ross, *Mission in the Twenty-First Century*, xiv).

30. Hunter, *To Change the World*, 237–54.

31. Koyama, "Neighbor," 24.

conceptual framework. The conceptual holistic framework attempted to provide theoretical and missiological indicators by which entrepreneurial church planters could measure their performances.

However, this study has several limitations. First, it lies within the interpretive tradition because it was conducted using a case study approach. Thus, there can be different interpretations of the same data which might be dissimilar to my interpretation. Given that this study was built upon subjective interpretation, the research findings while tentative provide a systematic examination of how these three ECPs operate.

Second, the research was conducted within the qualitative tradition with a focus on the individual perspectives of participants, minimizing the amount of generalization to other populations that is possible. The research engaged only those who were involved directly or indirectly in an ECP. It is possible that other community members within the same local communities who are not involved in the ECP may have different understandings of it.

Third, understandings of an ECP's economic context were not addressed as key concepts within this study. During my research, I was aware of the widely divergent economic climate of the west coast of San Francisco, impoverished Eastern Kentucky, and underdeveloped Selma, Alabama. I noticed that different circumstances made establishing a business significantly more challenging in the various locations. For example, when the main source of income (coal) is no longer being mined, as in Lynch, there was no economic foundation on which to build. Consequently, the development of an economic enterprise takes much more effort and produces fewer economic results quickly. In addition, Selma, with its violent and exploitative past related to the black population, takes a lot longer to bounce back with businesses that impact families and communities. San Francisco, on the other hand, so close to Silicon Valley, reflects some of the potential and cash flow from the locale.

Finally, this study paid little attention to leadership of the three ECPs. The three case studies made it evident that the direction in which the ministries developed were largely depended on the gifts and talents of the founding leaders. While the Holy Spirit gives new gifts to people for particular times and situations, the Holy Spirit often enhances the gifts and talents that the leaders already have. For example, the leaders of Redeemer Church and Dayspring Technologies developed ECPs to meet the needs of the community around them. Even though leadership determined the ministry, this study did not chiefly focus on their leadership in detail.

FUTURE RESEARCH

This study has explored how three ECPs, within the US attempt to measure the performance and the effectiveness of church-planting efforts combined with business models in order to assess ECP outcomes. Even though the three ministries did a modest job of measuring performance, they provided diverse possibilities for when and how an ECP could be operated to meet holistic transformation. Future research could explore global case studies from Africa, Latin America and Asia in order to broaden theological and missiological possibilities. In the light of post-Western Christianity, global case studies will re-attach United States church planting endeavors to spiritual roots in the Christian heritage. According to leading theologians and missiologists, Christian believers in the southern nations of Asia, Africa, and Latin America outnumber those in the northern nations.[32] That is, Southern Christianity is emerging as a powerful religious force in the twenty-first century. As a result, Newbigin pleaded that in order for the Western church to undertake an effective ministry in its own Western homeland, voices of post-Western Christians must be heard, appreciated, and taken seriously by the church.[33] Thus, future research should explore diverse case studies around the world.

SECTION SUMMARY

This study concludes by noting my personal reflections. This research project has been a great journey of learning and realizing how important it is for one to focus on a narrative of success that celebrates transformation of evangelical, economic, and social relationships. It has reminded me that the Kingdom of God doe not celebrate size, programs, or budgets, but rather is about holistically transformed relationships. By letting go of these old metrics for success, I had to ask myself, "Am I willing to abandon a goal of becoming a lead pastor in a mega church and go to the marketplace? Am I in tune with giving my resources, ability, and congregations away to bring life to others, so that they in turn could bring life to others? Am I focusing on what God is doing in local communities and people's vocations?" These questions do not mean deemphasizing what is happening inside the church. Rather, these help rediscover the church's God-given identity (love for God and neighbor) and its mission in the world.

---

32. Jenkins, *Next Christendom*, 1.
33. Newbigin, *Foolishness to the Greeks*, 146–47.

Appendix A

Informed Consent Letter

PhD in Intercultural Studies
Asbury Theological Seminary
Samuel Lee

Dear _____

I am a PhD in Intercultural studies program participant at Asbury Theological Seminary and I am conducting research on the topic of current practices of sustainable business and church planting models.

    Business and church planting have great potential. But it also has significant risks. For example, purely maximizing profits can limit the church planting impact. On the other hand, it is possible to only consider church planting as the main thing such that one recreates a secular-sacred duality, Church planting alongside an operating and viable for-profit business presents significant challenges. As a result, there is still a need for clear models that will provide a framework for how to navigate the tensions and show examples of successfully integrated business and ministry objective.

    If you agree to be in the study, you will be asked the following questions: (1) How do you define success?; (2) How do you measure the success and performance of Business as Church activities?; and lastly, (3) How do the measurements help you achieve your initial objectives? When it comes to the duration of participation, I will go to your office two times. Your family will know that you are in the study. If anyone else is given information about you, they will not know your name. A number or initials will be used instead of your name. If something makes you feel bad while you are in the study, please tell Samuel Lee. If you decide at any time you do not want to

Appendix A: Informed Consent Letter

finish the study, you may stop whenever you want. You can ask Samuel Lee questions any time about anything in this study.

I want to assure you that your responses will be kept confidential. I do not want to jeopardize your relationships in your business, so I will not ask for your name on the interview. The data will be collected using a code and all of the surveys will be collated to give a blended view rather than identify any one person. I believe the findings from this interview will allow me to identify fruitful practices that lead to the formation of new churches. My hope is that churches incorporating business from around the country will be helped because you and others like you have taken the time to participate. Once the research is completed in approximately one month, I will destroy the individual interview data and keep the data electronically, at least until my dissertation is written and submitted.

Please know that you can refuse to respond to any or all of the questions, and that you are free to withdraw from the research project at any time without consequence. I realize that your participation is entirely voluntary and I appreciate your willingness to consider being part of the study. Feel free to call or write me at any time if you need any more information.

If you are willing to assist me in this study, please sign and date this letter below to indicate your voluntary participation. Thank you for your help.

Sincerely,
Samuel Lee

I volunteer to participate in the study described above and so indicate by my signature below:

Your signature: _____

Date: _____

Please print your name: _____

Appendix B

Interview Questions

FOUNDER (business) QUESTIONS

1. What attracted you to this type of ministry? Why this community or what attracted you to this location. Did you consider other locations?
2. How did this business activity get started in the first place? What vision or challenges motivated you to start your company?
3. Do you see this ministry as primarily a church or a business or a comingling of the two? On what do you base your answer?
4. With regards to the business enterprise you have established, what is the mission or purpose of your business?
5. How do you know when this ministry is a success? If nothing is said about economic, then ask, in terms of economic considerations, when would you call this ministry/business a success? How would you like to see this neighborhood transformed?
6. When people talk about a program they are starting, they usually have a general idea of what they want to achieve as their purpose. "Do you have more specific goals for what you would like to see this business attain, that is, economic goals?" If the person says "No," then stop.
7. If the person says, "Yes," then ask what their goals are. Then ask, "Are these goals agreed upon in general, or are these the goals that come to your mind?" Then say, "I'm curious about the process you used for determining these goals. What led you to identify these goals? Were there any plans to determine if the goals were being met?" If "No," then

stop. If "yes," then, "What were the ways you used to determine if the goals were being met?"

8. When you told me why you selected this neighborhood, you indicated that there were some social problems [repeat any problems the person told you or problems that are obvious (boarded up buildings, litter, homeless people)]. I wonder, do you have any goals with regards to the social problems in this community? If no, then stop. If yes, then what plans are there to determine if these goals are being met? If yes, "What were the ways you planned to use to determine if the goals were being met?"

9. When you told me why you selected this neighborhood, you indicated that there were some spiritual problems. I wonder, do you have any goals with regards to the spiritual problems in this community? If no, then stop. If yes, then what plans are there to determine if these goals are being met? If yes, "What were the ways you planned to use to determine if the goals were being met?"

10. How often does the group of leaders sit down and review what is being achieved by this ministry? Does the group use the indicators to determine if the various goals are being met? If no, then stop. If yes, "What indicators are most commonly used? Do the indicators ever change the opinion of the group about what to do next?"

11. Since this is a business, I assume there is income. Are you at a break even point at this time? If yes, then how is the income allocated?

12. What did you want to create in terms of a business/church or church/business? Do you feel that this ministry is a good example of whichever option the person selected?

13. One of the common questions people ask each other is, "What do you do?" What do you say in response to that question? When you are with friends or people who are part of this community, what do you tell them about what you do? Is this ministry something that your family shares interest in or is it just you?

14. Not to get too personal here, but how do you spend your spare time?

15. What excites you the most about your ministry/business?

Appendix B: Interview Questions 183

FOUNDER (church) QUESTIONS

1. What attracted you to this type of ministry? Why this community or what attracted you to this location. Did you consider other locations?

2. How did this church activity get started in the first place? What vision or challenges motivated you to start your church?

3. Do you see this ministry as primarily a church or a business or a co-mingling of the two? On what do you base your answer?

4. With regards to the church you have established, what is the mission or purpose of your church?

5. How do you know when this ministry is a success? When would you consider this ministry a success from a spiritual perspective? How would you like to see this neighborhood transformed?

6. "When you told me why you selected this neighborhood, you indicated that there were some social problems [repeat any problems the person told you or problems that are obvious (boarded up buildings, litter, homeless people)]. I wonder, do you have any goals with regards to the social problems in this community?" If no, then stop. If yes, then what plans are there to determine if these goals are being met? If yes, "What were the ways you planned to use to determine if the goals were being met?

7. "When you told me why you selected this neighborhood, you indicated that there were some spiritual problems. I wonder, do you have any goals with regards to the spiritual problems in this community?" If no, then stop. If yes, then what plans are there to determine if these goals are being met? If yes, "What were the ways you planned to use to determine if the goals were being met?"

8. How often does the group of leaders sit down and review what is being achieved by this ministry? Does the group use the indicators to determine if the various goals are being met? If no, then stop. If yes, "What indicators are most commonly used? Do the indicators ever change the opinion of the group about what to do next?"

9. What did you want to create in terms of a business/church or church/business? Do you feel that this ministry is a good example of whichever option the person selected?

10. One of the common questions people ask each other is "What do you do?" What do you say in response to that question? When you are with friends or people who are part of this community, what do you tell

them about what you do? Is this ministry something that your family shares interest in or is it just you?

11. Not to get too personal here, but how do you spend your spare time?
12. What excites you the most about your ministry/business?

WORKER QUESTIONS

1. What do you do at your company?
2. How long have you worked here?
3. Where did you work before you started working here? For how long did you work at your former job? What did you do? Why did you leave that job to come here
4. How is working here different from where you worked before? Or how is this place different or the same from your previous job? OR if first job: What do you like about this job?
5. Do you feel good about working here? Why or why not?
6. Do you feel that you are respected on the job, (supervisor for employee and employee for supervisor is important)? Do you feel respected?
7. Do you think that this business is successful or not so successful? Why do you think that?
8. Do you feel that men and women are treated the same, paid the same for the same job? Do you feel that race makes a difference in hiring, promotions, type of job done? Why do you feel that way? Why do you think so?
9. What happens at work when you have a family emergency, e.g., your father has a heart attack and is rushed to the emergency room? Is it easy to get a little time off? Is your pay docked when you have to leave for a few hours?
10. Are some workers favored over others? If yes, "Why do you think so?"
11. Is there ever any talk about what this company wants to do for the community?
12. Is there ever any talk about what this company wants to do for you?

SUPERVISOR QUESTIONS

1. What do you do at your company?
2. How long have you worked here?
3. Were you initially hired to be a supervisor or were you promoted? If promoted, "Did you expect to be promoted into this job or did you think they would hire someone new for the supervisor's position? Why?"
4. Is this company like your previous place of employ or is it different? Why do you think this?
5. What do you like about this job?
6. How do you see yourself relative to the people you supervise?
7. Do you feel respected by your superiors? Why or why not?
8. Do you feel that you are just a worker or that you are part of the business? Why do you feel this way?
9. We know that some companies have a slogan. IBM's slogan for years was THINK. Does your company have a slogan? If yes, "What is it?"
10. Changing the focus from slogans to mission statements, does your company have mission or vision statements? If yes, do you think that the statements guide the actions taken by the company and its owners?
11. Do the statements guide you and your team? If yes, how do those mission statements guide you and your team in making decisions?
12. In this business, how is success determined? Please explain.
13. What does the vision of success in addressing your target economic/social/spiritual problem look like?

Community People

1. Do you live in this community? If yes, do you have a few minutes to answer a few questions about the community? If yes, ask number 2.
2. How long have you lived in this community?
3. If they moved to community, "Why did you move to this community?"
4. What do you think about this community? Prompt with, "Is this a good neighborhood in which to live?" Would this be a good community for me to live in? (needs to be a bit jokingly) You hear horror stories about people not knowing their neighbors. Is this a friendly neighborhood?

5. Are groceries and other stores nearby? Good schools?
6. What do you know about this business? Is there anything different about this business from other businesses in the community? Do you know that this business is a Christian business? If so, can you describe this business a little bit?
7. Does this business ever do anything for the community that you know about? If yes, what does the company do?
8. Do you know the owners of the business?
9. Do you know anyone who works at this company? What do they say about the company, if anything?
10. Has this business impacted your life? If so, tell him how.
11. What is the greatest thing or worst thing that has happened in the community since this business came into the community? What did the business do when this happened?
12. What do you think there is an economic, social problem or spiritual problem in this community?
13. Do you think that this business cares about the community? Why or why not?
14. Do you think this business is trying to meet needs in the community? If so, in what way(s) do you think is this business trying to meet needs in the community?
15. Has this company done anything for the community? What this company do you think have created change in the community? If yes, What did the company do? What change have you seen recently? Can you tell me about any changes in the community?
16. What kind of story did or do you hear about this business? What do you hear about this business within the community?
17. Does the company have a good effect, no effect, bad effect? Why?

Appendix C

Entrepreneurial Church Planting (ECP) Questionnaire

This questionnaire is part of a comprehensive study of ECP being conducted by Samuel Lee of Asbury Theological Seminary. The questions collect information from your background to your activity involvement with ECP. The goal is to assess ECP movement; its effectiveness. This research project is designed to measure three "bottom lines" of ECP: economic performance, social performance, and spiritual performance. Any identifiable information provided (age, type of business, etc.) will be held in strictest confidence. I appreciate your participation in my study. There are no right or wrong answers. Your answer should reflect your actual experience.

Thank you for your help.

Samuel Lee
PhD candidate in Intercultural Studies
Asbury Theological Seminary

Directions: Please answer each of the following questions. Place a check (√) in the box (☐) provided or on the line(s) provided. Some questions require a written answer. Please write/print your answer on the provided lines. When you have completed the survey, please return it to the researcher.

I. BACKGROUND INFORMATION

1. **Provide age categories:** 21 or below, 22–29, 30–39, 40–49, 50–59, 60–69, 70 and over.

2. **What is your gender?** ☐ Male ☐ Female

3. **What do you consider to be your nationality?**
   _____

4. **What do you consider to be your race/ethnicity?**
   _____

5. **Are you married?** ☐ Yes, I'm married ☐ Yes, I was married, but now I'm single ☐ No, but engaged ☐ No

6. **How many children do you have?** _____ children

7. **Does your husband or wife have a business experience?**

   ☐ Yes, in the area of my business ☐ Yes, in an area related to my business ☐ Yes, in an area unrelated to my business ☐ No ☐ Other, please explain: _____ ☐ Not married

8. **What is the highest level of formal education you have completed?**

   ☐ Less than high school   ☐ 4 years of college, e.g., Ba/Bs

   ☐ High School   ☐ Graduate school

   ☐ Some college   ☐ Graduate degree,
                                  Please specify _____

   ☐ 2-year degree, e.g., AA/AAS

9. **Are you associated with a mission agency?**

   ☐ Yes (If yes, which one?) ☐ Yes, full status ☐ Yes, short-term
   ☐ Yes, raising funds to go

   ☐ No

   With which mission agency? _____

10. In your organization, which areas do **you feel** that the mission leadership encourages you to succeed? Place one check (√) for each row (a, b, c)

Appendix C: Entrepreneurial Church Planting (ECP) Questionnaire

Leadership encourages	a lot	considerable emphasis	some emphasis	little emphasis	none
a Economic impact	_____	_____	_____	_____	_____
b Social Impact	_____	_____	_____	_____	_____
c Spiritual impact	_____	_____	_____	_____	_____

II. ABOUT YOUR ECP

11. **Did you start the business in which you are now working?**

    ☐ Yes, I started it

    ☐ Yes, I worked with others to start it

    ☐ No

12. **For how many years has this business been operating?** _____ years

13. **Who owns the business? Check one answer.**

    ☐ The founder   ☐ I, alone, own the business

    ☐ I and others on my team   ☐ My mission agency

    ☐ Outside investors (please explain) _____

    ☐ Other (please explain) _____

    ☐ I'm not sure (please explain) _____

14. **Where did the startup capital come from?**

    ☐ My own personal funds

    ☐ The founder's personal funds

    ☐ Loans from donors and other friends

    ☐ Equity stakes sold to investors

    ☐ My mission agency

    ☐ Grants/donations (please specify) _____

    ☐ Not sure

    ☐ Other (please specify) _____

15. **Does your business have a board of directors or advisory board?**

    ☐ Yes ☐ No

Frequency with which it meets?

☐ Monthly ☐ quarterly ☐ twice a year ☐ annually

☐ other (please specify)

Where does it meet?

☐ In the country where the business is located

☐ in the country of the mission agency

☐ Other (please specify) _____

The question on membership of the board. Check all that apply.

☐ Representative of sending organization

☐ the person who runs the business (you)

☐ pastor of local church

☐ representative of workers

☐ owner

☐ representative of investors

☐ local government official

☐ local supporter of the business

☐ technical expert associated with the business.

☐ Other (please specify) _____

16. **From where does your salary come? Check all that apply.**

    ☐ Entirely from income generated by the business

    ☐ Entirely from supporters of your ministry

    ☐ Mission Agency

    ☐ Family and relatives

    ☐ Your own retirement savings

    ☐ Other (please specify) _____

17. **Which of these *best* describes the industry you are in?**

    ☐ Restaurant/food services

    ☐ Consulting services

    ☐ Education/training

Appendix C: Entrepreneurial Church Planting (ECP) Questionnaire   191

☐ Computer programming

☐ Offshore provider of accounting, transcription, and other "back office" services

☐ Manufacturing (low technology production like crafts, clothing, toys, etc.)

☐ Manufacturing (high technology production like cell phones, medical equipment, etc.)

☐ Other (please specify) _____

18. **Perceived degree of cultural fit between the industry and the culture of the country**

    ☐ Exceptionally strong   ☐ Generally pretty good

    ☐ Okay, but could be better   ☐ Not very good

    Please explain your answer.

    _____

    _____

19. **Within the town/city where the business is located do most of your workers earn an amount**

    ☐ that is substantially more than the average of other employed workers

    ☐ that is more than the average of other employed workers

    ☐ that is about the same as other employed workers

    ☐ that is less than the average of other employed workers

    ☐ that is substantially less than the average of other employed works.

20. **Given the nature of the jobs that your workers do, do they go home dirty (clothes soiled by the work they do) or clean (clothes are relatively clean and unspotted)?**

    ☐ Most go home clean

    ☐ Some go home clean

    ☐ Few go home clean

    ☐ None go home clean.

21. **Are workers be able to read and write to do their jobs in your business?**

    ☐ Yes, most must be able to read and write

    ☐ Yes, many must be able to read and write

    ☐ Yes, some must be able to read and write

    ☐ Yes, a few must be able to read and write

    ☐ No, it doesn't matter if they are able to read and write.

22. **Where is the *primary* location of your business?**

    ☐ Middle East/North Africa ☐ South Asia

    ☐ East or Southeast Asia ☐ Central Asia/former USSR

    ☐ Europe (Western or Eastern) ☐ North America

    ☐ Central/South America ☐ Other (please specify) _____

III. SPECIFIC AREAS OF IMPACT—Among organizations that are interested in social enterprise, there is now emerging three "bottom lines" that a socially responsible business holds itself to: economic performance, social performance, and environmental performance. Many Christian organizations add a fourth bottom line: spiritual performance or spiritual impact. The following questions are intended to assess those four areas. Organizations vary depending on locale and resources; there are no right or wrong answers. Please answer these questions based on your experience.

23. Most organizations identify areas where they want to achieve. Some organizations go so far as compiling reports to see what they have accomplished. Others rely on anecdotal evidence. **Does your business have specific goals it is trying to achieve?**

    ☐ Yes, clearly defined goals

    ☐ Yes, understood goals

    ☐ Yes, vaguely understood goals

    ☐ No

    ☐ Other (please explain) _____

24. **Does your business have a way to measure each goal?**

    ☐ Yes, for most goals

    ☐ Yes, for many goals

☐ Yes, for some goals

☐ Yes, for a few goals

☐ No.

☐ Other (please explain) _____

25. **With regards to the four areas listed below, does your business have goals?**

	Yes clearly measurable goals	Yes some measurable goals	Yes vaguely measurable goals	No
Economic Performance	_____	_____	_____	_____
Social Impact	_____	_____	_____	_____
Spiritual impact	_____	_____	_____	_____

26. **Who reviews the goals of your business?**

    ☐ My board of advisors/directors   ☐ My sending agency

    ☐ My team members/leader   ☐ My home church

    ☐ Nobody (other than God)

27. **How important is it to you for your business to be financially self-sustaining, i.e., able to survive without subsidizing labor or capital?**

    ☐ It's already self sustaining. Go to the next question.

	Very Important	Quite Important	Somewhat Important	Not very important
The respondent	_____	_____	_____	_____
Sending agency	_____	_____	_____	_____
Supporters	_____	_____	_____	_____
Investors	_____	_____	_____	_____
Workers	_____	_____	_____	_____

28. **How would you rate the economic performance of your business over the past three years?**

    ☐ Exceptionally strong   ☐ Generally pretty good

    ☐ Okay, but could be better   ☐ Not very good

    ☐ We're not making a serious effort in this area

Appendix C: Entrepreneurial Church Planting (ECP) Questionnaire

29. **In what way(s) is your business actively trying to meet physical needs in the community? (Check all that apply)**

    ☐ Contribute support in time/money/knowledge to local groups

    ☐ Subsidize students by contributing to school expenses

    ☐ Contribute equipment to local play areas

    ☐ Contribute funds to local causes, e.g., clean water, road paving

    ☐ Political advocacy on the local level

    ☐ Political advocacy on the regional level

    ☐ Establish schools for otherwise uneducated students

    ☐ Provide computer training

    ☐ Organize community to achieve a social goal

    ☐ Support women's groups

    ☐ Help with orphans

    ☐ Other (please specify) _____

30. **With the coming of your business to the city/town, what problem(s) do you think your venture is solving?**

    _____

31. **Approximately how much money has your business spent over the last year in meeting physical needs or trying to remedy social problems in the community?**

    _____

    How typical is it that your business be involved in meeting physical needs in the community?

    _____

    Approximately how many team members were there in in trying to remedy social problems in the community?

    _____

    How much time did they donate to meeting those needs?

    _____

32. **Which of the following statements best describes your views about your business's social impact:**

☐ We are well known in the community for the care we have for the physical needs of the community

☐ We are actively seeking ways to meet social needs and have experimented with some ideas

☐ When social needs become apparent, we try to help

☐ We have talked about this, but not much has come of it yet

☐ We have made little effort to minister to their social needs.

33. **In what way(s) is your business actively trying to meet spiritual needs in the community? (Check all that apply)**

    ☐ Evangelism (Bible studies, youth outreach, etc.)

    ☐ Discipling new believers

    ☐ Equipping and/or mobilizing national church leaders

    ☐ Regular workplace devotionals and times of prayer

    ☐ Service to women

    ☐ Nothing

    ☐ Other (please specify) _____

34. **Over the last three years, how many people have been or are being discipled specifically because of your business's presence in that community?** _____

35. **Which of these best describes your business?**

    ☐ We are very open to outsiders about our faith and our desire to see others become followers of Christ.

    ☐ We are neither open nor secretive about it.

    ☐ We are very careful about who we talk to about spiritual matters.

    ☐ We generally do not discuss spiritual matters.

THANK YOU!

Appendix D

Description of Interviews

Table 1. Description of Goals of Blue Jean Church & Arsenal Place

Subject	Position	Goals of Blue Jean Church & Arsenal Place
Moses	Founder of BJC	Blue Jean Church aims to see people's lives transformed and our neighborhood renewed by becoming a good neighbor based on the love of Jesus & power of the Holy Spirit.
David	Worker at BJC	The vision is to see people alive to the Lord and the community transformed through relational, economic, and spiritual renewals.
Mary	Board member of BJC	Our vision is to build a Kingdom community by loving our neighborhood and making it a better place for everyone to live.
Daniel	Supervisor of BJC & APA	The vision is to transform people's lives and Selma Alabama through Jesus and into a Kingdom community of love and friendship.
Jonah	Board member of BJC & APA	I think Blue Jean Church and Arsenal Place operate to rebuild, review and restore community that has been destroyed by racism, extreme poverty, and unemployment.
Joshua	Founder of APA	Blue Jean and Arsenal Place seek to bring change to Selma and to help bring people out of poverty spiritually, socially, and economically through partnering with the Holy Spirit. (citation)

Appendix D: Description of Interviews 197

Subject	Position	Goals of Blue Jean Church & Arsenal Place
Abraham	Supervisor of APA	Blue Jean and Arsenal Place's vision is to see transformed lives and flourishing community by loving and blessing Selma through the three way integration of a church, a Dallas County district court initiative, and a business incubator.
Samuel	Worker at APA	I think Blue Jan Church and Arsenal Place are called to create a loving community.
Israel	Community Person of Integrity Worldwide	Blue Jean Church and Arsenal Place seem to seek to have a good effect on our community by becoming a neighbor, creating jobs, educating children at risk, and having broken relationships restored.
Ruth	Community Person of Integrity Worldwide	It appears to me that the vision of Blue Jean & Arsenal Place is to get people connected to God, neighbors, and job.
Esther	Community Person of Integrity Worldwide	To me, Blue Jean and Arsenal Place seem to aim to bring the community together and to work together for the renewal, rebuilding, and restoration of our neighborhood.

Table 2. Definitions of Success of Blue Jean Church & Arsenal Place

Subject	Position	Definition of Success
Moses	Founder of BJC	When we see people come alive in the Lord and when our whole community begins to be transformed and comes to new life.
David	Worker at BJC	We will know whether we are achieving these goals through relationships of mutual service, based on the formation of a strong transformation association.
Mary	Board member of BJC	Real success will involve how much kingdom value we create in networks of interdependence.
Daniel	Supervisor of BJC & APA	I think Blue Jean Church and Arsenal Place will be successful when they provide connected neighbors and connected neighborhood.

Appendix D: Description of Interviews

Subject	Position	Definition of Success
Jonah	Board member of BJC & APA	Success will be determined by how many people who once lived in the community move back or new people move into the community and by how many of those from the community have stayed and assumed positions of leadership such as starting a new business for the well-being of the community.
Joshua	Founder of APA	Success is determined when we help a small business become profitable and when we have influence with small businesses and gain more influence with helping establish larger industries in our whole neighborhood.
Abra-ham	Supervisor of APA	Through the changed lives that come from an encounter with Jesus Christ and through improved community conditions through concerted efforts.
Samuel	Worker at APA	I do not know well about how success will look like. But I think Blue Jean and Arsenal Place can generate value for the whole neighborhood by tangibly and intangibly manifesting the work of the Spirit in how they treat their neighbors; this will result in a more receptive response by community members to Blue Jean and Arsenal Place. They will also form genuine partnerships with neighbors, other churches, and organizations.
Israel	Local with Integrity Worldwide	Success will be found in mutual trust and responsibility, gender equity, sharing, family lives, and stewardship for the peace and prosperity of the community.
Ruth	Local with Integrity Worldwide	We will be fruitful when we bear the fruit of the Kingdom of God such as relationship restored, love incarnated through relationships in the neighborhood, and collaboration for the well-being of the neighborhood.
Esther	Local with Integrity Worldwide	I can tell that Blue Jean Church and Arsenal Place will be successful if living conditions are improved, people get connected to God and neighbors so that a sense of human dignity may be restored, and the community continues to sustain itself.

Appendix D: Description of Interviews

Table 3. Metrics of Success of Blue Jean Church & Arsenal Place

Subject	Position	Metrics of Success
Moses	Founder of BJC	To be honest, we just wanted to start loving people who were hurting & lost. So we didn't have a grand plan or metrics when we started. We just believe that the success of our ministry is connecting people to the Lord, a loving family community at BJ, and the local neighborhood.
David	Worker at BJC	The success of Blue Jean and Arsenal Place is found in improved self dignity, improved relationships between neighbors, improved community ownership. So the measure of success is breaking out of a poverty of being, a poverty of community, a poverty of stewardship, and a poverty of spiritual intimacy.
Mary	Board Member of BJC	Collaboration brought about Selma revival. Accordingly, the outcomes of Blue Jean and Arsenal Place may be weighed by shared purpose through a project such as a summer internship program or by the steady maintenance of the collaboration.
Daniel	Supervisor of BJC & APA	There is no tool to evaluate our ministry except relationship. It is because trust and transformation require a long time to develop.
Jonah	Board Member of BJC & APA	The purpose of Blue Jean Church and Arsenal Place is to make the love of Jesus incarnated by changing the socioeconomic situation of Selma and moving people out of spiritual poverty. So the real measure of success is in terms of people whose lives were connected to God, the faith community, and the larger neighborhood, the partnership and integration of faith (Blue Jean) and Arsenal Place (works).

Appendix D: Description of Interviews

Subject	Position	Metrics of Success
Joshua	Founder of APA	There are two metrics: number and change in a person and a community. First, we have numerical metrics such as financial bottom line, profitability, and sustainability. Secondly, we aim at developing people and neighborhood with the goal of holistic transformation. We try to measure all the small things such as meeting with the people, spending time with the people, and blessing our neighborhood that move a relationship and neighborhood toward transformation. I can see many people's lives transformed through spending time with them and lunch with them, words of encouragement. If you hear people say, "You have done so much in my life," it can indicate that some transformation took place. You can measure transformation by long term results that happen from ordinary things that you try to be faithful to; ordinary things such as opening the word of God with people, praying with them, being involved in their lives, helping people to create their businesses, blessing a neighborhood. God then does extra-ordinary things in their lives.
Abraham	Supervisor of APA	We believe revival must impact other areas of a community other than the church proper. For example, revival should help the economy and families that have single parents raising their kids. So we try to measure our success by launching five new companies a year. These companies may utilize our space or use a rented building outside our space. Additionally, we want them to be profitable by the third year. We measure these goals by holding annual reviews of their financials. Furthermore, we want to connect fathers to jobs so they can support their families better. We measure this goal by collecting data on the father's employment status each month, and their pay history with the court system. Lastly, as I mentioned earlier, our spiritual goal is to renovate our entire neighborhood for God's Kingdom. Especially, our block of the neighborhood will be the heart of the arts & entertainment district and we want to see it transformed to reflect God's vision and values.
Samuel	Worker at APA	The success of Blue Jean and Arsenal business can be evaluated through the changed lives and the neighborhood's cohesion, fluidity, and relationship prosperity. In other words, the measure of success for Blue Jean and Arsenal Place is how many of those from the community are connected to God, a community of faith and the whole community, how many of those from community become economic self-supporters and contribute to the wellbeing of their family and community, and how many times people congregate for community wellbeing and moments of collective action.

Appendix D: Description of Interviews 201

Subject	Position	Metrics of Success
Israel	Local Integrity World-wide	I believe that transformation starts with leadership. Wise, Spirit-filled, father figures like Judge Bob ignite a desire to make a difference in Selma. He formed a leadership team and networks of transformation. Then he shared the influence and resources that he had in the Dallas County with the leadership team. These networks influenced each other and the whole neighborhood. This in turn made possible for the leadership team to have a positive impact on our neighborhood. So the measure of Blue Jean is and Arsenal Place's success can be found in empowerment, participation, shared power.
Ruth	Local Integrity Worldwide	If people are connected to the Lord and receive a new life and become disciples of Jesus through Blue Jean Church and Arsenal Place, I can tell that they may succeed.
Esther	Local Integrity Worldwide	I do not know. There may be no specific metrics.

Table 4. Application of Success Indicators of Blue Jean Church & Arsenal Place: What Has Been Achieved

Subject	Position	Effectiveness of Success Indicators
Moses	Founder of BJC	God's manifest presence shows up every Sunday! Our worshipping community reconciles people to God and people to people by worshiping Jesus across ethnic boundaries such as black and white and socio-economic boundaries such as rich and poor. This enables people to form genuine friendship and partnerships for economic and social transformation of Selma. Such positive relationships help community members hold one another accountable and grow in their relationships with family members, neighbors, and God. We as a spiritual community try to work alongside our congregation and community members in relationships that lead to authentic community formation and holistic transformation.

Appendix D: Description of Interviews

Subject	Position	Effectiveness of Success Indicators
David	Worker at BJC	I get excited when I see Blue Jean Church serves as the prime mover of creating Kingdom value. Blue Jean Church is like the Kingdom leaven described in Matthew 13:33. They do not emphasize congregational rate of growth. Nor do they put Christianity in the center of society. They are not trying to build their own temple. Rather, they just seek, point to, serve, build and represent the kingdom of God in their words and deeds as Jesus embodied. As a result, they love and serve others so that God can transform and change the community. So Blue Jean Church is journeying towards Jesus, loving, serving, and blessing its neighbors and the whole community.
Mary	Board Member of BJC	We changed radically what we do and we intentionally started a church for those who have been marginalized. We went after people nobody wanted. The drug addicts, the homeless, the mentally ill. The framer whose name was Chuck. He was mentally ill, he is got real clinical needs, you know. He was just crazy, but we loved him. And so, yes, we've got challenges come every Sunday. People that are getting free from addiction, that's really weird, that's a weird mix, but we also have the doctor, the lawyer and the professional and blue collar worker. It just works because we are all valued by the Lord.
Daniel	Supervisor of BJC & APA	What excites me the most about Blue Jean Church and Arsenal Place was the integration of faith, work, and economics. Blue Jean Church serves as a central source of generating Kingdom values in partnership with Arsenal Place. Through their initiatives, we see juvenile prison commitments get down 93 percent. In 2008, ninety-three teens were sent to juvenile prison. Last year, the number was only three. We also see new businesses started here and there in our neighborhood. Arsenal Place connects them to thriving businesses and college campuses outside Selma to open their eyes to new possibilities and insights.

Appendix D: Description of Interviews 203

Subject	Position	Effectiveness of Success Indicators
Jonah	Board Member of BJC & APA	I want to tell you one exiting story. What happened was, I was in my shop the other day and I had a guy randomly come in the door. He started talking to me and he said, "I am a pastor, a bishop in Uganda." He said, "I have been in the United States for three weeks," and I said, "Do you have any connections with the Blue Jean Church or Arsenal Place?" He said, "No, I saw your program." They did a segment on Revival Coffee a year ago. That was the reason this guy was there because they recently showed it again. Anyway, he said, "A lot of the people in Uganda are coffee farmers. They have no resources outside of Uganda to sell their coffee." At this point I was looking at the company where I could go buy a container load of coffee. I said to myself, "Lord what's going on? It's really great. That was my prayer." The Lord starts doing stuff where you start seeing and making a connection. I did not know what it was, but I knew He was up to something. If I were moving the volumes to where I could go through a container load every year of every crop, that would be ideal because it really helps their economy. I believed that it would create more opportunities for jobs and bring food to the whole community.
Joshua	Founder of APA	I get excited when I see companies like GMommas Cookies or Revival Coffees do well with their business. It is exciting to see them gain new clients or when big name stores like Cracker Barrel or Wal-Mart carry their products. I also see a big difference that APA is having on the economic development of our city by building economic relationships that create Kingdom values in interconnected spheres of life.
Abraham	Supervisor of APA	God put me in all different kinds of boards for Selma revival and gave me Kingdom strategies that would bring reconciliation and prosperity. He gave me a place and boards to release them and got me connected to people who were interested in transformation of Selma. We as a community aspired to create and cultivate a new Kingdom culture and ethic within our own sphere of influence. This started a momentum. By creating Kingdom values and strategies, people came to collaborate with us for the reconciliation and welling-being of Selma. For example, I, as a foreigner and white guy have been invited to many African American churches and have spoken word of reconciliation every other week since I moved to Selma.

Appendix D: Description of Interviews

Subject	Position	Effectiveness of Success Indicators
Samuel	Worker at APA	Selma is the beginning of the civil rights movements. Lots of racial tensions still lives. Like 43 percent live below the poverty, 80 percent African American, lots of drugs, crimes, no jobs as a result. So Blue Jeans Church started Arsenal Place through which they provided jobs. Through a cooperative effort, crime and poverty has dropped significantly compared to the past. Children at risk are succeeding. People are getting clean of alcohol and drugs, because of our Kingdom networks. Arsenal Place and Blue Jean continue to invest in the community and to walk toward a new reality in Selma.
Israel	Local Integrity World-wide	It is hard when young business people come inside and start a business. They first need to build the relationships with people in the city. Even for me, the second time around, it has been a lot easier because I have been friends with one gate keeper. He introduced me with the other gate keepers. The term "gate keeper" is used in anthropology. So gate keepers are people in the community or the community leaders, who have established relationships. If I did not have that relationship with the gate keepers, it would be tough to start business here. But I see Blue Jean and Arsenal Place provide the opportunity to connect people to gate keepers. This gives people in need a sense of the community that they are seeking.
Ruth	Local Integrity Worldwide	Blue Jean Church brings the community together, all walks of life. We have doctors, we have homeless people, we have black and white. We are worshipping together. That helps us all understand each other better and love each other and accept each other again and get on common ground. That is one thing I love about Blue Jean. It is just everyone is welcome. The other thing I get excited about is the revitalization of the community. We as people of God were not indifferent to people in need outside our spiritual community. Rather, we got out in the marketplace and beyond the four walls and stood in solidarity with our neighbors to renew, rebuild, and restore Selma.

Subject	Position	Effectiveness of Success Indicators
Esther	Local Integrity Worldwide	I witness Selma is transforming. At the center of this change are Blue Jean Church and Arsenal Place. They are trying to make difference by seeking the peace and prosperity of Selma. Blue Jean Church and Arsenal Place take responsibility for neighbors and neighborhood spiritually, economically, and morally. Their collaborative efforts have united Selma and brought about revival. As a result, Dallas County now ranks tenth in the state in least violent crime. Also, by addressing moral problems such as poverty, inequality, and economic exclusion, they promoted spiritual, social responsibility and encouraged the development of Kingdom virtues in the lives of community members.

Table 5. Description of Goals of Meridzo Ministries

Subject	Position	Goals of Meridzo Ministries
Lonnie	Founder of Meridzo	Two things: when the Lord sent us here, He said two things, I want you to do in this order: Help people and share Jesus. In other words, help people first and then share Jesus.
Belinda	Founder of Meridzo	The vision of Meridzo is to daily live for Jesus by faith, let others see Jesus through a personal relationship, and recover the neighborhood to be a better place through relational, economic, and spiritual means. Simply put, help people and share Jesus.
Mary	Full-time Staff of Meridzo	The vision of Meridzo Ministries and Faithfully Fit is to help the community, now being together and being health; but to glorify God and help our temples to be an example. We want people to restore their relationships to God, others, and themselves.
Ruth	Full-time Staff of Meridzo	I think Meridzo Ministries seeks to restore the community that has been destroyed by extreme poverty and unemployment through living the faith-life and "creating lakes in which we can fish."
Hanna	Full-time Staff of Meridzo	Our ministry is to help people and share Jesus through God's people. So one of our ministries is to minster to short-term mission teams. Thus, it is just to make sure that not only as the community being ministered, but these teams are being ministered to.

Appendix D: Description of Interviews

Subject	Position	Goals of Meridzo Ministries
Elizabeth	Full-time Staff of Meridzo	Meridzo Ministries and Shekinah Village operate not only to change teenagers, but also the whole family atmosphere.
Gideon	Full-time Staff of Meridzo	Our goal is to help people and serve Jesus. The overarching teaching of the ministry is living in faith and watching for God to restore the broken community.
Joshua	Full-time Staff of Meridzo	The heart of the ministry, the purpose, and the reason why this ministry is here is to love on the people of Eastern Kentucky specifically, but love on people in general. We are here to help the community, love them as people and minster to its people just like Christ has loved us. I realize that the main goal is to find any way possible to instill hope and share God with them.
Abraham	Full-time Staff of Meridzo	The real reason behind this ministry is to share Jesus and help people. We are not here to make a profit. Whatever profits that the store makes, they will help fund other parts of the ministry. Our specific purpose is share and talk with and be a witness to this community. We also build a relationship and making friends by providing a convenience in the service to the community by having this place here.
Jonah	Full-time Staff of Meridzo	For me, the vision of this ministry is to love and help teenagers for Christ. Reaching teenagers is what is going to change this area because it is almost starting the cycle over a new generation.
Sarah	Full-time Staff of Freedom Center	It appears to me that the mission and purpose of Meridzo Ministries are to love God and neighbor. It seems to give expression in helping people by generating jobs and sharing the Good news by creating relational networks of assistance. Meridzo has sought the ultimate good and the common good individually, familially, and socially.
Israel	Community person of Lynch	It seems that Meridzo Ministries aims to help people and share the gospel through instilling hope, building vibrant communities, and creating jobs in the Promise Zone Region of Eastern Kentucky.
Luke	Community person of Lynch	The vision of Merizo Ministries seems to build a Kingdom-like community by showing neighbor love, restoring people to God, and bringing hope.
David	Community person of Lynch	Meridzo's mission appears to restore our community, bring hope and faith to the community, and serve others with Christ's love. Meridzo wants people to experience God.

Appendix D: Description of Interviews 207

Table 6. Definitions of Success of Meridzo Ministries

Subject	Position	Definition of Success of Meridzo Ministries
Lonnie	Founder of Meridzo	I define success by knowing God and walking with Him. That is what I term success. Now what would that look like? What that looks like is, God would be dealing with this stuff in you. God would be changing you and the people around you. He will be changing you with the quality. How would you term success is how well do you know the ways of God and how God's ways are now being funneled through your life to the world. We let God set the goals and learn how to walk with him in the process and God will be showing up every day. You know, Drew, who is one of the staff members, had his camp. He had five kids—that's the numbers and yet he was taught in seminary. He says to me, "How can we get more kids?" these numbers here. Now, in this right here I would have laid out for him a strategy. Right? You know what I said to him? I said to him, "Would you be satisfied if God only gave you five kids for the rest of your life? that you could pour your life into, that they could become what God wanted them to do." Then he came back two weeks later and said in tears. "I've settled this with God and I'll be content if God gave me one." Now this year we had over three thousand young people in the various youth camp. Do you see my point?
Belinda	Founder of Meridzo	We did not really know it was. Of course, when we got back home there was nothing here, there was no ministry. It began with a bag of groceries for a family because there was a need. Even at that point, I don't think we thought about a ministry like this. We could never have planned it. It evolved over time, and by word of mouth people heard that we were here. We didn't advertise, we didn't know anybody, but people called and said, "We'd like to do a mission trip there." As far as being fruitful and successful, I would suppose when we see the children, youth, people that we ministered to eighteen years ago who are now grown with their own children and serving the Lord. Also I am excited to see our community transformed. People care for one another and pray for one another.
Mary	Full-time Staff of Meridzo	For me, success is about people coming to faith in Christ, community glorifying the Lord, and praying together and celebrating together. That is where I gauge. We have one hundred thirty members, but that really doesn't translate to success. Of course, the success of it has to do with money because we're under that division of Meridzo that makes money, that funnels it back into the non-profit, but we have to pay rent on the building. It is $700 a month for the rent of that building. If we can do that, we're okay. It is exciting to see the community come together in purpose. I think it's just the joy of the Lord and the joy that's there.

Appendix D: Description of Interviews

Subject	Position	Definition of Success of Meridzo Ministries
Ruth	Full-time Staff of Meridzo	I think we can define success by fruit, as Jesus said. I look at the fact that Chris has prayed with customers; Dan is going to get baptized. The Exchange has people coming in there that are being ministered to. We're providing jobs to people that otherwise might not have jobs. We had one of the girls, that was one of our first employees, was a little sixteen-year-old girl. She came in with no job skills or anything. Now she is in Lexington, Kentucky managing two retail stories, because of the experience she got here. The training she worked here opened doors for her there. But more importantly, she wasn't in church and she came to us. We host thousands of people mission teams every year coming to do work in the community, come to the coffee shop. She came to me and said, "I want to know more about mission," She's not in church, but she said, "I see how these people are helping in my community. I might want to help someone in their community someday." She was affected by the missions even though she wasn't in church, but she saw what was going on in Meridzo Ministries. It moved her. I measure success by seeing God at work. People and community being affected for Christ.
Hanna	Full-time Staff of Meridzo	Every day is a success because we are working with and for God. As long as we're in His plan, it's a successful day. If one person comes to God, that is a success. As long as we're in God's will, it's a successful day.
Elizabeth	Full-time Staff of Meridzo	Meridzo Ministries defines success by the number of salvation. Also, we define success by relationships. I think success is all about reaching the people and build a relationship. Relationships are ongoing things. So it is about creating the relationship with each family, teenagers and the community as a whole.

Appendix D: Description of Interviews 209

Subject	Position	Definition of Success of Meridzo Ministries
Gideon	Full-time Staff of Meridzo	Success in our ministry is just honoring and following God and being content with whatever God provides and whatever God does. There's a level of contentment in there. Usually, worldly success, that's usually not a contentment in worldly success because you're always trying for more and more and more for me. But the faith walk is being content with what God wants. Second Corinthians 5:9 says, "Whether I'm present or absent"—talking about whether I'm with the Lord or here—"it is our ambition to be pleasing to him." Those are Paul's words. Holy ambition is simply to please God and follow His lead. Not to please myself, not to aspire for great numbers or fame. We do what's called responsive planning. We plan in response to the movement of God. God reveals. When a need comes, we pray about the need and then we watch God. We watch for him to move in that area and then when God opens the opportunities, we plan according what God reveals.
Joshua	Full-time Staff of Meridzo	The success of this ministry is by seeing different people in the community lives change. When community members come up and go to the coffee shop and tell the staff member, "This is what God has done for me," that is the success of the ministry. When people are getting saved and baptized and getting in church and are getting their life with Christ and neighbors, that is the success of the ministry. It is not only economic renewal, but also spiritual and social renewals. It is the lives that are changed and touched. The hope and the prayer is that, especially with the children, we measure to the children in hopes that those children go on to minister to their parents or grandparents or whoever they're living with. Then as they grow up and have children, that they minister to their children. When we minister to the parents, the hope is that the parents will then minister to their children and to their friends and that it just continues to go out and go beyond what we can see and know about. That is the success of the ministry. That is how we define the success of Meridzo Ministries.
Abraham	Full-time Staff of Meridzo	Success would be doing what God wants me to do so the results of it is not on me. If I can be around, if I can share somebody, what they do with it is not my thing. So it is to do what God called you to do, nothing less than that. A lot of Christians, especially in ministry, have a problem with it. It is also not to do more than He called you to do. Because if you're doing more than He called you to do, you're not doing what He told you to do.

Appendix D: Description of Interviews

Subject	Position	Definition of Success of Meridzo Ministries
Jonah	Full-time Staff of Meridzo	I think the only way we judge Meridzo Ministries being successful as long as we are in the will of God. If we stay in the will of God, we are successful because we are right where He wants us whether the fruit is small or large. It is just like in our own lives, there is never—until we get to heaven—there never going to be a point where we've arrived. We've done everything, we're always growing and the same with this ministry. It is always growing and we're always trying to seek God's will for this ministry and where he wants us to be. Thus, as long as we're in that, we're successful.
Sarah	Full-time Staff of Freedom Center	First, I think success might be defined by trusting our Heavenly Father, relying on Him. When we delight ourselves in the Lord and commit our ways to Him, He gives the desires of the heart. If you're fully surrendered to Him our desire is to serve Him. Our desire is to give everything all to Him and He gives us our needs, not our wants but He supplies our needs. Second, success will be determined by people's life that are transformed, or payer answered.
Israel	Community person of Lynch	For me, Meridzo Ministries is fruitful by setting Kingdom example. By Kingdom example I mean is to show people how to love on other people like Christ loves us. That way they know what a good healthy relationship looks like. That way they know what the love of Christ looks like when you take somebody who has not done what you've asked or had done wrong and you still love them and still help them. In many ways, Abraham and Ruth were like second parents to children. Of course, they do teach them how to ride a horse and how to groom a horse. They're learning service and how to serve others. That's what God has called us to do, to serve people and love on people.
Luke	Community person of Lynch	Success for me is to love God and neighbor. That is the most pleasing thing to God but yet the scripture says without faith it is impossible to please God. I think the greatest expression of love to God and neighbor is faith, because that is His great requirement. Doesn't that mean that faith, thinking about expression of love, faith is the greatest expression of love toward God? In our daily walk and work, we love God and neighbor.
David	Community person of Lynch	Success is not about economic restoration. I think personally, if a big industry came in and everybody in town could get good jobs if they wanted them. I think that would be great economically, but I think if that happens, we'd miss a lot of opportunity because when things are going good, God and neighbor's not really on your end.

Appendix D: Description of Interviews 211

Table 7. Metrics of Success of Meridzo Ministries

Subject	Position	Operation Metrics of Success
Lonnie	Founder of Meridzo	Metrics have to shift from quantity to quality. Our focus is not on quantity, but on quality, the quality of life for the individual that has been changed. I'd been used to the baptisms, the budgets, the buildings and all that. It doesn't make sense. Where is God? Is that ministry touching people with the quality of life? If you are talking about quality, only God can change your life. I want a guy that has a quality of difference in his life that God is actually doing something in him to do the same thing he did in me. He's providing for his family. He's sending in the right people to him that they might be discipled. People ask, how many people got saved? How many people did you baptize? How many people did you witness to? I say, what is the point in that? The point is what is God doing. So when I talk to a staff meeting, I say, "Tell me what's happening in your ministry? What's God doing in the community? A key question is, "What is God doing in people's lives, family, ministry, and community?" That changes from quantity to quality. Our whole life and ministry is being lived out in response to what God is doing and bringing for us.
Belinda	Founder of Meridzo	We were just thinking—helping people in whatever way that looked like. When people began to come and bring things, at that point people needed a helping hand with food or clothing or fixing their homes. Now they need a job. The Lord alerted us by bringing the thought of a coffee house in Cumberland. It never developed. We just waited patiently to see if God ever wanted to bring a coffee house. Several years ago, this building was mentioned to us; well we'd make a coffee house. Things began to come together and the building was complete. People came and for now they've been doing house coffee. So there's a time when you need to give a man a fish because that's the only way he can eat. There's a time when you need to teach him to fish but only if he's willing to learn. But there's a time when you create a pool so that you can teach people how to fish; they'll have a place in which they can fish.
Mary	Full-time Staff of Meridzo	People are used to missionaries coming and giving them everything. So they expect it. Also, they depend on the government. Either government or missionaries. But Meridzo Ministries is teaching them how to fish so that they can take care of themselves and their family and their community. The gym, as far as having a membership and paying, we could give it to them free. But if they have to put a little value into this and work a little bit to be there, they are going to appreciate it more.

Subject	Position	Operation Metrics of Success
Ruth	Full-time Staff of Meridzo	Our purpose for being here is to serve the community spiritually, economically, and relationally. If no one else got saved, if nothing else happened, that was worth it. One life was changed and he will hopefully change other lives. The parade, the morale and all that is good stuff. Anything to advance Christ or to glorify God. When we had that parade we won, there's one of the plaques on the wall, which is an award that we received for the restoration of this building. This was an old building and all dirty, and mission teams came in and fixed it up. The local Chamber of Commerce have made this building to be recognized for the fact that it was restored. We were able to go to the Governor of Kentucky's mansion in Frankfort Kentucky. We were probably about six people who received an award that day. One after the other they got up and said, "We received this government money," or "We paid for it this way." We went last and we stood up and we said, "God did this. The government didn't pay for anything. God built this place through mission teams." That, to me, is a measurement of success. We're glorifying God through what we are doing. We experience his presence and provision. There's no numbers attached to that. It does not matter how many people showed up for church. We glorified God through changed lives.
Hanna	Full-time Staff of Meridzo	With Meridzo coming in, we were able to get rid of a lot of the evil, the bad. God's kingdom in-breaking. Like for instance in Cumberland, there was bars everywhere in Cumberland. When an owner stopped and another owner came in, but because we had a building across the street, they weren't able to get their license. So a lot of that got pushed aside because we were coming into the picture. So we got some of that out of here. Instead, we've given people opportunities of work, of just a better way of life. Expanding opportunity creates a context for community building, spiritual reconciliation, and community flourishing.

Appendix D: Description of Interviews 213

Subject	Position	Operation Metrics of Success
Elizabeth	Full-time Staff of Meridzo	I do not know how to put it. Jonah and I invested in a young man. We built a relationship. Through that making Alan's relationship with the Lord stronger and that with other kids in the community. Alan has seen his mom probably once in the last eight years. His dad lives here but he's just not in the picture. So we took over that father role and mother role and raising him and he graduates from the high school this year. He's going into the military. So we're just pouring into him and making sure he's on the right track and right path. So for me personally, from learning over the years working with kids, it's all about giving a child value. When they're missing specifically their mother and father, they feel less valued. For us to love on them whether it's somebody living in his home or our youth kids, just loving on them, and letting them know that we love them, and that most of all God loves them. Through that, giving their life meaning so that hopefully they go into the world to make it a better place.
Samuel	Full-time Staff of Meridzo	Being successful is simply pleasing God. Some things are small, some things are big. Kind of the Asbury thing with the revival. The people who came and they had big aspirations. They were one hundred people coming down the alter. They only had one guy and he gets saved, but it is Lonnie, the founder of Meridzo Ministries. Look at what one guy, what God's done through him as an influence. We got the governor of Kentucky now coming to meet Lonnie to ask him, "Lonnie how can we create jobs in Eastern Kentucky?" So we don't try to measure success on what the American dream is or the numbers game kind of stuff. We just gauge success on, I guess, it is just being assured of what God's will is first and then trusting success is going to come if it's God's. Sometimes our expectations of what success is if well, it's going to be we're going to have a thousand member plus church and this kind of stuff. That's what we expect is success. So we no longer pray about methods, we pray simply about God's provision and then we watch for God's method of making that provision. When we are living in the relationship of communion with God, there is no failure. Whether the numbers out of it is small or large, if it's what God is calling me to do, then to me, it's successful. I can be content with being a sower. But someone thinks that you get to be the harvester and that's where sometimes our wordily ambition kicks in. we want to be the big harvester. We want to see the great big harvest living in the mode of being pleasing to God and do recall that's not doing pleasing things for God. If I wanted to please you in something, how would I know what pleases you unless in my relationship with you you've communicate that to me.

Subject	Position	Operation Metrics of Success
Joshua	Full-time Staff of Meridzo	The success or failure of each ministry is determined by God. We do not do anything to try and keep them going. We only do what God tells us to do and we use what God supplies. It is God's ministry and he does his will. We follow wherever he leads. We rely on each other to keep ourselves in check, to hold each other accountable on that book. We see God's success in everything. The success of the businesses, the success of the outreach ministries that would be the people they're being filled with hope in the Lord Jesus and getting saved. It is all about people. People you plant sow and reap. We might be the one to plant. We may never see the product of what we planted, but as long as that seed is planted, there will be evidence. May not be right then, but we may never see the evidence but there will be. That is just the success of the ministry is planting their seeds. Sometimes we are able, God uses the ministries to do all three to plant the seed, to cultivate, and to reap seed. That's rare but sometimes he does it. Sometimes we just plant the seed. Sometimes we've just sown into that life. Sometimes, God uses us to reap. That is the success. Planting, sowing, and reaping. This is how is this ordered in the Bible. There's a pattern to me in the Bible of threes: Father, Son, and the Holy Spirit. We were called to care and love on each other. And that community is that when God has planted us in this community, it is a natural thing when you're following Christ, to care for others and to love others and to love on the ones around you.
Abraham	Full-time Staff of Meridzo	Meridzo Ministries wants to provide for people a means to own that. When Meridzo builds industry, it's got one value to a person, a family, and the community. It really has an impact on people. All along, it's still based on the gospel of instilling hope. So creating jobs and business creation lead us to spiritual reconciliation and build vibrant community. It is all interconnected. This is important to increase the tax base. Without taxes, we don't function as a civil government.
Jonah	Full-time Staff of Meridzo	One of the success indicators is a transformed life. Their relationship with Christ once the youth accept him is the number one thing in their life. Another is God's presence and His provision in our ministry. We have communication with a staff meeting where we just let people know what God is doing and he's here so he sees it.

Appendix D: Description of Interviews 215

Subject	Position	Operation Metrics of Success
Sarah*	Full-time Staff of Freedom Center	The success of Meridzo Ministries is found in people's life stories. People tell us a lot here at the counter. They don't know what they would do without Meridzo ministries because it is such a huge blessing. They said that they would not have clothes for their children and for their neighbors, their grandkids, if we were not here. They say, "I hope you know how much Meridzo Ministries is a blessing to this community. Also through this ministry our lives are being transformed by volunteers. We are mutually growing in the Lord. Through prayer why God healed these or changed someone's life.
Israel*	Community person of Lynch	In word and action, Jesus ushered in the Kingdom of God, bringing the reality of God's rule, presence, and provision into the lives of those around him. This is Jesus-style success looks like. This is also what Meridzo seems to do. They desire to embody the Kingdom of God on earth by giving help, hope, and jobs to people and forming healthy community economically, relationally, and spiritually.
Luke*	Community person of Lynch	There are several ways of measuring Meridzo Ministries: first, Meridzo gives us opportunity such as job creation for the unemployed; secondly, they gives us the gift of ability such as skills training; thirdly, they give us emotional and practical support. The belief that God is at work was an essential antidote to a culture of hopelessness; Finally, they give us healing and forgiveness. So they strive to form a whole community.
David[1]	Community person of Lynch	God brings the people to you that you need the two-fold purpose. One is creating jobs. We live in the coal mining part of Kentucky and we have lost 18,000 jobs in the last years. The economy has taken a 1.2 billion dollar hit in our area. But God is resurfacing things like new businesses. Then they're able to help people. In the process of helping people, they hired people in those businesses. That's a good thing for us. They help people and then, because you helped them, you've earned the right to share what's on your heart, Jesus. As a result, Meridzo hopes, "Your Kingdom come, your will be done" by restoring community building such as family, neighborhood, and the church.

1. Non-Meridzo Ministries person

Table 8. Application of Success Indicators of Merizdo Ministries: What Has Been Achieved

Subject	Position	Effectiveness of Success Indicators
Lonnie	Founder of Meridzo	All I do is encourage and look for ways to connect opportunities with the things that God brings to us, with people, and with God, so we can match that up. People are so excited over that. The coffee shop now is in four different coffee shops in Kentucky. There are now five states who want a coffee shop in their state. I called it kingdom expansion. For eighteen years now, we respond to God. Our life has been catching up to what God says. God's success is allowing God to accomplish through you and his people what he designs. The spiritual climate and mindset of the people has changed. When we first came here, when people spoke about God or Jesus, it was in a curse word. Because everything was gone; no coal mines, no jobs, only poverty, illiteracy, hopelessness. Everything was gone. Now, when they talk about Jesus and God, it's positive. "Look what God has done, it's amazing what God has done." It's the whole mindset change over these eighteen years. God has changed the ecosystem; taking all the bad fish out and putting new fish in. Black bears. Plus, thousands of people, I probably couldn't count the number, but thousands of people have had their quality of life changed by receiving Jesus. We don't keep score, but churches are growing because of the transformed lives of people. Our church is growing, the African-American church growing, the Baptist church, is growing, all of them. Because God is making a change in people that's quality. That is Kingdom expansion. I do not count, because I can't keep up with a kingdom. God is changing so many. I saw many people come to serve the Lord here. Through discipleship and through the avenues that God has allowed them to serve, they just blossom and become. God provides an avenue through which their faith in God can be expressed in a way that they like. That's real joy to me. God uses me to connect the two, and then I get out of the way. The other thing that excites me is not only the people that God brings to us, how they blossom and grow, but second is how God brings new things into being to minister to people to help people to share Jesus, that we did not' think about. Like a fitness center. I never dreamed of that. Seeing new things come into being, that excites me because I know that there's going to be a new dimension of kingdom expansion out there somewhere.

Appendix D: Description of Interviews 217

Subject	Position	Effectiveness of Success Indicators
Belinda	Founder of Meridzo	I see this neighborhood being restored with a better quality of life for the people. The Lord has spoken to me. That was before we ever came back; that was probably in 1990. My mom lived here until 1990, and she no longer—didn't take care of herself. She was sick. I lived in Ohio and I came to take care of the house and get all of her things packed up, and then she came to live with me. I'd gone for a walk and I was in the alley down across from the church, very saddened by all that I saw. The decay of the town, it's just a very sad, depressing, kind of feeling. The Lord just spoke to me and told me that I would one day see people return. I have. Over the years, thousands of missionaries have come, but now I would like to see the local people filling the houses, and that I would be a constant for them. Also, the problem in this community is drug addiction. It is a definite spiritual path. They're so consumed that they don't see beyond their drugs. That's all they think about, or their alcohol. It was something that was brought to us through our C3 Church through the Christian Center, that we're going to begin Celebrate Recovery. Over the past six or seven years, so many have received Christ. So I am excited when I see people go on to be what God wants them to be. You never know who God is going to send and for what reason. It's exciting God speak to people about what he can do and how he can provide. We are always concerned about the people, and their hearts, and them knowing the Savior, and a personal relationship and communal relationship. We are excited when people have a better-quality life, personal relationship with God and communal relationship with other.
Mary	Full-time Staff of Meridzo	It is exciting to see that community come together and enjoying the Lord. It is through five new businesses that we hired seventeen people and work together.

Appendix D: Description of Interviews

Subject	Position	Effectiveness of Success Indicators
Ruth	Full-time Staff of Meridzo	What I found exciting is that lives were changed and making friends. Just watching what God's doing. Whether it's with people or with the area and how God is bringing change about in a place that everybody had given up on. One of the things we started doing as a church was Fall Festival at the Shekinah Village at the farm. We've got a group of kids that were in County care. All these kids have been abused in some parts. Some sexually abused, some physically abused. They'd all been taken out of their houses and they were in the care of the County Government. Since we had a bunch of children playing kick ball out the field and they were giggling and laughing. They were safe and happy because we had extended God's love to them. I need more moments like this. I need to feel God's presence like that. It's that touch of God that is the most exciting thing. We've seen the difference that God makes. I believe there's going to be a massive explosion, a good kind of explosion. There's going to be a population explosion, there's going to be a revival. We really see that on the horizon. We see ourselves as in the foundational stages. It's literally reached worldwide what God's doing here.
Hanna	Full-time Staff of Meridzo	It is through Meridzo that our community is becoming healthy. People are invigorated in their faith. When you first came here a long time ago, everybody felt the devil owned this place. Prostitutes would run out on the road trying to stop you. Now people come and they think, "God is in this place." Several of the ministries around here that are not under the Meridzo umbrella at one time were, but they flourish so well. The majority of ministries have had some kind of Meridzo influence. Now we are involved with one another, in this town. Some local churches also cooperate with us.
Elizabeth	Full-time Staff of Meridzo	I am watching people back home who are seeing what God is doing in my life and it's changing their life. God's changing things and he's changing the kingdom.

Subject	Position	Effectiveness of Success Indicators
Samuel	Full-time Staff of Meridzo	One of the local pastors here who was coal miner said it very eloquently. He said that when the coal mines here and prosperity was here, because of the coal mines, he said, "I believe coal became the God of the people." He said, "Now that false God has been taken away, the transformation we're seeing here in Lynch is that the real God is replacing the false God." He felt like the coal had to move out in order to show the people who the true God was. However, after the coal mines went out, there was no real income. To make things worse, people began to live off a welfare check and entitlements. They think there's no hope for this economic chasm that they feel like they're in. They don't think there's any hope of coming out of it. So some of the things we're doing as a ministry is trying to create jobs in various ways and having a coffee shop is to instill hope. "Hey, this community still is not dead. If we believe God and trust in Him, he gives us hope through other means of employment and revitalization in the community can came." We need to combat that culture of no hope. Last week they had over a hundred-people going through there, which is amazing. It is growing. We haven't even got to the peak seasons yet, and they're already getting a hundred people here in one day. All of this plays into this, trying to get them out of that socio-economic pit that they feel like that they're fit. But as we're doing that, we're letting them know this is God. This is not just a couple of people that are trying to rescue your community, this is something God is doing. When you can get them to connect the dots that this is God doing this. Did you see the Ebenezer stone at Black Mountain gas station? It has Ebenezer written across it. We had somebody who if you go back to the transformation that has happened here. It all comes back to four prayer meetings. It all began with the prayers of the people. We've got that down there. All of what God is doing, even when Lonnie came here, people had been praying that God would bring somebody that would care for the people, Meridzo care, would care for the people and bring hope back to them. We try to remind people that God loves them and that God has not forgotten them. A big part in bringing hope is letting people know God has not forgotten Lynch and he cares for them as his family. With the things that are happening and people are starting to see, they're seeing evidence that God has not forgotten, That God still has a plan for a community that some thought was a dying community.

Subject	Position	Effectiveness of Success Indicators
Joshua	Full-time Staff of Meridzo	God used the missionaries to restore and to re-instill hope. That is the thing that has really happened. People are starting to see that they are worthy of being loved. They're starting to see that other people care about them and love them and want to help them. That gives them the love of themselves, that gives them the love for their own community, that encourages them to want to better themselves both in the natural world and in the spiritual world. There's the spiritual side and the physical side. There's a restoration. God's even restored the ecosystem here. There's just been a whole restoration. God continues to build His Kingdom.
Abraham	Full-time Staff of Meridzo	For them to have a gas station so they don't have to go all the way to Cumberland to get gas. It kind of brings back a little sense of something going on here, but a lot of them need somebody to talk to. We have guys. One guy was in for about an hour today. A couple of them, several of them come in and sit down on a stool over there. If it's lunch time we sit there and have lunch. I like the people that come here. They are not merely customers or neighbors but brothers.
Jonah	Full-time Staff of Meridzo	God has supplied all the finances and the food that we need for our ministries. It's just through praying and trusting God that he did that. God is in the details. It is watching God meet the everyday needs. It's watching the student out here fish for the first time, the excitement and the joy in their eye. It's leading somebody to Christ. It's watching a family living with hope. There's a lady down the road that used to clean the cabins for us and she's got three kids. Her husband left her after their youngest was born so she was a single mom, three kids, no job. We found that out and brought here her and she started cleaning cabins for us and through that process, we helped her get into the local college, into the nursing program. She made it all the way through the nursing program and now is an ER nurse and being able to provide for her family. Things like that we see changed, lives changed, that brings excitement.
Sarah	Full-time Staff of Freedom Center	Through their ministry, our lives and their lives are being transformed by God. We are growing in the Lord, keep growing, trusting the Lord more and more. I see God bringing a lot of people back to Lynch that used to live here. They're coming home maybe in their older years, but I also see God bringing new people to Lynch. Most of the people that have moved into this community are Christians and are coming here as missionaries. They're coming together to give Him the glory.

Appendix D: Description of Interviews 221

Subject	Position	Effectiveness of Success Indicators
Israel	Community person of Lynch	I get excited when the community works together. After we built relationships with people, it gave us the opportunity as a marketplace missionary, to share, to build Kingdom relationships. We create and secure the markets. We're using the resources that are here and the people that are already in place to do that. We train and equip those operators so that they have the best opportunity for success. Everybody wants them to succeed, provide for them. Also provide continued support along continued education to make sure that they're staying up on all that they need to. That's all done by those strategic partners that are in the area. It is all for the benefit of the operations because it's coming along and holding them and saying, "We're going to walk through this together and make sure that we are together.
Luke	Community person of Lynch	What it all boils down to me for me, is love. They love like Christ loved, which means they love people, they love animals, they love His creation. If you love all those, you take care of all those. You'll preserve them, you'll help them, and that is what it boils down into Meridzo Ministries.
David	Community person of Lynch	It is exciting to me to see how the neighborhood is changing and coming together. Meridzo is a key player in this. They do not follow the lust of the flesh, the lust of the eyes, and the pride of life. It is the physical part of us, the sustainability. "How is this going to occur? How can we provide for this? All of us do, because we are in the same boat, that's the flesh rising up to speak to you, instead of God. There is the lust of the eyes, that is the senseless things that you feel. Am I sure about this, or not sure about this? Am I right? There is a pride of life that's probably the culmination of the whole thing. Why did they do what they do? What kind of ministry can they produce, that everybody will look at them and say, "Look how wonderful this is. Did you see how the pride in your life can be a distraction from the direction that God wants you to have. The direction that God gives to you is for kingdom extension, not your personal gratification. When people give Meridzo accolades, or things like that, that's not the end result of that, Rather, the end result is change, a corner of the Kingdom of God.

Appendix E

Operational Indicators of Four Relational Changes

Action	Indicator
Evangelistic Activities	• Distributing useful items: soap, toothpaste & brush, backpacks • Charitable outreach: meals, snacks • Shelter for homeless • Music Outreach • Getting to know the names of your neighbors • Helping neighbors—provide rides when needed • Taking in meals during stressful times (death, birth, loss of job, family member arrested) • Medical services • Rallies, e.g., Luis Palau type of sessions • Rake leaves • One-on-one witnessing • Prayer meetings • Bible distribution • Alcohol/Drug rehab • Distribution of tracts • Mobile churches

Appendix E: Operational Indicators of Four Relational Changes

Action	Indicator
Evangelistic Activities *(continued)*	• Sunday services • Small group meetings • Sunday school • Spiritual counseling • Impromptu preaching sessions • Revival services • Pre-marital counseling • Accountability sessions
Economic Development	• Starting a business • Hiring a part-time employee • Hiring a full-time employee • Paying workers a living wage • Signing a contract with a local business • Teaching employees new skills • Supporting people who are starting a new business • Hiring local people
Social Development	• Helping preschoolers become prepared for school • Providing medical care • Providing recreational activities for teens • Providing sex education to teenagers • Providing housing for homeless • Providing alcohol & drug counseling • Helping people apply for jobs, social security card • Helping people get their GEDs • Having child care program for working parents • Providing programs to encourage teens to stay in school • Working with teens released from jail and prison
Becoming a Good Neighbor	• Getting to know the names of your neighbors • Helping neighbors—provide rides when needed • Raking leaves • Taking in meals during stressful times (death, birth, loss of job, family member arrested) • Helping out with child care

Appendix E: Operational Indicators of Four Relational Changes

Action	Indicator
Becoming a Part of God's Family	• Spending time with other Christians at church • Socializing with church people in different settings • Participating on a church sport's team • Visiting in the homes of other Christians (not just the people who go to your church) • Attending Christian activities at other churches or Christian venues • Visiting church people in the hospital • Providing child care for other people in your church • Taking food to a family when family members are ill or for a death in the family or a birth of a child • Providing transportation for those in need • Being involved in compassionate activities—sending birthday cards to people, sending get-well card to people
Economic Vitality	• # of job fairs for the unemployed • # of space for people to learn how to find, apply for, and keep a job • # of mentoring assistance for people to become self-supporting • Monitoring increased economic dynamism based on employment numbers • Resume-training and job follow-up
Enhancing Human Capital	• # of people who got GED • # of people who took computer classes • # of teens who graduated from HS • Monitoring teen pregnancy rates • # of people who attend AA meetings • # of people who learn how to read • # of parents who help out at their children's school • Monitoring rates of spousal abuse • Monitoring rates of child abuse • # of teens jailed • # of teens in prison • # of people employed who were previously unemployed • Monitoring recidivism rates for those released from jail and/or prison • # of deaths due to overdose of drugs and DUIs

Bibliography

Alabama Department of Early Childhood Education. "Children's Policy Council." September 10, 2016. http://children.alabama.gov/cpc.
Alabama Fatherhood Initiative (AFI). *Alabama Fatherhood Directory: Information About Fatherhood Programs in Your Community*. Montgomery, AL: Alabama Department of Human Resources, 2013. https://brettwmartin.com/wp-content/uploads/2013/11/FatherhoodDirectory.pdf.
Anderson, Gerald H. *Biographical Dictionary of Christian Missions*. Grand Rapids: Eerdmans, 1999.
Appalachian Regional Commission. "Appalachia Then and Now: Examining Changes to the Appalachian Region since 1965." February 23, 2015. https://www.arc.gov/wp-content/uploads/2020/06/AppalachiaThenAndNowCompiledReports.pdf.
Aprem, Mar. *Nestorian Missions*. Golden Jubilee Publications 2. Trichur, Kerala: Mar Narsai, 1976.
Armstrong, Bob. "A Proposal for the Millennial Project." 2016. Unpublished.
Arntzen, Arnliot Mattias. *The Apostle of Norway: Hans Nielsen Hauge*. Eugene, OR: Wipf & Stock, 2011.
Babbie, Earl. *The Practice of Social Research*. 12th ed. Belmont, CA: Wadsworth, Cengage Learning, 2010.
Bainton, Roland Herbert. *Here I Stand: A Life of Martin Luther*. New York: Abingdon, 1950.
———. *The Reformation of the Sixteenth Century*. Boston: Beacon, 1952.
Ballor, Jordan J. *Ecumenical Babel: Confusing Economic Ideology and the Church's Social Witness*. Grand Rapids: Christian's Library, 2010.
Banchoff, Thomas, and Jose Casanova, eds. *The Jesuits and Globalization: Historical Legacies and Contemporary Challenges*. Washington, DC: Georgetown University Press, 2016.
Barram, Michael D. *Missional Economics: Justice and Christian Formation*. Grand Rapids: Eerdmans, 2018.
Bell, Daniel M. *The Economy of Desire: Christianity and Capitalism in a Postmodern World*. The Church and Postmodern Culture. Grand Rapids: Baker Academic, 2012.

Benesh, Sean. *The Multi-Nucleated Church: Towards a Theoretifcal Framework for Church Planting in High-Density Cities.* Metrospiritual Book Series. Portland, OR: Urban Loft, 2012.

Bergeron, Josh. "Accelerator's Business Picking Up." *Made in Alabama*, July 22, 2014. https://www.madeinalabama.com/news/sba/accelerators-business-picking.

Bevans, Stephen B., and Roger Schroeder. *Constants in Context: A Theology of Mission for Today.* American Society of Missiology Series 30. Maryknoll, NY: Orbis, 2004.

Bimba, Namie. "Business as Ministry Assessment." *Transform: Regent University Journal of Kingdom Business* 1 (2012). https://regententrepreneur.org/wp-content/uploads/2015/12/NamieBimba.pdf.

Blank, Steve. "Why the Lean Start-Up Changes Everything." *Harvard Business Review* 91.5 (2013) 63–72.

Bornstein, Erica. *The Spirit of Development: Protestant NGOs, Morality, and Economics in Zimbabwe.* Stanford, CA: Stanford University Press, 2005.

Bosch, David Jacobus. *Transforming Mission: Paradigm Shifts in Theology of Mission.* American Society of Missiology Series 16. Maryknoll, NY: Orbis, 1991.

Branson, Mark Lau. *Starting Missional Churches: Life with God in the Neighborhood.* Downers Grove, IL: InterVarsity, 2014.

Bronkema, David, and Christopher M. Brown. "Business as Mission Through the Lens of Development." *Transformation* 26.2 (2009) 82.

Brown, Callum G. *The Death of Christian Britain: Understanding Secularisation, 1800–2000.* Christianity and Society in the Modern World. New York: Routledge, 2009.

Bruce, Frederic Fyvie. *The Spreading Flame: The Rise and Progress of Christianity from Its First Beginnings to the Conversion of the English.* Grand Rapids: Eerdmans, 1973.

Bryman, Alan, and Emma Bell. *Business Research Methods.* Oxford: Oxford University Press, 2003.

Business as Mission (BAM) Global. "Business as Mission and Church Planting: Fruitful Practices for Establishing Faith Communities." Think Tank Report. January 2014. http://bamglobal.org/wp-content/uploads/2015/12/BMTT-IG-BAM-and-CP-Final-Report-January-2014.pdf.

———. "The Current State of Business as Mission Research." Think Tank Report. May 2014. https://www.bamglobal.org/wp-content/uploads/2015/12/BMTT-IG-BAM-Scholarship-and-Research-Final-Report-May-2014.pdf.

Campo-Flores, Arian. "Selma, Fifty Years After 'Bloody Sunday,' Still Struggles with a Divided Identity." *Wall Street Journal*, March 10, 2015. http://www.wsj.com/articles/selma-50-years-after-bloody-sunday-still.

Cardoza-Orlandi, Carlos F. *Mission: An Essential Guide.* Nashville: Abingdon, 2002.

Casarella, Peter J. *Jesus Christ: The New Face of Social Progress.* Grand Rapids: Eerdmans, 2014.

"Children's Policy Council Makes a Difference in Selma, Dallas County." *Selma Times-Journal*, July 16, 2006. https://www.selmatimesjournal.com/2006/07/16/childrens-policy-council-makes-a-difference-in-selma-dallas-county.

Children's Policy Councils (CPC) of Alabama. "What Is a CPC." http://www.alcpc.org/whatisacpc.

Cnaan, Ram A., and Stephanie C. Boddie. *The Invisible Caring Hand: American Congregations and the Provision of Welfare.* New York: New York University Press, 2002.

Collins, James C. *Good to Great and the Social Sectors: Why Business Thinking Is Not the Answer.* New York: HarperCollins, 2005.

Corbett, Steve, and Brian Fikkert. *When Helping Hurts: How to Alleviate Poverty without Hurting the Poor—and Yourself.* Chicago: Moody, 2009.

Cray, Graham, et al., eds. *New Monasticism as Fresh Expressions of the Church.* Norwich: Canterbury, 2010.

Creswell, John W. *Research Design: Qualitative, Quantitative, and Mixed Methods Approaches.* Thousand Oaks, CA: SAGE, 2014.

Danker, William John. *Profit for the Lord: Economic Activities in Moravian Missions and the Basel Mission Trading Company.* Christian World Mission. Grand Rapids: Eerdmans, 1971.

Dayton, Donald W. *Discovering an Evangelical Heritage.* Peabody, MA: Hendrickson, 1988.

DellaMea, Chris. "Lynch, KY." *Coalfields Of The Appalachian Mountains*, January 2007. http://www.coalcampusa.com/eastky/harlan/lynch-kentucky-coal-camp/lynch-kentucky-coal-camp.htm.

Deshazo, Alaina Denean. "Hope Academy Recognized at BOE Meeeting." *Selma Times-Journal*, September 3, 2015. https://selmatimesjournal.com/2015/09/03/hope-academy-recognized-at-boe-meeeting.

Dixon, Chris. "Eric Ries On 'Vanity Metrics' and 'Success Theater.'" *TechCrunch*, September 24, 2011. https://techcrunch.com/2011/09/24/founder-stories-eric-ries-vanity-metrics.

Edwards, Jamus. "Authority, Autonomy, and Healthy Communication: Embracing the Organizational Complexities of the MultiSite Church." *Great Commission Research Journal* 5.2 (2014) 182–94.

Eisenhardt, Kathleen M. "Building Theories from Case Study Research." *Academy of Management Review* 14.4 (1989) 532–50.

Eldred, Kenneth A. *God Is at Work.* Ventura, CA: Regal, 2005.

Engen, Charles Edward van, et al., eds. *The Good News of the Kingdom: Mission Theology for the Third Millennium.* Maryknoll, NY: Orbis, 1993.

Fanning, Don. "Brief History of Methods and Trends of Missions" *Trends and Issues in Missions* 1 (2009). https://digitalcommons.liberty.edu/cgm_missions/1.

Fitch, David E. *The Great Giveaway: Reclaiming the Mission of the Church from Big Business, Parachurch Organizations, Psychotherapy, Consumer Capitalism, and Other Modern Maladies.* Grand Rapids: Baker, 2005.

Forster, Greg. *Joy for the World: How Christianity Lost Its Cultural Influence and Can Begin Rebuilding It.* Wheaton, IL: Crossway, 2014.

———. "Theology That Works: Making Disciples Who Practice Fruitful Work and Economic Wisdom in Modern America." *Oikonomia Network*, August 5, 2013. http://oikonomianetwork.org/wp-content/uploads/2014/02/Theology-that-Works-v2-FINAL.pdf.

Fresh Expressions. "Starting Our Journey: Where Do I Begin?" https://freshexpressions.org.uk/starting-our-journey-where-do-i-begin.

Garber, Steven. *Visions of Vocation: Common Grace for the Common Good.* Downers Grove, IL: InterVarsity, 2014.

Gascoigne, Bamber. "History of Monasticism." *HistoryWorld.* http://www.historyworld.net/wrldhis/PlainTextHistories.asp?gtrack=pthc&ParagraphID=eje#eje.

Getu, Makonen. "Measuring Transformation: Conceptual Framework and Indicators." *Transformation* 19.2 (2002) 92.

Gibbs, Eddie, and Ryan K. Bolger. *Emerging Churches: Creating Christian Community in Postmodern Cultures*. Grand Rapids: Baker Academic, 2005.

Graham, Gordon. *The Kuyper Center Review*. Grand Rapids: Eerdmans, 2010.

Grenz, Stanley J. *The Social God and the Relational Self: A Trinitarian Theology of the Imago Dei*. Louisville, KY: Westminster John Knox, 2001.

Hahn, Scott. *A Father Who Keeps His Promises: God's Covenant Love in Scripture*. Ann Arbor: Servant, 1998.

Halter, Hugh, and Matt Smay. *The Tangible Kingdom: Creating Incarnational Community: The Posture and Practices of Ancient Church Now*. San Francisco: Jossey-Bass, 2008.

Hays, Richard B. *The Moral Vision of the New Testament: Community, Cross, New Creation: A Contemporary Introduction to New Testament Ethics*. San Francisco: HarperSanFrancisco, 1996.

Heelas, Paul. *The Spiritual Revolution: Why Religion Is Giving Way to Spirituality*. Religion and Spirituality in the Modern World. Malden, MA: Blackwell, 2005.

Hemphill, Kenneth S. *The Bonsai Theory of Church Growth*. Nashville: Broadman, 1991.

Heuertz, Christopher L., and Christine D. Pohl. *Friendship at the Margins: Discovering Mutuality in Service and Mission*. Resources for Reconciliation. Downers Grove, IL: InterVarsity, 2010.

Hock, Ronald J. "Paul's Tentmaking and the Problem of His Social Class." In *Tentmaking: Perspectives on Self-Supporting Ministry*, edited by James M. M. Francis and Leslie J. Francis, 4–13. Leominster: Gracewing/Fowler Wright, 1998.

———. "The Workshop as a Social Setting for Paul's Missionary Preaching." In *Tentmaking: Perspectives on Self-Supporting Ministry*, edited by James M. M. Francis and Leslie J. Francis, 14–25. Leominster: Gracewing/Fowler Wright, 1998.

Hoekendijk, Johannes Christiaan. "The Church in Missionary Thinking." *International Review of Mission* 41.163 (1952) 324–36.

Hull, John M. "'Come Back, Christianity—All Is Forgiven': Public Theology and the Prophetic Church." *Theology* 119.2 (2016) 83.

Hunter, George G. *The Celtic Way of Evangelism: How Christianity Can Reach the West Again*. Nashville: Abingdon, 2000.

Hunter, James Davison. *To Change the World: The Irony, Tragedy, and Possibility of Christianity in the Late Modern World*. New York: Oxford University Press, 2010.

Irvin, Dale T., and Scott Sunquist. *History of the World Christian Movement*. Maryknoll, NY: Orbis, 2001.

Jacobson, Louis. "Is Today's Poverty Rate In Selma, AL, Nine Times Higher for Blacks Than Whites?" *PolitiFact*, March 10, 2015. https://www.politifact.com/factchecks/2015/mar/10/henry-sanders/todays-poverty-rate-selma-ala-nine-times-higher-bl.

James, Christopher B. *Church Planting in Post-Christian Soil: Theology and Practice*. New York: Oxford University Press, 2018.

Jenkins, Philip. *Next Christendom: The Coming of Global Christianity*. Oxford: Oxford University Press, 2002.

Jennings, Theodore W. *Good News to the Poor: John Wesley's Evangelical Economics*. Nashville: Abingdon, 1990.

Johnson, Charles Neal. *Business as Mission: A Comprehensive Guide to Theory and Practice*. Downers Grove, IL: InterVarsity, 2009.

———. "God's Mission to, within, and through the Marketplace: Toward a Marketplace Missiology." PhD diss., Fuller Theological Seminary, 2004.
Jones, Scott J. *The Evangelistic Love of God & Neighbor: A Theology of Witness and Discipleship*. Nashville: Abingdon, 2003.
Joo, Sang Rak. "Entrepreneurial Church Planting (ECP) as a Model of Fresh Expressions in the South Korean Context: Case Studies Exploring Relationships between Church Planting and Social Capital." PhD diss., Asbury Theological Seminary, 2017.
Keller, Timothy J. *Generous Justice: How God's Grace Makes Us Just*. New York: Dutton, 2010.
Keplinger, Ksenia, et al. "Entrepreneurial Activities of Benedictine Monasteries—A Special Form of Family Business?" *International Journal of Entrepreneurial Venturing* 8.4 (2016) 317.
Kim, Sangkeun. *Strange Names of God: The Missionary Translation of the Divine Name and the Chinese Responses to Matteo Ricci's Shangti in Late Ming China, 1583-1644*. Studies in Biblical Literature 70. New York: Peter Lang, 2004.
Kim, Sebastian C. H., and Kirsteen Kim. *Christianity as a World Religion*. New York: Continuum, 2008.
Kirk, J. Andrew. *What Is Mission?: Theological Explorations*. Minneapolis: Fortress, 2000.
Kisskalt, Michael. "Mission as Convivence—Life Sharing and Mutual Learning in Mission: Inspirations from German Missiology." *Journal of European Baptist Studies* 11.2 (2011) 5-14.
Koyama, Kōsuke. "Neighbor: The Heartbeat of Christ-Talk." *The Living Pulpit* 11.3 (2002) 24-25.
Lai, Patrick. *Tentmaking: The Life and Work of Business as Missions*. Colorado Springs, CO: Authentic, 2005.
Latourette, Kenneth Scott. *A History of the Expansion of Christianity*. London: Harper, 1937.
Lausanne Movement. "Lausanne Statement on Tentmaking." Statement issued at Lausanne II: International Congress on World Evangelization, Manila, Philippines, July 11-20, 1989. https://fazendotendas.files.wordpress.com/2014/10/lausanne-statement-on-tentmaking.pdf.
Lee, Samuel. "Assessing the 'Success' of Business as Mission: A Case Study from Central Asia." *Evangelical Missions Quarterly* 52.1 (2016) 56-64.
———. "Can We Measure the Success and Effectiveness of Entrepreneurial Church Planting?" *Evangelical Review of Theology* 40.4 (2016) 327-45.
———. "An Eschatological Framework for Assessing the Effectiveness of Business as Mission Companies." *The Asbury Journal* 72.1 (2017) 95-109.
———. "Historical Perspectives on Entrepreneurial Church Planting." In *Entrepreneurial Church Planting: Missional Innovation in the Marketplace*, edited by Frederick Long and W. Jay Moon, 101-20. Nicholasville, KY: GlossaHouse, 2018.
———. "A Holistic Framework for Measurement of Entrepreneurial Church Planting." *Great Commission Research Journal* 9.2 (2018) 151-72.
———. "Living Out Being a Public Church in Selma, Alabama." *International Journal of Public Theology* 13.3 (2019) 360-73.

———. "Transformative Metrics for Holistic Ministry in the Marketplace." *Missiology* 47.2 (2019) 121–39.

Lee, Samuel, and Mary E. Conklin. "Conceptualization of the Relational Proximity Framework in Christian Missions." *Journal of Asian Mission* 17.1 (2016) 17–40.

Leshem, Dotan. "Retrospectives: What Did the Ancient Greeks Mean by Oikonomia?" *Journal of Economic Perspectives* 30.1 (2016) 225–38.

Lim, David S. "Norway: The Best Model of a Transformed Nation Today." *Davidlim53's Blog* (blog), September 2, 2011. https://davidlim53.wordpress.com/2011/09/02/norway-the-best-model-of-a-transformed-nation-today.

Lingenfelter, Sherwood G., and Marvin Keene Mayers. *Ministering Cross-Culturally: A Model for Effective Personal Relationships*. Grand Rapids: Baker Academic, 2016.

Long, Frederick, and W. Jay Moon, eds. *Entrepreneurial Church Planting: Missional Innovation in the Marketplace*. Nicholasville, KY: GlossaHouse, 2018.

Lovejoy, Shawn. *The Measure of Our Success: An Impassioned Plea to Pastors*. Grand Rapids: Baker, 2012.

Lowery, James L. *Case Histories of Tentmakers*. Wilton, CT: Morehouse-Barlow, 1976.

Lupton, Robert D. *Toxic Charity: How Churches and Charities Hurt Those They Help (and How to Reverse It)*. New York: HarperOne, 2011.

Madhani, Aamer. "Selma Anniversary Puts Spotlight on Deep Poverty." *USA Today*, March 8, 2015. http://www.usatoday.com/story/news/2015/03/08/selma-poverty-bloody-sunday-50th-anniversary/24603599.

Martin, R. W. Hiebl, and Birgit Feldbauer-Durstmuller. "What Can the Corporate World Learn from the Cellarer?: Examining the Role of a Benedictine Abbey's CFO." *Society and Business Review* 1 (2014) 51. https://doi.org/10.1108/SBR-12-2012-0050.

McDonald, Robin, et al. *Visions of the Black Belt: A Cultural Survey of the Heart of Alabama*. UPCC Book Collections on Project MUSE. Tuscaloosa: University Alabama Press, 2015.

McKnight, John. *The Careless Society: Community and Its Counterfeits*. New York: Basic, 1995.

———. "Why 'Servanthood' Is Bad: Are We Service Peddlers or Community Builders?" *The Other Side* 31.6 (1995) 56–59.

McNeal, Reggie. *Missional Renaissance: Changing the Scorecard for the Church*. San Francisco: Jossey-Bass, 2009.

Meeks, M. Douglas. *Trinity, Community, and Power: Mapping Trajectories in Wesleyan Theology*. Nashville: Kingswood, 2000.

Merriam, Sharan B. *Qualitative Research and Case Study Applications in Education*. A Joint Publication in the Jossey-Bass Education Series and the Jossey-Bass Higher Education Series. San Francisco: Jossey-Bass, 1998.

Miller, Donald E. *Spirit and Power: The Growth and Global Impact of Pentecostalism*. Oxford: Oxford University Press, 2013.

Mission and Public Affairs Council (MPAC), Church of England. *Mission-Shaped Church: Church Planting and Fresh Expressions of Church in a Changing Context*. London: Church House, 2009.

Moffett, Samuel H. *A History of Christianity in Asia*. Maryknoll, NY: Orbis, 1998.

Moltmann, Jürgen. *The Church in the Power of the Spirit: A Contribution to Messianic Ecclesiology*. New York: Harper & Row, 1977.

———. *God for a Secular Society: The Public Relevance of Theology*. Minneapolis: Fortress, 1999.
Moltmann, Jürgen, et al. *A Passion for God's Reign: Theology, Christian Learning, and the Christian Self*. Grand Rapids: Eerdmans, 1999.
Moon, W. Jay. "Entrepreneurial Church Planting: A Missional Approach to Engage the Marketplace." *Send Institute*, January 17, 2019. https://www.sendinstitute.org/entrepreneurial-church-planting.
———. *Intercultural Discipleship: Learning from Global Approaches to Spiritual Formation*. Encountering Mission. Grand Rapids: Baker Academic, 2017.
Moon, W. Jay, et al., eds. *Case Studies in Social Entrepreneurship*. Nicholasville, KY: DOPS, 2017.
Morris, Thomas V. *If Aristotle Ran General Motors: The New Soul of Business*. New York: H. Holt, 1998.
Moynagh, Michael. *Being Church, Doing Life: Creating Gospel Communities Where Life Happens*. Oxford: Monarch, 2014.
———. *Church for Every Context: An Introduction to Theology and Practice*. London: SCM, 2012.
———. *Church In Life: Innovation, Mission and Ecclesiology*. London: SCM, 2017.
Murray, Stuart. *Planting Churches: A Framework for Practitioners*. Milton Keynes: Paternoster, 2008.
Myers, Bryant L. *Walking with the Poor: Principles and Practices of Transformational Development*. Maryknoll, NY: Orbis, 2011.
Neill, Stephen, and Owen Chadwick. *A History of Christian Missions*. Vol. 6 of *The Penguin History of the Church*. New York: Penguin, 1990.
Nel, Malan. "Congregational Analysis: A Theological and Ministerial Approach." *HTS Teologiese Studies/Theological Studies* 65.1 (2009) 1–17.
Newbigin, Lesslie. *Foolishness to the Greeks: The Gospel and Western Culture*. Grand Rapids: Eerdmans, 1986.
———. *The Gospel in a Pluralist Society*. Grand Rapids: Eerdmans; Geneva: WCC, 1989.
———. *The Open Secret: An Introduction to the Theology of Mission*. Grand Rapids: Eerdmans, 1995.
———. "What Is a Local Church Truly United." *The Ecumenical Review* 29.2 (1977) 115–28.
Offutt, Stephen. "New Directions in Transformational Development." *The Asbury Journal* 67.2 (2012) 35–50.
Oikonomia Network. "A Christian Vision for Flourishing Communities." 2014. https://oikonomianetwork.org/wp-content/uploads/2014/02/EWP-NewVersion.pdf.
Ott, Craig, and Gene Wilson. *Global Church Planting: Biblical Principles and Best Practices for Multiplication*. Grand Rapids: Baker Academic, 2011.
Pachuau, Lalsangkima. "Engaging the 'Other' in a Pluralistic World: Toward a Subaltern Hermeneutics of Christian Mission." *Studies in World Christianity* 8.1 (2002) 63–80.
———. "Missiology in a Pluralistic World: The Place of Mission Study in Theological Education." *International Review of Mission* 89.355 (2000) 539–55.
Paeth, Scott R. "Jürgen Moltmann's Public Theology." *Political Theology* 6.2 (2005) 215–34.

Perkins, John. *Restoring At-Risk Communities: Doing It Together and Doing It Right*. Grand Rapids: Baker, 1995.

Phan, Peter C. "Crossing the Borders: A Spirituality for Mission in Our Times from an Asian Perspective." *SEDOS Bulletin* 35.1–2 (2003) 8–19.

Pocock, Michael, et al. *The Changing Face of World Missions: Engaging Contemporary Issues and Trends*. Encountering Missions. Grand Rapids: Baker Academic, 2005.

Poll, Evert van de, and Joanne Appleton. *Church Planting in Europe: Connecting to Society, Learning from Experience*. Eugene, OR: Wipf & Stock, 2015.

Preece, Gordon. "The Threefold Call: A Trinitarian and Reformed Theology of Vocation in Response to Volf's 'Work in the Spirit.'" PhD diss., Fuller Theological Seminary, 1998.

———. "Vocation in Historical-Theological Perspective." *Theology of Work Project*, July 28, 2010. https://www.theologyofwork.org/auxiliary-pages/vocation-depth-article.

Pulliam, Alison. "Gas Station Fuels Spiritual Life in Eastern Kentucky Town of Lynch." *Kentucky Today*, June 29, 2016. https://www.kentuckytoday.com/stories/gas-station-ministry-fuels-spiritual-life-in-eastern-kentucky,4554.

Ramachandra, Vinoth. *The Recovery of Mission: Beyond the Pluralist Paradigm*. Grand Rapids: Eerdmans, 1997.

Ready Ratios. "DuPont Formula." https://www.readyratios.com/reference/profitability/dupont_formula.html.

Redeemer Community Church. "Gospel Partners." https://www.redeemersf.org/gospel-partners.

———. "Vision Statement." May 3, 2011. https://static1.squarespace.com/static/55d64ac7e4b0e91cf1a359e5/t/567894bba976af9f4de1bf8f/1450742971805/vision-statement.pdf.

Rendle, Gilbert R. *Doing the Math of Mission: Fruits, Faithfulness, and Metrics*. Lanham, MD: Rowman and Littlefield, 2014.

Riley, Lonnie. "Testimony: Miracle In The Mountain." *Expedition Church*, February 3, 2012. http://expeditionchurch.org/wp-content/uploads/2012/02/Lonnie-Riley-Testimony-Completed-Outline.pdf.

Riley, Lonnie, et al. *Miracle in the Mountains: Experiencing the Transforming Power of Faith in the Heart of Appalachia*. Bloomington, IN: Crossbooks, 2010.

Robb, Carly. "Ubuntu: I Am Because You Are—The Foreign Philosophy We Need to Explore Now More Than Ever Before." *Thrive Global*, March 14, 2017. https://journal.thriveglobal.com/ubuntu-i-am-because-you-are-66efa03f2682.

Robert, Dana Lee. *Christian Mission: How Christianity Became a World Religion*. Blackwell Brief Histories of Religion Series. Chichester, UK; Malden, MA: Wiley-Blackwell, 2009.

Roxburgh, Alan J., et al. *Introducing the Missional Church: What It Is, Why It Matters, How to Become One*. Allelon Missional Series. Grand Rapids: Baker, 2009.

Rundle, Steven L. "Does Donor Support Help or Hinder Business as Mission Practitioners? An Empirical Assessment." *International Bulletin of Missionary Research* 38.1 (2014) 21–26.

Russell, Mark. *The Missional Entrepreneur: Principles and Practices for Business as Mission*. Birmingham, AL: New Hope, 2010.

———. "The Use of Business in Missions in Chiang Mai, Thailand." PhD diss., Asbury Theological Seminary, 2008.

Saxby, Trevor. "Revival-Bringer: Hans Nielsen Hauge's Remarkable Labors in Nineteenth-Century Norway." *Mining for Gold* (blog), April 14, 2020. https://makinghistorynow.wordpress.com/2020/04/14/the-country-boy-who-fathered-a-nation-part-1.

Scherer, James A. *Gospel, Church & Kingdom: Comparative Studies in World Mission Theology*. Eugene, OR: Wipf & Stock, 2004.

Scherer, James A., and Stephen Bevans, eds. *Theological Foundations*. Vol. 2 of *New Directions in Mission and Evangelization*. Maryknoll, NY: Orbis, 1994.

Schmidt, Ann. "Decline of the Town That Coal Built: 100 Years after It Sprang up to Fuel the Steel Industry, Attracting 10,000 Residents from 38 Nations, Lynch Is Home to Just 650 People and Struggles to Survive." *Daily Mail*, March 27, 2017. https://www.dailymail.co.uk/news/article-4332054/Lynch-Kentucky-turns-100-year-fights-survive.html.

Seasoltz, R. Kevin. "Benedictines." In *The Encyclopedia of Religion*, edited by Mircea Eliade, 96–98. Complete and unabridged ed. New York: Macmillan, 1993.

Second Vatican Council. *Ad Gentes: On the Mission Activity of the Church*. Decree promulgated by Pope Paul VI, December 7, 1965. http://www.vatican.va/archive/hist_councils/ii_vatican_council/documents/vat-ii_decree_19651207_ad-gentes_en.html.

Sedmak, Clemens. "Mission as Kinship on the Margins." Paper presented at the 59th Annual Meeting of the Midwest Missions Studies Fellowship, South Bend, IN, November 11, 2016.

Self, Charlie. *Flourishing Churches and Communities: A Pentecostal Primer on Faith, Work, and Economics for Spirit-Empowered Discipleship*. Biblical Faith, Work, & Economics Series. Grand Rapids: Christian's Library, 2012.

Sentinel Group. "Putting Feet on Jesus in Lynch, Kentucky." *Pray.Network*, November 1, 2013. http://praynetwork.ning.com/forum/topics/the-sentinel-group-lynch-ky.

Sherman, Amy L. *Kingdom Calling: Vocational Stewardship for the Common Good*. Downers Grove, IL: InterVarsity, 2011.

Sherman, Doug, and William D. Hendricks. *Your Work Matters to God*. Colorado Springs: Nav, 1990.

Sider, Ronald J. *Churches That Make a Difference: Reaching Your Community with Good News and Good Works*. Grand Rapids: Baker, 2002.

———. *One-Sided Christianity? Uniting the Church to Heal Alost and Broken World*. Grand Rapids: Zondervan, 1993.

———. *Rich Christians in an Age of Hunger: Moving from Affluence to Generosity*. Dallas: Word, 1997.

Siemons, Ruth E. "The Vital Role of Tentmaking in Paul's Mission Strategy." *International Journal of Frontier Missions* 14 (July 1997) 121–29.

Skeie, Karina Hestad. *Building God's Kingdom: Norwegian Missionaries in Highland Madagascar, 1866–1903*. Studies in Christian Mission 42. Leiden: Brill, 2013.

Smither, Edward L. *Mission in the Early Church: Themes and Reflections*. Eugene, OR: Cascade, 2014.

Snyder, Howard A. "The Babylonian Captivity of Wesleyan Theology." *Wesleyan Theological Journal* 39.1 (2004) 7–34.

———. *Liberating the Church: The Ecology of Church & Kingdom*. Downers Grove, IL: InterVarsity, 1983.

———. *Models of the Kingdom*. Eugene, OR: Wipf & Stock, 2001.

———. "Salvation Means Creation Healed: Creation, Cross, Kingdom and Mission." *The Asbury Journal* 62.1 (2007) 9–47.

———. *Yes in Christ: Wesleyan Reflections on Gospel, Mission, and Culture.* Tyndale Studies in Wesleyan History and Theology 2. Toronto: Clements Academic, 2010.

Spaugh, Herbert. "A Short History of the Moravian Church. Touching on its History, Theology, Customs and Practices." 1957. Revised by Worth Green. *New Philadelphia Moravian Church*, 1996. https://newphilly.org/pdf/moravian.ashorthistory.pdf.

Sperling, Bert. "Lynch, Kentucky." *BestPlaces.* https://www.bestplaces.net/people/city/kentucky/lynch.

Steffen, Tom A., and Mike Barnett. *Business as Mission: From Impoverished to Empowered.* Evangelical Missiological Society Series 14. Pasadena, CA: William Carey, 200

Stevens, R. Paul. *Liberating the Laity: Equipping All the Saints for Ministry.* Downers Grove, IL: InterVarsity, 1985.

———. *The Other Six Days: Vocation, Work, and Ministry in Biblical Perspective.* Grand Rapids: Eerdmans, 1999.

Strauss, Anselm L., and Juliet M. Corbin. *Basics of Qualitative Research: Techniques and Procedures for Developing Grounded Theory.* Thousand Oaks, CA: SAGE, 1998.

Sunde, Joseph. "All Is Gift: How Our Work Sings of God's Presence." *Acton Institute Powerblog* (blog), May 14, 2014. https://blog.acton.org/archives/68815-gift-work-sings-gods-presence.html.

Swanson, Eric, and Sam Williams. *To Transform a City: Whole Church, Whole Gospel, Whole City.* Grand Rapids: Zondervan, 2010.

Swarr, Sharon Bentch, and Dwight Nordstrom. *Transform the World: Biblical Vision and Purpose for Business.* Kona, HI: Center for Entrepreneurship and Economic Development, University of the Nations, 1999.

Taylor, Mark C. *After God.* Religion and Postmodernism. Chicago: University of Chicago Press, 2007.

Terry, John Mark, and Robert L. Gallagher. *Encountering the History of Missions: From the Early Church to Today.* Grand Rapids, MI: Baker Academic, 2017.

Thurow, Lester C. *Investment in Human Capital.* Wadsworth Series in Labor Economics and Industrial Relations. Belmont, CA: Wadsworth, 1970.

Tillmanns, Walter G. "The Lotthers: Forgotten Printers of the Reformation." *Concordia Theological Monthly* 22.4 (1951) 260–64.

Torrance, Thomas Forsyth. *The Trinitarian Faith: The Evangelical Theology of the Ancient Catholic Church.* Edinburgh: T. & T. Clark, 1988.

Tunehag, Mats, et al. "Business as Mission." 2005. Lausanne Occasional Paper 59. https://www.lausanne.org/content/lop/business-mission-lop-59.

United States Census Bureau. "QuickFacts: San Francisco, California." https://www.census.gov/quickfacts/fact/table/sanfranciscocitycalifornia,US/PST045219.

———. "QuickFacts: Selma, Alabama." https://www.census.gov/quickfacts/fact/table/selmacityalabama/PST045219#flag-js-X.

Veith, Gene Edward, Jr. *Working for Our Neighbor: A Lutheran Primer on Vocation, Economics, and Ordinary Life.* Grand Rapids: Christian Library, 2016.

Villagomez, Cynthia Jan. "The Fields, Flocks, and Finances of Monks: Economic Life at Nestorian Monasteries, 500–850." PhD diss., UCLA, 1998.

Volf, Miroslav. "A Vision of Embrace: Theological Perspectives on Cultural Identity and Conflict." *Ecumenical Review* 47.2 (1995) 195–205.

———. *Work in the Spirit: Toward a Theology of Work.* New York: Oxford University Press, 1991.

Volland, Michael. *The Minister as Entrepreneur: Leading and Growing the Church in an Age of Rapid Change*. London: SPCK, 2015.
Walls, Andrew F. *The Cross-Cultural Process in Christian History: Studies in the Transmission and Appropriation of Faith*. Maryknoll, NY: Orbis, 2002.
———. *The Missionary Movement in Christian History: Studies in the Transmission of Faith*. Maryknoll, NY: T. & T Clark, 1996.
Walls, Andrew F., and Cathy Ross. *Mission in the Twenty-First Century: Exploring the Five Marks of Global Mission*. London: Darton, Longman & Todd, 2008.
Wan, Enoch. "The Paradigm of 'Relational Realism.'" *Occasional Bulletin* 19.2 (2006) 1–8. https://www.westernseminary.edu/files/documents/faculty/wan/Relational%20realism-EMS-OB-Spring2006.pdf.
Weber, Max. *The Protestant Ethic and the Spirit of Capitalism*. Translated by Talcott Parsons. New York: Routledge, 1930.
Wee, M. O. *Haugeanism: A Brief Sketch of the Movement and Some of Its Chief Exponents*. St. Paul: n.p., 1919.
Weeks, Lee. "Unemployment, Poverty Gripped Their Hearts for Appalachia." *Baptist Press*, December 15, 2004. https://www.baptistpress.com/resource-library/news/unemployment-poverty-gripped-their-hearts-for-appalachia.
Wesley, John. *The Works of the Reverend John Wesley, AM*. Vol. 5. Oxford: J. Emory and B. Waugh, 1833.
———. *The Works of the Reverend John Wesley, AM*. Vol. 10. New York: J. & J. Harper, 1827.
White, Charles Edward. "Four Lessons on Money from One of the World's Richest Preachers." *Christian History*, January 1, 1988.
Winter, Ralph D., et al. *Perspectives on the World Christian Movement: A Reader*. Pasadena, CA: William Carey, 2009.
Winter, Ralph D., and Bruce A. Koch. "Finishing the Task: The Unreached Peoples Challenge." *International Journal of Frontier Missions* 16 (1999) 67–76.
Winter, Ralph D., and Beth Snodderly. *Foundations of the World Christian Movement: A Larger Perspective: Course Reader*. Pasadena, CA: William Carey, 2012.
Witherington, Ben, III. *Work: A Kingdom Perspective on Labor*. Grand Rapids: Eerdmans, 2010.
Wright, Christopher. "Biblical Reflections on Land." *Evangelical Review of Theology* 17.2 (1993) 153–67.
Wright, David. *How God Makes the World a Better Place: A Wesleyan Primer on Faith, Work, and Economic Transformation*. Grand Rapids: Christian's Library, 2012.
Yamamori, Tetsunao, and Kenneth A. Eldred. *On Kingdom Business: Transforming Missions through Entrepreneurial Strategies*. Wheaton, IL: Crossway, 2003.
Yates, Paula, and Joris van Eijnatten. *The Churches: The Dynamics of Religious Reform in Northern Europe, 1780–1920*. The Dynamics of Religious Reform in Church, State and Society in Northern Europe, 1780–1920. Leuven: Leuven University Press, 2010.
Yin, Robert K. *Case Study Research: Design and Methods*. Applied Social Research Methods Series 5. Thousand Oaks, CA: SAGE, 2003.
Yong, Amos. *Spirit-Word-Community: Theological Hermeneutics in Trinitarian Perspective*. Ashgate New Critical Thinking in Religion, Theology, and Biblical Studies. Burlington, VT: Ashgate, 2002.
Zizioulas, Jean. *Being as Communion: Studies in Personhood and the Church*. Contemporary Greek Theologians 4. Crestwood, NY: St. Vladimir's Seminary, 1985.

Index

f after page locator refers to figures; *t* after page locator refers to tables; *n* as part of page locator refers to a note

abolitionists, 29
accelerator, vs. incubator, 138n8. *See also* Arsenal Place Accelerator (APA)
accountability, 100, 106
Ad Gentes: On the Mission Activity of the Church (Paul VI, pope), 162
African community, and Chinese investors, 75
African slaves, mission for, 27
African-Americans
    absence in Meridzo Ministries, 117
    empowerment of, 107
    MM and, 127–28
Agribusiness Center, 113
Alabama, incarceration percent change for selected counties, 2000-2015, 90f, 91t
Alopen, 24
analysis unit, 47
Anderson, Rufus, 41
anonymity, 60, 61
APA. *See* Arsenal Place Accelerator (APA)
apothecary shops, 28
Appalachian Mountains, 110
Aquila and Priscilla, 15

Arbela Kingdom, 24
Armstrong, Bob, 52, 89–90, 91, 94, 108
Arsenal Place Accelerator (APA), 48, 49, 86–102, 103, 138, 196–97t
    background information, 87–94
    description of selection criteria, 50t
    interplay with BJC and CPC, 105
    network of affiliations, 93, 93f
    success definitions, 197–98t
    success indicators, 201–5t
    success metrics, 199–201t
Asbury Marketplace Summit, 57n19
Asbury Theological Seminary, 52
    Institutional Review Board, 61
Asbury University, 52
Asbury, Francis, 29
Asia, Christianity introduced, 24
assessment tools, lack of, 4
attendance statistics, 66
Augustine of Canterbury, 23
awareness, lack of, 98–99

BAM. *See* Business as Mission (BAM)
Bayview/Hunters Point (San Francisco, California), 64, 78
Becoming a Good Neighbor, measuring, 107

237

Index

BED. *See* Business for Economic Development (BED)
belonging, 77, 81
    ECP and, 80–81t
Benedictines, 30
    daily activities, 23–24
Benesh, Sean, 101n22
Bergeron, Ryan, 92–93
Berry, Mark, 9
Bevans, Stephen B., *Constants in Context: A Theology of Mission for Today*, 31
Bible. *See* scripture
biblical relationships, 133
biblical stewardship, 120
Bishop of Rome (Gregory), 23
bi-vocational approach, 48
BJC. *See* Blue Jean Church (BJC)
Black Mountain Exchange, 124
    gas station, 53
Blank, Steve, 38n84
blessing, 79, 81–82
    ECP and, 80–81t
    as success measure, 72–74
blood kinship, 130, 132
Blue Jean Church (BJC), 48, 49, 52, 59, 86–102, 137, 174
    advantage, 139
    background information, 87–94
    church attendance and, 88
    description of selection criteria, 50t
    evaluation, 170
    and evangelism, 138
    goals, 196–97t
    Holistic Transformation applied, 140t
    interplay with APA and CPC, 105
    interviews, 95–101
    network of affiliations, 93, 93f
    percentage of parishioners who live within 1 mile, 102f
    recommendations, 106–7
    research findings of goals, 141t
    research procedure at, 94–96
    site visits and interviews, 54
    success indicators, 201–5t
    success metrics, 98, 199–201t
body of Christ, 37

Bolger, Ryan, 125
bonding, 106
bonsai tree, and church planting, 135
Boren, Scott, *Introducing the Missional Church*, 163
Bosch, David, 18n73
Bread of Life, 112
broken relationships, 130
Bronkema, David, 4
Brown, Christopher M., 4
business
    and the church, historical overview, 22–30
    Meridzo Ministries creation, 113
Business as Mission (BAM), 3n16, 7–8, 15, 17, 31, 35–37
    characteristics, 16–17
    practitioners, 3
    theoretical perspective, 6
Business for Economic Development (BED), 36f, 37. *See also* Business as Mission (BAM)
    characteristics, 43t
    characteristics of faith/work interaction, 40
    emphasis, 32, 41
    measures of spiritual success, 44
    similarities with tentmaking, 42

calling, 30, 33, 37
Camp House (Chattanooga, Tennessee), 48
case study method, 46. *See also* Dayspring Technologies; Redeemer Community Church
    information collection, 57
    to research methodology, 10–11
Catholic Church, need for ecclesial reform, 26
Celtic missionaries, 22–23, 30
Changan (Tang dynasty capital), 24
change indicators, 170
    for ECP, 164
    sorting into categories, 171
Chien, Chi-Ming, 51, 64, 68
Children's Policy Council (CPC), 89–90, 99

Index 239

interplay with APA and BJC, 105
network of affiliations, 93, 93f
China, Christianity introduced, 24
Christianity
 lay people in, 33
 need for standard to measure performance, 5
church, 3n17, 14, 42
 as agent for God's universal outreach, 35
 BAM's approach as downplaying, 37
 beyond structural walls, 86
 change in concept, 22
 defining relationships, 38
 economic activities and, 66
 as institution and organism, 174–75
 meaning of, 174
 mission as extending, 31–32
church growth, 65–66
church planting, 15, 37, 52
 and economic activity, 21
 economic strategies and, 2
 as goal, 44
 holistic outreach to the community, 101
 three-self principle, 41
civic responsibility, 39
Claiborne, Shane, 9
coal mining industry, 110
coding process, 60
collaboration, 105
Columba, 22–23
communion formation, 123, 129, 134
 in MM, 122
community, 75
 holistic outreach to, 86
 Perkin's three-fold strategy of development, 173
 size of, 141
 true, 18
community building, 129, 134
 MM and, 123–24
Community Christian Center, 53
Community-for-a-community, 114, 133, 134
compassion, 131
confidentiality, 60, 61

connection, and communion formation in MM, 122–23
Consent Form, 59, 61
Constants in Context: A Theology of Mission for Today (Bevans and Schroeder), 31
content analysis, 60
Copper River Grill (Nicholasville, Kentucky), 48
Corbin, Juliet, 60
Cornerstone Missionary Baptist Church, 65
countercultural communities of faith, 135n3
covenantal relationships, 120, 123
CPC. *See* Children's Policy Council (CPC)
crafts, in medieval period, 21–22
Creation Commission, 13, 17, 27, 31, 133
 mission strategies, 108
 MM and, 118
 Moravians and, 31
 stewardship as goal, 4
creation ethics, 133
Creswell, John W., 46
Crisis Aid International, 93
Cuius regio, eius religio, 27n39
Cultural Mandate. *See* Creation Commission

Dallas County District Court and Juvenile Court, BJC collaboration with, 104
Dallas County Workforce Investment Act, 104
data, constant comparison, 46
Dayspring Technologies, 51, 71, 76, 81, 137, 166, 173
 background information, 64–70
 case study, 63–85
 community and, 139–40
 description of selection criteria, 50t
 and evangelism, 138
 goal and outcomes, 77f
 measurements and objectives, 83–84
 outcomes of operation, 71–76

Dayspring Technologies *(continued)*
  outcomes of the operation, 71–76
  political environment, 67
  relational approach, 73
De Rhodes, Alexander, 26
dechurched, reaching, 3
dependent variables, 55
design, 46
development, 87n4
disciples, 31
discipleship
  accountability and, 39
  whole-life, 13n47, 136
DuPont formula, 37n81

economic activity, and church planting, 21
economic assistance, company startups as, 103
economic development
  APA and, 100
  operational indicators, 223t
economic distribution, scriptural vision of, 67
economic fruitfulness, 11
  as goal, 44
economic growth, 160
economic justice, 28
economic revitalization, 92
economic strategies, and church planting, 2
economic sustainability, 48, 137
economic symbiosis, 103
economic Trinity, 163
economic vitality, 168
  operational indicators, 224t
ECP. *See* Entrepreneurial Church Planting (ECP)
ECWA Theological Seminary, 65
Edessa, 24
effectiveness, 6n24, 10
  determining, 10
  of ministries, 1
Egede, Hans, 27
Ekklesia Project, 65
Eldred, Kenneth A., 15, 41
employment, 29
entrepreneur, 13
  Hauge as, 30

Entrepreneurial Church Planting (ECP), 2, 16, 19, 136, 136n5
  analysis of ministries, 136–40
  assessment of outcomes, 170–72
  background, 3–6
  characteristics, 16–17
  cross-case analysis, 140–46
  focus of, 133
  goals, 141–43
  growth factors, 165, 165f
  love for God and neighbor as goal, 162
  measure of success and effectiveness, 159
  measuring outcomes, 108
  missional assessment of performance, 164
  operation of, 169f
  operationalization of outcomes, 80–81t
  potential for problems, 4
  programs, 47
  questionnaire, 187–95
  recommendations, 83
  relational view of, 164
  relevance to other missional issues, 172–75
  social/developmental aspects, 83
  specific criteria, 47
  statement of problem, 6
  stewarding capabilities of, 2
  success for, 79
  theoretical foundation, 6–9
entrepreneurship, 165, 165f
  operationalization of, 166
environment, nurturing Christian, 68
environmental factors, 11–12
Ethelbert (King of Kent), 23
evangelical economics, 28
Evangelical Revival, 27
evangelism, 17, 138
  MM and, 139
  operational indicators, 222–23t
evangelistic-economic continuum for measuring success, 1

faith, integration with work and *oikonomia*, 109
faithfulness, as success measure, 72–74

Family Crisis Center, 140
family crisis program, at BJC, 89
family of God, operational indicators, 224t
Father, 13, 31, 161. *See also* God
    human messengers, 164n10
Fatherhood Initiative, 104
fellowship, at BJC, 89
financial sustainability, 37
Finney, Charles, 29
First Presbyterian Church of Selma, 87–88
Fong, Danny, 51, 64, 73, 84
    key issues and responses, 71t
food bank, 53, 112
foreign contexts, appeal of ECP, 3
formation, 134
40-hour work week limit, 68–69
Freedom Center, 115
Fresh Expressions of Church (FXC), 3, 9, 17
    characteristics, 16–17
    theoretical perspective, 6
friends, borrowers and lenders as, 69
FXC. *See* Fresh Expressions of Church (FXC)

G Momma's Cookies, 92
G Mommas Cookies, 138
Genesis, 37n80
Gibbs, Eddie, 125
global case studies, 177
Global Reporting Initiative (ISO 2600), 41
goals
    determined by measuring, 134
    holistic transformation as, 172
    identification for BJC, 97
    love for God and neighbor as, 162
    of Meridzo Ministries (MM), 205–6t
God, 13. *See also* Father; Holy Spirit
    Chinese terms for, 26
good neighbors, equip the people of the church, 102
Good news, Meridzo Ministries sharing, 119
Good Samaritan, 103
gospel, sharing, 53

Grace Fellowship Community Church, 64, 66
Grace Urban Ministries, 64
Great Commandment, 13, 18, 31, 128
    commitment to, 136
    mission strategies, 108
    Moravians and, 27
    social transformation as goal, 4
Great Commission, 13, 17, 85, 133
    mission strategies, 108
    MM and, 118
    reconciliation/discipleship, 4
Gregory (Bishop of Rome), 23
growth and development, 160

Hahn, Scott, 120, 123
Hauge, Hans Nielsen, 27, 29–30, 31, 33
heart, transformation of, 133
Heaven's Door Chapel, 113
Hock, Ronald, 7
holistic approach to success, 98
holistic community development, 8
holistic ministry, 1, 160
    concern for, 162
    in MM, 118
holistic transformation, 94
    as goal, 172
    measuring, 164
    model applications, 140t
    relationship between marketplace missional engagement, 172–73
Holistic Transformation Business Model (HTB), 31, 37–40, 39f, 42, 135–58. *See also* Entrepreneurial Church Planting (ECP)
    characteristics, 43t
    characteristics of faith/work interaction, 40
    emphasis, 32
    evaluation approach, 41–42
    measures of spiritual success, 44
    value of metrics, 5
Holy Spirit, 13, 31, 94, 102, 121, 161, 164
    gifts, 176
hope, 104, 167
    in Lynch, 114
Hope Academy, 92, 94, 104
hospitality, 9

house churches, 22
HTB. *See* Holistic Transformation Business model (HTB)
human capital, 168
    operational indicators for enhancements, 224t

identity transformation, 125
IN relationships, 14
in-betweenness, 165, 165f
    operationalization of, 166
incubator, vs. accelerator, 138
independent variables, 55–56
individualism, 38
Industrial Revolution, 22
information collection, ethical considerations, 60
informed consent letter, 179–80
institution, church as, 174–75
Institutional Review Board, 61
Integrity Worldwide, 95, 97
interpersonal relationships, in new monasticism, 8
interviews, 115
    with BJC, 95–101
    content analysis of, 101
    data collection, 59
    description, 196–97t
    description of subjects, 115–17
    development, 58
    questions, 181–86
Isaiah 40 policy, 51, 67
ISO 2600, 41

Jennings, Theodore, 28
Jesuits (Society of Jesus), 23
Jesus Christ, 31
    continuing missions of, 161
    personal relationship with, 34
Jubilee Immigration Advocates, 65
Judge Bob, 105
Justo Mwale Theological University College, 65
Juvenile Court of Dallas County, 89
juvenile incarcerations
    drop in, 100
    selected counties in Alabama, 2000-2015, 90f

Kentucky, economic climate, 176
kingdom business, 8
Kingdom of God, 163
    in-breaking metrics of success at MM as, 121
    outlook, 48
    understandings of, 39
Kingdom proximity, 104, 105
    measuring, 107
Kingdom Transformation, 18–19. *See also* Great Commandment
Kingdom-like community, goal of BJC, 97
kingdom-shaped church, 38
kinship model, 110, 130
    transformation between levels, 131t
Kirk, Andrew, 5
koivonia, 14
Kuyper, Abraham, 174

laity, role in outreach, 42
Lamp House Coffee Shop, 53
Lausanne Tentmaking Statement, 33
leadership, 176
    training for others, 163
lean start-up, 38n84
The Lean Startup (Ries), 159
less developed countries, economic opportunities for disenfranchised, 3
living wage, 73
loans, 51, 69
Louisville, Kentucky, United Methodist Church of the Promise, 5
Lovejoy, Shawn, 120
Loyola, Ignatius, 26
Lupton, Robert, 106
    Toxic Charity, 106n37
Luther, Martin, 25–26, 30, 33
Lynch, KY, 110, 138. *See also* Meridzo Ministries (MM)
    economic growth in, 160–61
    redevelopment in, 161
    redistribution in, 173
    transformation in, 114

marketplace, 8, 14
marketplace missional engagement, 173–74

relationship between holistic
    transformation and, 172–73
materialism, 38
McNeal, Reggie, 73
Meridzo Ministries (MM), 48, 49,
    52–54, 59, 110–34, 111n10, 137,
    138, 166
  community, 126
  description, 113–14
  description of selection criteria, 50t
  evaluation, 170
  and evangelism, 139
  goals, 117–19, 205–6t
  grassroots definition of success,
    126–27
  historical overview, 110–12
  holistic praxes, 129–33, 129f
  holistic transformation, 128–33
  Holistic Transformation applied,
    140t
  identity transformation leading to
    oikonomia, 125–26
  renewal associated with, 114–15
  research findings of goals, 141t
  research procedure at, 115–18
  "responsive planning," 127
  site visits and interviews, 54
  success definition, 119–20, 207–10t
  success metrics, 121–22, 211–15t
  volunteer facilitation, 113
messengers of God, 164n10
Methodists. *See also* Wesley, John
  circuit riders, 29
metrics, 6, 10
  for Blue Jean Church success,
    199–201t
  for missional church, 163
  performance and effectiveness for
    church-planting efforts, 45
  for success, 71t
milk kinship, 130, 132
Miller, Donald, 122
minority voices, need for, 127–28
missio Dei, 9, 103, 168, 169
  Bosch definition, 18n73
  church engagement in, 109
  Community and, 108
  community of faith and, 18
  and human participation, 74

Kingdom culture maintenance, 85
marketplace workers in, 31
Trinity and, 12
Willingen Conference (1952) and,
    35
missional activities, relationality and,
    160
missional church, 163
missional witness, 6
missionaries, 127–28
  God's use of, 167
missions
  as business, 32
  development, 1
  earliest view of, 32
  evangelistic-socio-economic
    dimensions, 19
  Moravian economic model for, 27
  theocentric conceptualization of, 35
  theology of, 31
Mission-Shaped Church, 14
  report, 15
MM. *See* Meridzo Ministries (MM)
Moltmann, Jürgen, 103
Moon, Jay, 16, 135n1
Moravians, 26–27, 30, 33
  Wesley and, 28n46
Moynagh, Michael, 14, 164
  on four dimensions, 164n11
multiple-case approach, 46–47
mutual indwelling/act of divine self-
    giving, 102n25
Myers, Bryant, 18

narrative, 83
Neighbor Fund, 51, 66, 69, 74–75, 81,
    84, 140
neighborhood
  BJC, APA, and the CPC, and
    change, 100
  Blue Jean Church and, 139
  operational indicators, 223t
  revitalization, 107
  spiritual responsibility for, 103
Neighborly Collaboration, measuring,
    107
Neighborly Love, 99–100
  measuring, 107
Nestorians, 24–25, 30

Index

neutral spaces (third space), 3, 124
New Creation Commission, 13
New Creation, MM and, 118
new monasticism, 8
Newbigin, Lesslie, 162, 162n7, 164, 166n13, 177
NGOs, social services, 7
Nobili, Roberto, 26
nonprobability-based sampling, 54
Northern Picts, 22

observations, data from, 59
OF relationships, 14
oikonomia, 119, 120, 123, 125–26, 128, 129, 134, 165, 165f, 168n18
    integration with faith and work, 109
    MM and, 118
    operationalization of, 167
Oikonomia Network, 13n47
Open Door Legal, 65
organism, church as, 174–75
ostracism, 3
OUT relationships, 14
outcomes assessment
    of ECP, 170–72
    indicators, 171t
outreach, laity role in, 42
Oxford Center for Mission Studies, 15

participant observation, 58–59
Paul, 7, 15, 33
    missionary strategy, 21
Paul VI, pope, *Ad Gentes: On the Mission Activity of the Church*, 162
performance, 6n24
perichoresis, 102n25, 105
perichoretic (mutual indwelling) Trinity, 38
perichoretic relationships, 132
perichoretic view of ECP, 107–8
Perkins, John, 102n23
Persia, Christianity introduced, 24
personal commitment, 29
personal relationships
    within business, 48
    with Jesus, 34
personhood, 165
physical proximity, 102

measuring, 107
poverty, in Selma, 88
prayer, 89
prayer meeting, 111
Presbyterian Church, 51
pride, in Lynch, 114
priesthood of all believers, 25, 26
"Primitive Physick" (Wesley), 28
printing shop
    Luther and, 25, 30
    Wesley and, 28
Priscilla and Aquila, 15
privacy, 60
process, study of, 10
profitability, 11
Protestant Reformation, 25
Providence Baptist Church, 65

quantification, 83
questionaire, for ECP, 187–95
questions, 177
    interview, 181–86

racially-related issues, 12
"rank and yank" workplace structure, 67
rational reconciliation, 71
reconciliation, 79
Redeemer Community Church, 48, 49, 51, 71, 76, 137, 174
    background information, 64–70
    case study, 63–85
    description of selection criteria, 50t
    goal and outcomes, 77f
    Holistic Transformation applied, 140t
    key issues and responses, 71t
    leadership, 176
    measurements and objectives, 83–84
    outcomes of the operation, 71–76
    relational approach, 73
    research findings of goals, 141t
    site visits and interviews, 54
    success measurement, 72
    surveys, 59
redemption, 31
redevelopment, in Selma and Lynch, 161
redistribution, absence in Selma, 173
reflected love, 79, 81

ECP and, 80–81t
Reformed churches, 26
relational ministry, 136
relational proximity, 103, 108
  measuring, 107
relational restoration, 18
relational strategy, 134
relational transition, 129
relationality, 160
relationship building orientation, 77
relationships, 14, 42, 83, 98, 120, 132
  in BJC, 98
  in Holistic Transformation Business
    model (HTB), 42
  from one-on-one contact, 53
  proximities, 108
  of trust, MM and, 124
relief, 87n4
relocation, 102n23
replication logic, 47
research
  delimitations and limitations, 11–12
  findings, 160–163
  future, 177
  implications of study, 163–175
  limitations, 176
  purpose of, 10
  significance of, 11
  sub-reach questions, 6
research methodology, 10–11, 45–61
  case study, 46–47
  data analysis, 60
  data collection, 59
  research design, 46
  site visits and interviews, 54
  unit of analysis and sample
    selection, 47–55
  use of triangulation of methods, 57
  variables and operationalization,
    55–56
responsive planning, 127
restoration, 167
return on equity (ROE), 37n81
Revival Coffee Company, 92–93, 138
Ricci, Matteo, 26, 30, 33
Ries, Eric, 38n84
  The Lean Startup, 159
Riley, Belinda, 111

Riley, Lonnie, 52–54, 111. *See also*
  Meridzo Ministries (MM)
Rise University Preparatory, 66, 83n13
Roxburgh, Alan, Introducing the
  Missional Church, 163
"Rule of St. Benedict," 23
Rundle, Steve, 57
Russell, Lowery, 58
Russell, Mark L., 15

Sabbath, 68–69
Saint Thomas (Caribbean island), 27
salary scale, 73
salvation, 164, 166
sample size, 47
San Francisco. *See also* Redeemer
  Community Church
  economic climate, 176
Sassanid Persia, 24
school for troubled teens, in Selma, 91
Schreiter, 162
Schroeder, Roger, *Constants in Context:*
  A Theology of Mission for Today,
  31
scripture
  Genesis 1:26, 31
  Genesis 1:26–28, 173
  Genesis 1:27–30, 13
  Isaiah 41:17–20, 111
  Matthew 6:33, 100
  Matthew 28:19–20, 13, 31
  Luke 10, 78
  Luke 10:30–37, 103
  John 1:8, 15
  John 1:13, 125
  John 4:34, 12
  John 5:30, 12
  John 8:29, 12
  1 Corinthians 3:6–10, 15
  1 Corinthians 12:13, 172
  2 Corinthians 2:14, 88
  2 Corinthians 5:18, 71
  Galations 3:28, 172
  Ephesians 1:3–14, 15
  Ephesians 4, 174
  Philippians 2:4–10, 15
  Peter 2:4–10, 15
  Peter 3, 15
  Revelations 21, 105

Sedmak, Clemens, kinship model, 110, 130
Seed and Light International Sunrise Ministries, 65
self-centerdness, 38
Selma Life Ministries, 93
Selma, AL, 86, 87, 138. *See also* Blue Jean Church (BJC)
    economic climate, 176
    economic growth in, 160–61
    percentage income distribution vs. Alabama, 88t
    redevelopment in, 161
    redistribution absent in, 173
Shang Ti, 26
Shekinah Christian Fellowship, 65
Sherman, Amy, 80n12
Sider, Ron, 1, 87n4, 118
slavery, Wesley and, 29
Smedley, Sheryl, 92
Snyder, Howard, 18, 39, 166, 166n13
social development
    evangelism and, 139
    operational indicators, 223t
social front, 87n4
social justice, transformative networks, 174
social responsibility, 48
social transformation, 86
Society of Jesus (Jesuits), 23
socio-economic engagement, 3
socio-economic reconciliation, 51
Son, 31. *See also* Jesus Christ
specific criteria, 47
Spirit of Capitalism (Weber), 2
spiritual community, building, 77
spiritual kinship, 130
spiritual reconciliation, 81
spiritual transformation, 80
startup capital, initial source, 55–56
startup companies, success and failure, 159
stereotypes, 104
Stevens, R. Paul, 13, 31
stewarding capabilities of ECP, 2
stewardship, 136, 173n23
    of money, 28
Stoess, Larry, 5

Strauss, Anselm, 60
structural change, 87n4
success, 71t
    for Dayspring, 76
    definitions for Blue Jean Church, 97–98, 197–98t
    definitions for Meridzo Ministries, 119–20, 207–10t
    for ECP, 79
    God's definition, 120
    indicators for Blue Jean Church, 201–205t
    indicators for Meridzo Ministries, 216–221t
    measuring, 85, 115
    metrics, 106
    metrics for Blue Jean Church, 199–201t
    metrics for Meridzo Ministries, 211–215t
    for RCC, 76
    theoretical definition, 72
Suriname, 27, 28
survey construction, 57

Table Café (Louisville, Kentucky), 48
taxing, 112
Teen Challenge Center, 90, 93, 94
tent-making, 7, 15, 17, 27, 31
    characteristics, 16–17, 43t
    characteristics of faith/work interaction, 40
    downside to, 34
    emphasis, 32
    measures of spiritual success, 44
    model, 33–35, 34f
    personal relationship with Jesus, 34
    preliminary research, 48
    similarities with BED, 42
    theoretical perspective, 6
Tentmaking Statement, 33
third space, 3, 124
Thoughts Upon Slavery (Wesley), 29n52
T'ien, 26
transformation, 18, 39, 97, 103
    in Lynch, 114
    mission as commitment, 31–32

transformational change, 159
　measure to access, 159
transformational development, 8, 9
transformed business practices, 71
Trinitarian mission, 13
Trinity, 12–13
　economic, 163
　perichoretic, 38
Triune God, 163
true community, 18
trust, 78, 81
　in God, 68
truth
　mission as discovery of, 32
　mission as extending, 31–32

unchurched, 33, 174
　reaching, 3
　softer approach for, 139
unemployment, 78
　rate in Selma, 88
United States Steel Corp, 110
University of Alabama, 52
UP relationships, 14
urban/suburban/rural issues, 12

variables
　dependent, 55
　independent, 55–56
Venn, Henry, 41

vocation, 25
vocational identity, 120
vocational stewardship, 80n12, 165f
Volf, Miroslav, 37, 38, 38n82
Volland, Michael, 13

walkable churches, 101n22
water-based kinship, 130, 131n51
wealth, 25
Weber, Max, 2
Wesley, John, 28–29, 31, 33
Wesleyan/Evangelical revival, 27
Whitefield, Dayton, 29
whole-life discipleship, 13n47, 136
Willingen Conference (1952), 35
wine-based kinship, 130
work, 38
　in "business for human
　　development" view, 37n80
　changes in understanding of, 22
　as holy calling, 26
　importance to Benedictines, 23
　integration with faith and
　　oikonomia, 109
　in tentmaking, 34–35
workplace, redemptive qualities, 64

Yamamori, Tetsunao, 15, 41
Yin, Robert, 46, 47, 64, 84
Yong, Amos, 161